handwritten notes:
RPM
(Pridmore)
(805)
648-2894
(213) 549-3551 / Brad
(213) 305-2980
(800) 673-211 byens
Carla Harmon
mid notch
P/J: 45 50
M/J: 160 170
N/J: 2,64 2.66

# *MW*

## 0-1000cc TWINS • 1970-1982
### SERVICE • REPAIR • PERFORMANCE

**ERIC JORGENSEN**
*Editor*

**JEFF ROBINSON**
*Publisher*

# CLYMER PUBLICATIONS

World's largest publisher of books devoted exclusively to
automobiles and motorcycles.

*12860 MUSCATINE STREET • P. O. BOX 20 • ARLETA, CALIFORNIA 91331*

---

FIRST EDITION
Published July, 1978

SECOND EDITION
*Revised by Mike Bishop to include 1979 models*
First Printing October, 1979

THIRD EDITION
*Revised by David Sales to include 1980 models*
First Printing July, 1982

FOURTH EDITION
*Revised by Ron Wright to include 1981-1982 models*
First Printing September, 1983
Second Printing July, 1984

---

Printed in U.S.A.

ISBN: 0-89287-225-X

*Production Coordinator, Blesilda Jacinto*

*Technical assistance by Bob Brown, Brown Motor Works, Pomona, California and William B. Bledsoe.*

*Performance chapter by Chris Bunch.*

*COVER: Photographed by Michael Brown Photographic Productions, Los Angeles, California.*

# CONTENTS

# QUICK REFERENCE DATA

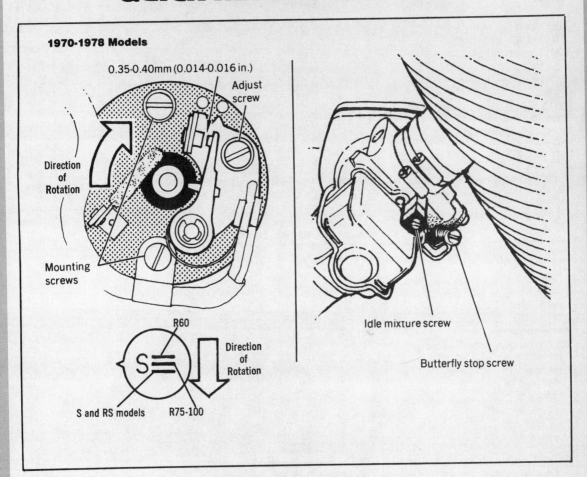

**1970-1978 Models**

0.35-0.40mm (0.014-0.016 in.)

Adjust screw

Direction of Rotation

Mounting screws

R60

S

R75-100

S and RS models

Direction of Rotation

Idle mixture screw

Butterfly stop screw

## TUNE-UP SPECIFICATIONS

| | |
|---|---|
| **Ignition point gap** | |
| 1970-1980 models | 0.35-0.40 mm (0.014-0.016 in.) |
| 1981-on | Electronic ignition |
| **Ignition timing** | |
| 1970-1978 | "S" mark static or @ idle |
| 1979-on | "S" (middle line) mark @ idle |
| | "Z" mark @ 3,500 rpm |
| **Valve clearance** | |
| 1970-1978 | |
| Intake | |
| /7 | 0.10 mm (0.004 in.) |
| All other models | 0.15 mm (0.006 in.) |
| Exhaust | |
| /7 | 0.15 mm (0.006 in.) |
| All other models | 0.20 mm (0.008 in.) |
| 1979-on | |
| Intake | 0.10 mm (0.004 in.) |
| Exhaust | 0.15 mm (0.006 in.) |
| **Idle speed** | |
| 1970-1978 | 500-750 rpm |
| 1979 | 800-1,000 rpm |
| 1980-on | 800-1,100 rpm |
| **Spark plug gap** | 0.6-0.7 mm (0.024-0.028 in.) |

## RECOMMENDED SPARK PLUGS*

| Model | Bosch | Champion |
|---|---|---|
| **1970-1978** | | |
| R100S, RS; R100T, RT; | | |
| R100/7; R90/6; R90S | W5D | N6Y |
| R75/5, /6, /7 | W6D | N7Y |
| R50/5; R60/5, /6, /7 | W5D | N6Y |
| R80/7 | W7D | N10Y |
| **1979-1980** | | |
| R80/7 | W7D | N10Y |
| R100S, R100RT, R100RS, | W5D | N6Y |
| R100T | | |
| **1981-on** | W6D | N7Y |

* Higher number in Bosch spark plugs indicates a colder heat range. Higher number in Champion plugs indicates a hotter heat range.

## APPROXIMATE REFILL CAPACITIES

| | | |
|---|---|---|
| **Fork oil** | | |
| 1970-1980 | 265 cc | 9.0 oz. |
| 1981-on | 220 cc | 7.44 oz. |
| **Engine oil** | | |
| 1970-1978 | 2.3 liters | 2.4 qt. |
| 1979-on* | 2.4 liters | 2.6 qt. |
| **Transmission oil** | 800 cc | 27 oz. |
| **Final drive gear case** | | |
| 1970-1978 | 250 cc | 8.5 oz. |
| 1979-on | 350 cc | 11.83 oz. |
| **Drive shaft housing** | | |
| 1970-1978 | | |
| /5 models | 100 cc | 3.4 oz. |
| /6 & /7 models | 150 cc | 5.1 oz. |
| 1979** | 350 cc | 11.83 oz. |

* Check engine oil level with dipstick resting on top of threads.
** On models equipped with the torsion damper driveshaft, it is impossible to check the oil level in the driveshaft housing. Instead, drain and refill with 150 cc (5.1 oz.) with the correct weight hypoid gear oil.

## RECOMMENDED FUEL AND LUBRICANTS

| | |
|---|---|
| Fuel | 85-95 octane |
| **Engine oil** | |
| 75° F and above | SAE 40; SAE 20W-50 |
| 32-75° F | SAE 20W-40; SAE 20W-50 |
| 32° F and below | SAE 10W-30; SAE 10W-40 |
| **Transmission oil** | |
| 75° and above | SAE 90 hypoid gear oil |
| Below 75° F | SAE 80 hypoid gear oil |
| Fork oil | SAE 5W fork oil |
| Final drive gear oil | SAE 90 hypoid gear oil rated GL-5 |
| Brake fluid* | Rated DOT 3 or DOT 4 |

*WARNING: Use only glycol based brake fluid rated DOT 3 or DOT 4. Mixing silicon or petroleum based fluids can cause brake component damage leading to brake system failure.

# CHAPTER ONE

# GENERAL INFORMATION

BMW opposed twins have a deserved reputation for strong performance and long service life. Their potential can best be realized through careful, periodic maintenance. This handbook covers all service operations — from changing a spark plug to overhauling the engine — in a format intended to be understandable to a hobbyist mechanic.

## MODELS

This handbook covers all BMW models built from 1970 on—the /5, /6, and /7 series. Included are R50, R60, R75, R80, R90, and R100 series.

To accurately identify a given motorcycle, examine the serial number and the manufacturer's plate (**Figure 1**).

## MANUAL ORGANIZATION

The service procedures in this manual are grouped by major subassembly (e.g., engine, transmission, fuel system, etc.) to speed work. In addition, an easy-to-use troubleshooting guide is provided. Common maintenance tasks and tune-up are covered in a single chapter because they are the most frequently performed tasks.

Dimensions, capacities, and weights are expressed both metrically and in terms familiar to American mechanics. When working with critical dimensions (cylinder-to-piston clearance, crankshaft journal diameters, oil pump rotor clearances, etc.), the metric values should be used to ensure accuracy.

## SERVICE HINTS

Most of the service procedures described can be performed by anyone reasonably handy with tools. However, carefully consider your own capabilities before attempting any operation which involves major disassembly of the engine or transmission.

Some operations, for example, require the use of a press. It would be wiser to have them performed by a shop equipped for such work, rather than to try to do the job yourself with makeshift equipment. Other procedures require precision measurements, and unless you have the skills and equipment to make them, it would be better to have a motorcycle shop help in the work.

Repairs can be made faster and easier if the motorcycle is clean before you begin work. There are special cleaners for washing the engine and related parts. Just brush or spray on the solution, let it stand, then rinse it away with a garden hose. Clean all oily or greasy parts with cleaning solvent as you remove them.

### WARNING
*Never use gasoline as a cleaning agent. It presents an extreme fire hazard.*

Always work in a well-ventilated area when using cleaning solvent. Keep a fire extinguisher, rated for gasoline fires, handy just in case.

Special tools are required for some service procedures. Some of these may be purchased through BMW dealers. If you are on good terms with the dealer's service department, you may be able to borrow or rent some.

Much of the labor charge for repairs made by dealers is for removal and disassembly of other parts to reach the defective one. It is frequently possible to do all of this yourself, then take the affected subassembly to the dealer for repair.

Once you decide to tackle a job yourself, read the entire section in this handbook pertaining to it. Study the illustrations and the text until you have a thorough idea of what's involved. If special tools are required, make arrangements to get them before you begin work. It's frustrating to get part way into a job and then discover that you are unable to complete it.

Collect the necessary tools, parts, lubricants, and cleaning supplies before starting a job. It's to your advantage to have your work area scrupulously clean to reduce the possibility of contamination of precision parts and critical surfaces. You'll also find that a few metal baking pans or sandwich bags and tape are worth their weight in gold for organizing and storing nuts, bolts, washers, and small bits and pieces as they are removed from the motorcycle.

## TOOLS

To properly service your motorcycle, you will need an assortment of ordinary hand tools. As a minimum, these include:

1. Combination wrenches (metric)
2. Socket wrenches (metric)
3. Plastic mallet
4. Small hammer
5. Snap ring pliers
6. Phillips screwdrivers
7. Slot screwdrivers
8. Impact driver
9. Allen wrenches (metric)
10. Pliers
11. Feeler gauges
12. Spark plug gauge
13. Spark plug wrench
14. Dial indicator
15. Drift

An original equipment tool kit, like the one shown in **Figure 2**, is available through most

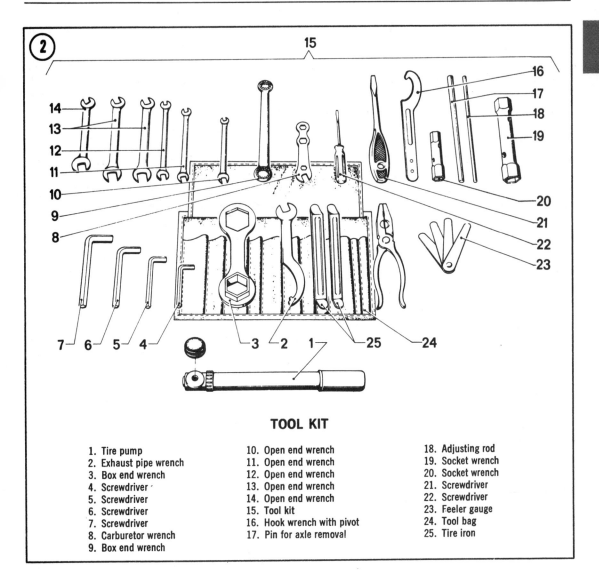

## TOOL KIT

1. Tire pump
2. Exhaust pipe wrench
3. Box end wrench
4. Screwdriver
5. Screwdriver
6. Screwdriver
7. Screwdriver
8. Carburetor wrench
9. Box end wrench
10. Open end wrench
11. Open end wrench
12. Open end wrench
13. Open end wrench
14. Open end wrench
15. Tool kit
16. Hook wrench with pivot
17. Pin for axle removal
18. Adjusting rod
19. Socket wrench
20. Socket wrench
21. Screwdriver
22. Screwdriver
23. Feeler gauge
24. Tool bag
25. Tire iron

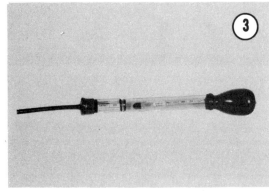

BMW dealers and it is suitable for minor servicing.

Special tools necessary are shown in the chapters covering the particular repair in which they are used.

Electrical system servicing requires a voltmeter, ohmmeter, or other device for determining continuity and a hydrometer for assessing battery condition.

Engine tune-up and troubleshooting procedures require a few more tools.

### Hydrometer

This instrument (**Figure 3**) measures state of charge of the battery and tells much about battery condition. Such an instrument is available at any auto parts store or motorcycle shop and through most large mail order outlets.

### Multimeter or VOM

This instrument (**Figure 4**) is invaluable for electrical system troubleshooting and service. A few of its functions may be duplicated by locally fabricated substitutes, but for the serious hobbyist it is a must. Its uses are described in the applicable sections of this book.

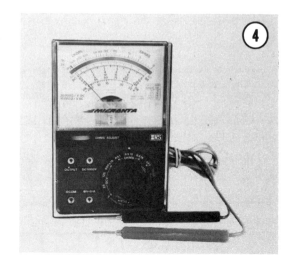

### Compression Gauge

An engine with low compression cannot be properly tuned and will not develop full power. A compression gauge (**Figure 5**) measures engine compression. Compression gauges are available at auto and motorcycle stores or by mail order from large catalog order firms.

### Impact Driver

This tool (**Figure 6**) might have been designed with the motorcyclist in mind. It makes removal of tight nuts and screws easy, and eliminates damaged screw heads.

### Ignition Gauge

This tool (**Figure 7**) measures point gap. It also has round wire gauges for measuring spark plug gap.

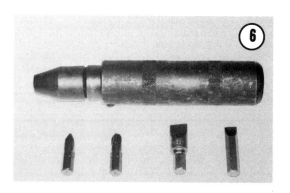

### EXPENDABLE SUPPLIES

Certain expendable supplies are also required. These include grease, oil, gasket cement, wiping rags, cleaning solvent, and distilled water. Ask your dealer for the special locking compounds, silicone lubricants, and commercial cable lube products which make motorcycle maintenance simpler and easier. Solvent is available at most service stations and distilled water for the battery is available at most supermarkets.

### SAFETY HINTS

A professional mechanic can work for years and never sustain a serious injury. If you

observe a few rules of common sense and safety, you can enjoy many hours safely servicing your own machine. You can also hurt yourself or damage your motorcycle if you ignore these rules.

1. Never use gasoline as a cleaning solvent.

2. Never smoke or use a torch around flammable liquids, such as cleaning solvent.

3. Never smoke or use a torch in areas where batteries are being charged. Highly explosive hydrogen gas is formed during the charging process. And never arc the terminals of a battery to see if it has a charge; the sparks can ignite the explosive hydrogen as easily as an open flame.

4. If welding or brazing is required on the motorcycle, remove the fuel tank and set it a safe distance away — at least 50 feet.

5. Always use the correct size wrench for turning nuts and bolts, and when a nut is tight, think for a moment what would happen to your hand if the wrench were to slip.

6. Keep your work area clean and uncluttered.

7. Wear safety goggles in all operations involving drilling, grinding, the use of a chisel, or an air hose.

8. Don't use worn tools.

9. Keep a fire extinguisher handy. Be sure it is rated for gasoline and electrical fires.

**1**

# CHAPTER TWO

# TROUBLESHOOTING

Diagnosing mechanical problems is relatively simple if you use orderly procedures and keep a few basic principles in mind.

The troubleshooting procedures in this chapter analyze typical symptoms, and show logical methods of isolating causes. These are not the only methods. There may be several ways to solve a problem, but only a systematic, methodical approach can guarantee success.

Never assume anything. Don't overlook the obvious. If you are riding along and the bike suddenly quits, check the easiest, most accessible problem spots first. Is there gasoline in the tank? Is the gas petcock in the ON or REVERSE position? Has a spark plug wire fallen off? Check ignition switch. Sometimes the weight of keys on a key ring may turn the ignition off suddenly.

If nothing obvious turns up in a cursory check, look a little further. Learning to recognize and describe symptoms will make repairs easier for you or a mechanic at the shop. Describe problems accurately and fully. Saying that "it won't run" isn't the same as saying "it quit on the hghway at high speed and wouldn't start," or that "it sat in my garage for 3 months and then wouldn't start."

Gather as many symptoms together as possible to aid in diagnosis. Note whether the engine lost power gradually or all at once, what color smoke (if any) came from the exhaust, and so on. Remember that the more complicated a machine is, the easier it is to troubleshoot because symptoms point to specific problems.

After the symptoms are defined, areas which could cause problems are tested and analyzed. Guessing at the cause of a problem may provide the solution, but it can easily lead to frustration, wasted time, and a series of expensive, unnecessary parts replacements.

You don't need fancy equipment or complicated test gear to determine whether repairs can be attempted at home. A few simple checks could save a large repair bill and time lost while the bike sits in a dealer's service department. On the other hand, be realistic and don't attempt repairs beyond your abilities. Service departments tend to charge heavily for putting together a disassembled engine that may have been abused. Some won't even take on such a job — so use common sense, don't get in over your head.

## OPERATING REQUIREMENTS

An engine needs three basics to run properly: correct gas/air mixture, compression, and a spark at the right time. If one or more are missing, the engine won't run. The electrical system is the weakest link of the 3 basics. More problems result from electrical breakdowns than from any other source. Keep that in mind before you begin tampering with carburetor adjustments and the like.

If a bike has been sitting for any length of time and refuses to start, check the battery for a charged condition first, and then look to the gasoline delivery system. This includes the tank, fuel petcocks, lines, and the carburetors. Rust may have formed in the tank, obstructing fuel flow. Gasoline deposits may have gummed up carburetor jets and air passages. Gasoline tends to lose its potency after standing for long periods. Condensation may contaminate it with water. Drain the old gas and try starting with fresh fuel.

## TROUBLESHOOTING INSTRUMENTS

Chapter One lists many of the instruments needed and detailed instructions on their use.

## STARTING DIFFICULTIES

Check gas flow first. Remove the gas cap and look into the tank. If gas is present, remove the float bowl from the carburetor and see if gas flows freely. If none comes out, the fuel tap may be shut off, blocked by rust or foreign matter, or the fuel line may be stopped up or kinked. If the carburetor is getting usable fuel, turn to the electrical system next.

Check that the battery is charged by turning on the lights or by beeping the horn. Refer to your owner's manual for starting procedures with a dead battery. Have the battery recharged if necessary.

Pull off a spark plug cap, remove the spark plug, and reconnect the cap. Lay the plug against the cylinder head so its base makes a good connection, and turn the engine over with the kickstarter. A fat, blue spark should jump across the electrodes. If there is no spark, or only a weak one, there is electrical system trouble. Check for a defective plug by replacing it with a known good one. Don't assume a plug is good just because it's new.

Once the plug has been cleared of guilt, but there's still no spark, start backtracking through the system. If the contact at the end of spark plug wire can be exposed, it can be held about $\frac{1}{8}$ inch from the head while the engine is turned over to check for a spark. Remember to hold the wire only by its insulation to avoid a nasty shock. If the plug wires are dirty, greasy, or wet, wrap a rag around them so you don't get shocked. If you do feel a shock or see sparks along the wire, clean or replace the wire and/or its connections.

If there's no spark at the plug wire, look for loose connections at the coil and battery. If all seems in order there, check next for oily or dirty contact points. Clean points with electrical contact cleaner, or a business card, With the ignition switch turned on, open and close the points manually with a screwdriver. Look for spark across the point gap.

No spark at the points with this test indicates a failure in the ignition system. Refer to Chapter Three for checkout procedures for the entire system and individual components. Refer to the same chapter for checking and setting ignition timing.

Note that spark plugs of the incorrect heat range (too cold) may cause hard starting. Set gaps to specifications. If you have just ridden through a puddle or washed the bike and it won't start, dry off plugs and plug wires. Water may have entered the carburetor and fouled the fuel under these conditions, but wet plugs and wires are the more likely problem.

If a healthy spark occurs at the right time, and there is adequate gas flow to the carburetor, check the carburetor itself at this time. make sure all jets and air passages are clean, check float level, and adjust if necessary. Check that the carburetors are mounted snugly and no air is leaking past the manifold.

NOTE: *For this check, the engine must be started and run at idle. Spray WD-40 around the manifold joints and listen for changes in engine idle speed. Changes indicate an air leak.*

### Check for a Clogged Air Filter

Compression, or the lack of it, usually enters the picture only in the case of older machines. Worn or broken pistons, rings, and cylinder bores could prevent starting. Generally a gradual power loss and harder starting will be readily apparent in this case.

Compression may be checked in the field by turning the kickstarter (pre-1975) by hand and noting that an adequate resistance is felt.

An accurate compression check gives a good idea of the condition of the basic working parts of the engine. To perform this test, you need a compression gauge. The motor should be warm.

1. Remove the plug on the cylinder to be tested and clean out any dirt or grease.

2. Insert the tip of the gauge into the hole, making sure it is seated correctly.

3. Open the throttle all the way and make sure the chokes on the carburetors are open.

4. Crank the engine several times and record the highest pressure reading on the gauge. Run the test on each of the cylinders.

5. The normal compression is 125-147 psi. If the readings are significantly lower than 125 psi as a group, or if they vary more than 15 psi between cylinders, proceed to the next step.

6. Pour a tablespoon of motor oil into the suspect cylinder and record the compression. (Horizontal cylinders often make this test inconclusive.)

If oil raises the compression significantly — 10 psi in an old engine — the rings are worn and should be replaced.

If the compression does not rise, one or both valves are probably not seating correctly.

Valve adjustments should be checked next. Sticking, burned, or broken valves may hamper starting. As a last resort, check valve timing.

## STARTER

Starter system troubles are relatively easy to isolate. The following are common symptoms and causes.

1. *Engine cranks very slowly or not at all.* Turn on the headlight. If the light is very dim, the battery or connecting wires are probably at fault. Check the battery. Check the wiring for breaks, shorts, or dirty connections.

If the battery or connecting wires are not at fault, turn the headlight on and try to crank the engine. If the light dims drastically, the starter

is probably shorted to ground. Remove it and test as described.

If the light remains bright, or dims only slightly when trying to start the engine, the trouble may be in the starter, relay, or wiring. Perform the following steps to isolate the cause.

WARNING
*Disconnect the coil wire to prevent accidental starting. Keep away from moving parts when working near the engine.*

a. If the starter doesn't respond at all, connect a 12-volt test lamp between the starter terminal and ground. Turn the ignition key to START. If the lamp lights, the starter is probably at fault. Remove it and test the unit. If the lamp doesn't light, the problem is somewhere in the starting circuit. Perform the next steps.

b. Connect a jumper wire between the battery and starter terminals on the starter relay. If starter doesn't respond at all, the relay is probably defective. If the starter cranks normally, perform the next step.

c. Connect a test lamp between the starter terminal on the stater relay and ground. Turn the ignition key to START. If the lamp doesn't light, check the ignition switch and associated wiring. Turn the key to START and work it around in the switch. If the lamp lights erratically, the ignition switch is probably defective.

d. If the problem still has not been isolated, check all wiring in the starting circuit with an ohmmeter or other continuity tester. See the wiring diagrams in Chapters Eight and Fourteen.

2. *Starter turns, but does not engage.* This problem may be caused by a defective starter drive mechanism, or broken gear teeth. Remove and inspect starter as described in Chapter Eight.

3. *Loud grinding noises when starter runs.* This may mean the teeth are not meshing properly, or it may mean the starter drive mechanism is damaged. In the first case, remove the starter and examine the gear teeth. In the latter case, remove the starter and replace the starter drive mechanism.

## POOR IDLING

Poor idling may be caused by incorrect carburetor adjustment, incorrect timing, or ignition system defects. Check the gas cap vent for an obstruction. Check for low compression.

## MISFIRING

Misfiring can be caused by a weak spark or dirty plugs. Check for fuel contamination. Run the machine at night to check for spark leaks along plug wires and under spark plug cap.

### WARNING
*Do not run engine in dark garage to check for spark leaks. There is considerable danger of carbon monoxide poisoning.*

If misfiring occurs only at certain throttle settings, refer to Chapter Six for the specific carburetor circuits involved. Misfiring under heavy load, as when climbing hills or accelerating, is usually an indication of bad spark plugs, plug wires or plug connectors.

## FLAT SPOTS

If the engine seems to die momentarily when the throttle is opened and then recovers, check for a dirty main jet in the carburetor, water in the fuel, or an excessively lean mixture. Check the metering rod position.

## POWER LOSS

Poor condition of rings, pistons, or cylinders will cause a lack of power and speed. Ignition timing should be checked.

## OVERHEATING

If the engine seems to run too hot all the time, be sure you are not idling it for long periods. Air-cooled engines are not designed to operate at a standstill for any length of time. Heavy stop and go traffic is hard on a motorcycle engine. Spark plugs of the wrong heat range can burn pistons. An excessively lean gas mixture may cause overheating. Check ignition timing. Don't ride in too high a gear. Broken or worn rings may permit compression gases to leak past them, heating cylinders excessively.

Check oil level and use the proper grade lubricants.

## ENGINE NOISES

Experience is needed to diagnose accurately in this area. Noises are hard to differentiate and harder yet to describe. Deep knocking noises usually mean main bearing failure. A slapping noise generally comes from loose pistons. A light knocking noise during acceleration may be a bad connecting rod bearing. Pinging should be corrected immediately or damage to pistons will result. Compression leaks at the head-cylinder joint will sound like a rapid on-and-off squeal.

## PISTON SEIZURE

Piston seizure is caused by incorrect piston clearances when fitted, fitting rings with improper end gap, too thin an oil being used, incorrect spark plug heat range, or incorrect ignition timing. Overheating from any cause may result in seizure.

## EXCESSIVE VIBRATION

Excessive vibration may be caused by loose motor mounts, worn engine or transmission bearings, loose wheels, worn swinging arm bearings, a generally poor running engine, broken or cracked frame, or one that has been damaged in a collision. See also *Poor Handling*.

## CLUTCH SLIP OR DRAG

Clutch slip may be due to incorrect clutch adjustment, a worn pressure plate, or a glazed disc. Clutch drag may be caused by incorrect adjustment, a warped pressure plate, or oil on the disc.

All clutch problems, except adjustments or cable replacement, require removal to identify the cause and make repairs.

1. *Slippage* — This condition is most noticeable when accelerating in high gear at relatively low speed. To check slippage, drive at a steady speed in 4th or 5th gear. Without changing the throttle position, pull in the clutch lever just long enough to let engine speed increase. Then

let the clutch out rapidly. If the clutch is good, engine speed will drop quickly or the bike will jump forward. If the clutch is slipping, engine speed will drop slowly and the bike will not jump forward.

Slippage results from insufficient clutch lever free play, worn disc or weak diaphragm spring. Riding the clutch can cause the disc surfaces to become glazed, resulting in slippage.

2. *Drag or failure to release* — This trouble usually causes difficult shifting and gear clash especially when downshifting. The cause may be excessive clutch lever free play, warped pressure plate, stretched clutch cable, or broken or loose disc linings.

3. *Chatter or grabbing* — Check for worn or misaligned disc, or warped pressure plate.

> NOTE: *Clutch wear is accelerated if the transmission is habitually left in gear with the clutch disengaged while waiting for long-duration traffic lights. Instead, shift the transmission to* NEUTRAL *and release the clutch until the cross-traffic amber light indicates that the light is about to change. In addition to reducing clutch wear, a measure of safety is gained in that it precludes a cable failure, most certain to occur when the clutch lever is pulled in.*

## TRANSMISSION

Transmission problems are usually indicted by one or more of the following symptoms.

   a. Difficult shifting gears

   b. Gear clash when downshifting

   c. Slipping out of gear

   d. Excessive noise in NEUTRAL

   e. Excessive noise in gear

Transmission symptoms are sometimes hard to distinguish from clutch symptoms. Be sure the clutch is not causing the trouble before working on the transmission.

## POOR HANDLING

Poor handling may be caused by improper tire pressures, a damaged frame or swinging arm, worn shocks or front forks, weak fork springs, a bent or broken steering stem, misaligned wheels, loose or missing spokes, worn tires, bent handlebar, worn wheel bearing, or dragging brakes.

Poor handling is also caused by the steering head, being adjusted too tight or too loose, or by the races and balls being excessively worn. Also, if the frame has been recently repainted, overspray on the bearing races will prevent the bearings from seating correctly and make accurate adjustment impossible.

Worn or frozen swing arm bearings will also cause handling problems. They can be checked by removing the swing arm and rotating the bearings by hand. They should turn freely and smoothly. If they do not, replace them.

> NOTE: *A worn or loose swing arm pivot will usually be felt through a tendency for the motorcycle to weave from side to side. A high-rate wobble indicates front-end trouble.*

In addition to the checks mentioned, make certain the tires are mounted correctly and that the beads are seated evenly on the rims. Tires have alignment indicator ribs around the bead and an incorrectly seated bead will be visually apparent. If this condition exists, deflate the tire and reseat the bead before inflating it.

The increasingly common practice of cutting rain grooves into road surfaces has added a totally new handling problem for most motorcycles no matter how well tuned the suspension. It is most easily solved by using tires that do not have a center groove. If the motorcycle tends to snake, as though the swing arm pivot were loose or worn, the problem usually lies with the rear tire. If the steering is imprecise and mushy, the front tire is at fault. If all other handling factors are correct, a change of tread pattern will almost always correct the situation.

## BRAKE PROBLEMS

Sticking brakes may be caused by broken or weak return springs, improper cable or rod adjustment, or dry pivot and cam bushings. Grabbing brakes may be caused by greasy linings which must be replaced. Brake grab may also be due to out-of-round drums or linings which have broken loose from brake shoes. Glazed linings or glazed brake pads will cause loss of stopping power.

Stopping power is also greatly reduced with drum brakes when the angle of the cable and the brake arm exceed 90° with the brake fully applied. This adjustment is covered in Chapter Ten.

## ELECTRICAL PROBLEMS

Bulbs which continuously burn out may be caused by excessive vibration, loose connections that permit sudden current surges, poor battery connections, installation of the wrong type bulb, or a faulty voltage regulator.

A dead battery, or one which discharges quickly, may be caused by a faulty alternator or rectifier. Check for loose or corroded terminals. Shorted battery cells or broken terminals will keep a battery from charging. Low water level will decrease a battery's capacity. A battery left uncharged after installation will sulphate, rendering it useless.

A majority of light and horn or other electrical accessory problems are caused by loose or corroded ground connections. Check those first, and then substitute known good units for easier troubleshooting.

## TROUBLESHOOTING GUIDE

The following summarizes the troubleshooting process. Use it to outline possible problem areas, then refer to the specific chapter or section involved.

### Loss of Power

1. *Poor compression* — Check piston rings and cylinder, cylinder head gasket, and valve leaks.

2. *Overheated engine* — Check lubricating oil supply, air leaks, ignition timing, clogged cooling fins, slipping clutch, and carbon in the combustion chamber.

3. *Improper mixture* — Check for dirty air cleaner, restricted fuel flow-jets, clogged gas cap vent hole.

### Gearshifting Difficulties

1. *Clutch* — Check clutch adjustment, clutch spring, and pressure plate. Look for oil on the clutch.

2. *Transmission* — Check oil quantity and type, oil grade, gearshift mechanism adjustment, return spring, and gear change forks.

### Brake Troubles

1. *Poor brakes* — Check brake adjustment, brake drum out-of-round, oil or water on brake linings, and loose brake linkage or cables.

2. *Noisy brakes* — Check for worn or scratched linings, scratched drums, and dirt in brakes.

3. *Unadjustable brakes* — Check for worn linings, drums, and brake cams.

4. *Miscellaneous* — Check for dragging brakes and tight wheel bearings.

### Steering Problems

1. *Hard steering* — Check steering head bearings, steering stem head, and tire pressures.

2. *Pulls to one side* — Check for worn swing arm bearings and make sure they are properly adjusted. Check also for bent swing arm, bent steering head, and bent frame. Check the alignment of the front and rear wheels. If the motorcycle is fitted with a fairing, check its alignment with the motorcycle to make sure it is not offset to one side or the other.

3. *Shimmy* — check for loose, broken or missing spokes, deformed wheel rims, worn wheel bearings and incorrect wheel balance.

Low-speed shimmy is usually caused by the steering head adjustment being too loose. This is a critical adjustment (see Chapter Eight) and if you are unsure of your ability to accurately carry it out, refer the matter to a dealer.

NOTE: If you own a 1979 or later model, first check the Supplement at the back of the book for any new service information.

# CHAPTER THREE

# PERIODIC MAINTENANCE AND TUNE-UP

Regular maintenance is the best guarantee of a trouble-free, long-lasting motorcycle. An afternoon spent now, cleaning and adjusting, can prevent costly mechanical problems in the future and unexpected breakdowns on the road.

The tune-up procedures presented in this chapter should hold no terror for an owner with average mechanical skills. The operations are outlined step-by-step and are easy to follow.

Instruments and measuring devices calibrated to the metric system, rather than the inch-foot system, will be easier to work with when measuring parts and comparing them to the specifications, and when tightening critical-torque nuts and bolts. The text gives specifications in both systems, but inch-foot equivalents of standard metric values are occasionally awkward.

## MAINTENANCE INTERVALS

The factory recommends a tune-up every 4,000 miles, but 6,000 miles is acceptable for most situations. Many BMW specialists feel that the factory-recommended lube and oil change intervals are too long and that this work should be carried out every 2,000 miles. Maintenance schedules are shown in **Table 1**.

## TOOLS AND PARTS

In addition to the basic tools suggested in the introduction to this handbook (Chapter One), a tune-up requires a strobe timing light — or a buzz box — and a set of flat feeler gauges, preferably calibrated in millimeters.

> NOTE: *The feeler gauge set in the original-equipment tool kit works better than aftermarket gauges in that it is shaped so that the sliding resistance of the gauge feels only the clearance and not resistance of rubbing on the head casting when adjusting the valves.*

Parts required for a tune-up are 2 spark plugs, a set of points, a condenser, and an air filter.

## SERVICING

The following pages cover servicing or replacement of the oil and filter, spark plugs, ignition breaker points and condenser, static and advanced timing, valve clearances, air cleaner, fuel valve, carburetors, clutch, and battery. The tune-up should be performed in the order the operations are listed.

Other routine service procedures, such as adjusting the brakes, the headlight, and adjusting

Table 1    MAINTENANCE SCHEDULE

### MINOR SERVICE

1. Check compression
2. Change engine oil and filter
3. Grease rear swing arm
4. Grease and adjust brake and clutch levers and throttle assembly
5. Grease foot brake and clutch arm
6. Check cables for condition
7. Service battery and check for drain
8. Clean or replace air filter (Check fuel line for condition)
9. Change transmission oil
10. Change driveshaft oil
11. Change rear drive oil
12. Check wheel bearing for side-play
13. Check for broken or bad spokes
14. Check tire pressure
15. Check spark plugs
16. Check plug cap connections
17. Adjust contact breaker cap (lubricate felt)
18. Adjust ignition timing
19. Check alternator output
20. Adjust rocker arm end play and center pushrods
21. Torque heads and adjust valve clearance
22. Clean fuel filters
23. Clean float bowls and jets
24. Adjust fuel air mixtures and balance throttle cables
25. Check all electrical functions
26. Tighten nuts and bolts
27. Test drive and final inspection

### MAJOR SERVICE

1. Check compression
2. Change engine oil and filter
3. Grease rear swing arm bearings
4. Grease and adjust brake and clutch levers and throttle assembly
5. Grease foot brake and clutch arm
6. Check all cables for condition
7. Service battery and check for ground drain
8. Clean or replace air filter (Check fuel line for condition)
9. Change transmission oil
10. Change driveshaft oil
11. Change rear drive oil
12. Change telescopic fork oil
13. Pack wheel bearings
14. Check tire pressure
15. Check for broken or bad spokes
16. Check brakes for condition
17. Adjust rocker arm end play and center pushrods
18. Torque cylinder heads and adjust valve clearance
19. Check spark plugs
20. Check plug cap connections
21. Adjust contact breaker gap (Lubricate felt)
22. Adjust ignition timing
23. Check alternator output
24. Clean fuel filters
25. Clean float bowls and jets
26. Adjust fuel air mixture and balance throttle cables
27. Check all electrical functions
28. Tighten nuts and bolts
29. Test drive and final inspection

and lubricating the swing arm bearings and controls, are covered in other chapters.

## ENGINE OIL AND FILTER

### Frequency

The engine oil should be changed every 2,000 miles or 60 days, whichever occurs first. These recommendations assume operation in moderate climates. In extremely cold climates change oil every 30 days regardless of the mileage. The time interval is more important than the mileage interval because acids formed by gasoline and water vapor from condensation will contaminate the oil even if the motorcycle is not run for several months. Also, if the motorcycle is operated under dusty conditions the oil will get dirty more quickly, so change it more frequently.

Use only a detergent oil with an API rating of SE, SD (formerly MS) or SC (formerly MM). These quality ratings are stamped on the top of the can. Always try to use the same brand of oil. The use of oil additives is not recommended.

SAE 30 oil is recommended for normal operation in moderate climates. The factory recommends the alternate weights shown in **Table 2**, according to prevailing temperatures.

### Draining Oil

1. Run the engine for a few minutes. Warm oil drains faster and carries more sludge with it than cold oil.
2. Place a drip pan of at least 3 quart capacity beneath the drain plug located at the bottom rear of the oil pan. Remove the dipstick from the engine.
3. Remove the oil drain plug from the oil pan (**Figure 1**), allow the oil to drain and clean the plug.
4. Unscrew the bolts and remove the filter cover (**Figure 2**). On 1976 and earlier models, unscrew the filter cap (**Figure 3**). Remove the filter (**Figure 4**) with a piece of thin wire bent into a hook.
5. Inspect the small inner O-ring, cover gasket (through 1976) or large outer O-ring (1977 and later) and replace them if they are damaged. Install the internal O-ring, a new filter

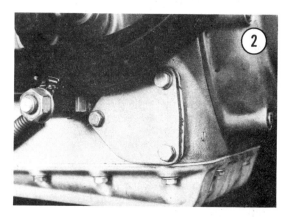

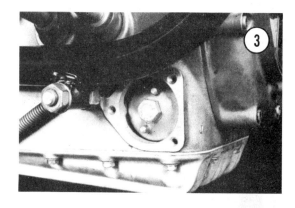

cartridge, the cap and the bolt. Install the outer cover and gasket.

*NOTE*
*American Parts Distributors' Power Flo filter No. 854 (approximately $2.85) is identical to the BMW original equipment filter.*

6. For 1974 and earlier models, crank the engine several times with the kickstarter to force out any oil trapped in the engine's internal recesses. On 1975 and later models, disconnect the spark plug leads and crank the engine with the starter button.

*NOTE*
*Pour the used oil into plastic bottles such as those used for laundry bleach. Cap tightly and discard them in the trash.*

## Filling With Oil

1. Install the drain plug in the oil pan.
2. Fill the engine with 2 U.S. quarts (1.7 Imp. quarts) of recommended oil and check the level with the dipstick.

*NOTE*
*Insert the dipstick all the way into the hole but do not screw it in when checking the level.*

3. Run the engine at about 1,000 rpm for a couple of minutes, shut it off and check for seepage from the drain plug and around the filter cover. Recheck the oil level with the dipstick and top up if necessary.

## TRANSMISSION OIL

It is suggested that the transmission oil be changed at the same time as the engine oil. Refer to **Table 2** and **Table 3** for transmission capacity and recommended type of oil.
1. Ride the motorcycle sufficiently to warm up the transmission oil.
2. Place the motorcycle on the centerstand and place a drain pan (2-3 quart capacity) under the transmission.
3. Remove the transmission filler plug (Allen head) located slightly above the gearshift lever (**Figure 5A**).

Table 2    RECOMMENDED FUEL AND LUBRICANTS

| | |
|---|---|
| Fuel | 85-95 octane |
| Engine oil | |
|   75° F and above | SAE 40; SAE 20W-50 |
|   32-75° F | SAE 20W-40; SAE 20W-50 |
|   32° F and below | SAE 10W-30; SAE 10W-40 |
| Transmission oil | |
|   75° and above | SAE 90 hypoid gear oil |
|   Below 75° F | SAE 80 hypoid gear oil |
| Fork oil | SAE 5W fork oil |
| Final drive gear oil | SAE 90 hypoid gear oil rated GL-5 |
| Brake fluid* | Rated DOT 3 or DOT 4 |

* WARNING: Use only glycol based brake fluid rated DOT 3 or DOT 4. Mixing silicon or petroleum based fluids can cause brake component damage leading to brake system failure.

Table 3    CAPACITIES

| | | | |
|---|---|---|---|
| Engine oil | 2.3 liters | 2.4 U.S. qt. | 2.0 Imp. qt. |
| Transmission oil | 800 cc | 27 U.S. oz. | 28 Imp. oz. |
| Drive shaft housing | | | |
| /5 models | 100 cc | 3.4 U.S. oz. | 3.5 Imp. oz. |
| /6 and /7 models | 150 cc | 5.1 U.S. oz. | 5.3 Imp. oz. |
| Final drive gear case | 250 cc | 8.5 U.S. oz. | 8.8 Imp. oz. |
| Fork oil capacity | | | |
| Refill only | 265 cc | 9.0 U.S. oz. | 9.3 Imp. oz. |
| After disassembly | 280 cc | 9.5 U.S. oz. | 9.9 Imp. oz. |

*NOTE*
*The filler plug opening also indicates the correct transmission oil level.*

4. Remove the transmission drain plug (large plug toward the rear of the transmission). Allow several minutes for the transmission oil to drain completely.

*CAUTION*
*Ensure that only the larger rear plug is removed to drain the transmission oil. The smaller plug (farther forward) should be removed only during transmission disassembly.*

5. Wipe the drain plug with a clean rag and install in the transmission.
6. Fill the transmission with the recommended type and quantity of oil as specified in **Table 2** and **Table 3**. Ensure that the transmission oil is at the bottom edge of the filler plug opening. Slowly add more oil if necessary. Install the filler plug.

## TUNE-UP

A complete tune-up should be performed every 6,000 miles of normal riding (combination of highway and city). More frequent tune-ups may be required if the motorcycle is used primarily in stop-and-go city traffic.

For maximum performance and fuel economy, the expendable ignition parts (spark plugs, points and condenser) should be replaced during the tune-up and you should have them on hand before beginning. The old parts can be reused once if replacement is impractical and if their condition is satisfactory, as described later.

Because different systems in an engine interact, the procedures should be done in the following order:
1. Tighten cylinder head bolts.
2. Adjust valve clearances.
3. Work on ignition system.
4. Adjust carburetors.
Refer to **Table 4** for tune-up specifications.

## HEAD BOLT TORQUE AND VALVE ADJUSTMENT

Incorrect clearances between the tappets and valve stems can damage the valves and mar performance. To forestall premature wear and a costly regrind, adjust the clearances regularly.

Table 4    TUNE-UP SPECIFICATIONS

| | |
|---|---|
| Spark plug gap | 0.6-0.7 mm (0.024-0.028 in.) |
| Ignition point gap | 0.35-0.40 mm (0.014-0.016 in.) |
| Ignition timing (1978 and earlier) | "S" mark static or at idle |
| | "F" mark at 2,600 rpm |
| Ignition timing (1979 and later models) | "S" mark at idle |
| | "Z" mark at 3,500 rpm |
| Valve clearance | |
| Intake (rear valves) /7 models | 0.10 mm (0.004 in.) |
| All other models | 0.15 mm (0.006 in.) |
| Exhaust (front valves) /7 models | 0.15 mm (0.006 in.) |
| All other models | 0.20 mm (0.008 in.) |
| Idle speed | |
| 1979 and later models | 800-1,000 rpm |
| 1978 and earlier models | 500-750 rpm |

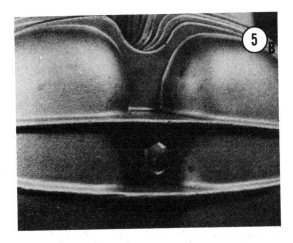

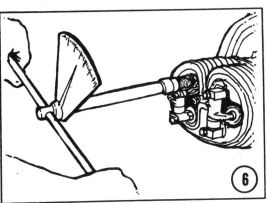

*NOTE*
*This procedure is performed with the engine cold. The factory recommends that the valves be adjusted every 4,000 miles.*

1. Unscrew the cap nuts in the center of the rocker covers and the 2 nuts inboard of the large fins on the heads. Remove the covers, the cover gaskets and the washers (**Figure 5B**).
2. Check torque of cylinder head bolts (**Figure 6**). It should be 3.5-3.9 mkg (25-28 ft.-lb.).
3. Remove the spark plugs from the cylinders. Rotate the crankshaft until the cylinder to be adjusted is at TDC on the compression stroke. This is evident when both valve springs are fully extended and play can be felt in the pushrods and rockers. If the motorcycle is equipped with a kickstarter, the starter can be used to rotate the crankshaft. If it is not equipped with a kickstarter, shift the transmission into second gear and rotate the crankshaft by turning the rear wheel.

*NOTE*
*When the cylinder is at TDC on the compression stroke, the OT mark on the flywheel should line up with the pointer (Figure 7). On some early /5 and /6*

*models the OT mark may not line up exactly at the point at which the clearance is the greatest. Slowly rock the flywheel back and forth over the OT mark and check the clearance by feeling the play in the rockers. The clearance should be checked and set at the widest point (see below). When the clearance is correct, line up the OT mark and check the pushrods to make sure some clearance is present. If not, increase the clearance slightly until the pushrod has slight play.*

4. Use a flat-blade feeler gauge and check the clearances between the valve stem and the rocker arm on each valve. Refer to **Table 4** for correct valve clearances. If the valve clearances are not as specified, perform the following steps:

5. Loosen the 12 mm locknut (**Figure 8**). To decrease the clearance, turn the adjusting screw clockwise; to increase it, turn it counterclockwise. The gap is correct when there is a slight drag on the feeler blade.

6. When the clearance is correct, tighten the locknut and then recheck the clearance to make sure the tightening did not upset the setting.

7. The adjustment steps must be performed on both valves on each cylinder with the engine at TDC.

8. Rotate the crankshaft 360° to bring the other cylinder to TDC on the compression stroke and check and adjust the clearances in the same manner.

9. Before reinstalling the rocker covers, check the gaskets for damage and replace them if necessary. Clean the sealing surfaces carefully and reinstall the covers.

## SPARK PLUGS

### Removal

1. Blow out any debris from the recesses around the spark plugs.

2. Carefully remove the spark plug leads. Do not jerk them; the wires could be pulled out of the insulator caps. Check the wires for broken or cracked insulation. Replace them if their condition is in doubt.

3. Unscrew the spark plugs with a socket that has a rubber insert to grip the insulator.

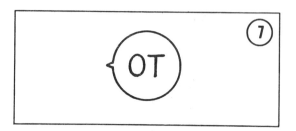

### Inspection

The normal color of the tip of the spark plug insulator ranges from light tan to chocolate brown, depending on the concentration of lead in the gas being used.

**Figure 9** shows some of the abnormal tip conditions, along with probable causes.

### Plug Types

Recommended spark plugs are shown in **Table 5**.

### Old Plugs

If the old plugs are to be used, inspect them for cracked insulators, damaged threads or eroded electrodes. Discard both plugs if any of these conditions are present.

### Cleaning

Clean the tips of the plugs with a sandblasting machine—some gas stations have them—or with a wire brush and solvent, followed by compressed air.

*CAUTION*
*When blowing solvent and debris out of the plug with compressed air, hold the plug so the electrode end is pointed away from you.*

**⑨** SPARK PLUG CONDITION

**NORMAL**
- Identified by light tan or gray deposits on the firing tip.
- Can be cleaned.

**GAP BRIDGED**
- Identified by deposit buildup closing gap between electrodes.
- Caused by oil or carbon fouling. If deposits are not excessive, the plug can be cleaned.

**OIL FOULED**
- Identified by wet black deposits on the insulator shell bore electrodes.
- Caused by excessive oil entering combustion chamber through worn rings and pistons, excessive clearance between valve guides and stems, or worn or loose bearings. Can be cleaned. If engine is not repaired, use a hotter plug.

**CARBON FOULED**
- Identified by black, dry fluffy carbon deposits on insulator tips, exposed shell surfaces and electrodes.
- Caused by too cold a plug, weak ignition, dirty air cleaner, too rich a fuel mixture, or excessive idling. Can be cleaned.

**LEAD FOULED**
- Identified by dark gray, black, yellow, or tan deposits or a fused glazed coating on the insulator tip.
- Caused by highly leaded gasoline. Can be cleaned.

**WORN**
- Identified by severely eroded or worn electrodes.
- Caused by normal wear. Should be replaced.

**FUSED SPOT DEPOSIT**
- Identified by melted or spotty deposits resembling bubbles or blisters.
- Caused by sudden acceleration. Can be cleaned.

**OVERHEATING**
- Identified by a white or light gray insulator with small black or gray brown spots and with bluish-burnt appearance of electrodes.
- Caused by engine overheating, wrong type of fuel, loose spark plugs, too hot a plug, or incorrect ignition timing. Replace the plug.

**PREIGNITION**
- Identified by melted electrodes and possibly blistered insulator. Metallic deposits on insulator indicate engine damage.
- Caused by wrong type of fuel, incorrect ignition timing or advance, too hot a plug, burned valves, or engine overheating. Replace the plug.

3

Table 5    RECOMMENDED SPARK PLUGS

| Model | Bosch | Champion |
|---|---|---|
| R100S, RS; R100T, RT | W225T30 (W5D) | N6Y |
| R100/7; R90/6; R90S; | | |
| R75/5, /6, /7 | W200T30 (W6D) | N7Y |
| R50/5; R60/5, /6, /7 | W225T30 (W5D) | N7Y |
| R80/7 | W175T30 (W7D) | N9Y |

*NOTE: Higher number in Bosch spark plugs indicates a colder heat range. Higher number in Champion spark plugs indicates a hotter heat range.

## Gapping and Installation

1.  Referring to **Figure 10**, adjust the spark plug gap to 0.7 mm (0.028 in.). If the engine is hard to start when it is cold, close the plug gap to 0.6 mm (0.024 in.).

> *NOTE*
> *Vary the gap by bending only the outside electrode. The gap is correct when the gauge slips through with a slight amount of drag.*

2.  Use new gaskets and screw the plugs back into the cylinder heads, turning the socket by hand until the plugs are seated. Then tighten 1/2 to 3/4 of a turn more.

> *CAUTION*
> *Overtightening can change the gap, damage the threads and make the plug hard to remove the next time. If new plugs are being installed in a warm engine, allow time for the plugs to reach engine temperature before tightening.*

## BREAKER POINTS

### Inspection

1. Disconnect the battery ground cable to protect the ignition from a dead short during cover removal and inspection.
2. Remove the front engine cover. Three Allen bolts hold the cover in place (**Figure 11**).
3. Insert a 6 mm Allen wrench into the front of the alternator rotor bolt and rotate the engine clockwise until the points are fully open (**Figure 12**).

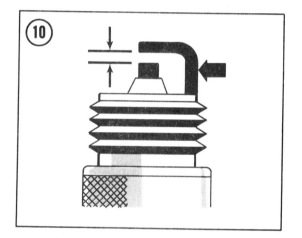

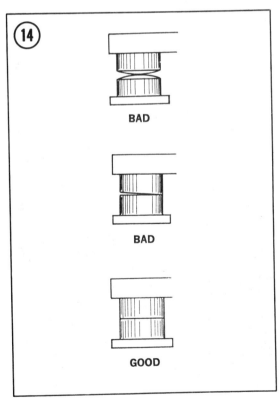

*CAUTION*
*Do not attempt to rotate the engine by turning the nut that holds the advance mechanism in place (Figure 13). The camshaft can be easily damaged.*

**Figure 14** shows what to look for. Replace the points if they are severely pitted or worn.

Gray discoloration is normal. Dress the contact surfaces with a point file. Never use sandpaper or emery cloth—they tend to round the edges of the contacts, creating a condition that is much like extreme wear.

Blow away the residue and then clean the contacts with a chemical contact cleaner or a piece of unwaxed, stiff paper, such as a clean business card. Make certain the contact surfaces are absolutely clean. Even oil from a fingerprint can affect performance.

If the condition of the points is good enough for them to be reused, skip the next section outlining replacement.

**Replacement**

*NOTE*
*The condenser should be routinely replaced with the points. Parts are usually sold in sets.*

1. Unscrew the hex nut from the advance unit and remove the unit (**Figure 15**).

2. Remove the slotted screw, disconnect the condenser wire and remove the point plate (**Figure 16**).

3. Apply a small amount of distributor cam grease to the felt pad that rubs against the distributor cam and grease the advance unit shaft (**Figure 17**).

4. Install the new points, making sure the brass axle for the breaker cam is located in the correct hole in the mounting plate (**Figure 18**).

5. Before installing the advance mechanism, check to see that it moves freely and that the springs return it quickly. Slip the unit into place, aligning the flat in the opening with the flat on the shaft (**Figure 19**). Install the nut and lockwasher.

*CAUTION*
*Do not overtighten the nut; the cam is easily snapped and very expensive to replace.*

**Adjusting the Gap**

1. Insert a 6 mm Allen wrench into the front of the alternator rotor bolt and rotate the engine clockwise until the points are fully open (**Figure 20**).

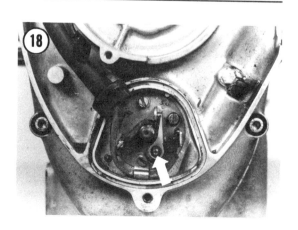

*CAUTION*
*Do not attempt to rotate the engine by turning the nut that holds the advance mechanism in place (Figure 21).*

2. Loosen the lock screw on the stationary point plate (**Figure 22**).
3. Place the blade of a screwdriver between the two small pins on the mounting plate and apply pressure to the breaker plate (**Figure 23**) until gap is between 0.35-0.40 mm (0.014-0.016 in.).
4. Tighten the lock screw and recheck the gap. If it changed when the lock screw was tightened, reset it as just described.

*NOTE*
*If the engine is to be timed, do not install the front engine cover.*

## IGNITION TIMING

There are two ways to time the engine—the static method and the more precise method using a stroboscopic light.

The static method requires something that can signal when an electric circuit is opened and closed. This can be a buzz box, an ohmmeter or a continuity light. The latter is the easiest to use.

A light can be made at home from a bulb, a socket to hold it and two wires with alligator clips at the ends attached to the socket.

### Static Timing

1. Connect one lead of the light or buzz box to the condenser and the other lead to ground (**Figure 24**). Turn the ignition on.
2. With the spark plugs removed from the cylinders, rotate the crankshaft until the "S" mark on the flywheel lines up with the reference mark on the inspection hole on the left side of the engine (**Figure 25**). This is the basic timing.

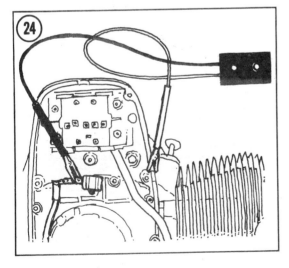

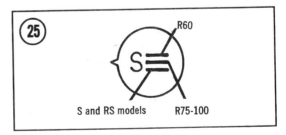

S and RS models    R75-100

*CAUTION*
*Rotate the crankshaft with a 6 mm Allen wrench inserted into the bolt in the alternator rotor; do not turn the engine over with the nut that holds the advance unit in place.*

*NOTE*
*Although probably not intended by the factory, the three marks adjacent to the "S" indicate optimum timing for different models. The top mark should be used for R60 models, the middle one for R65 to R100 models and the bottom one for sport models.*

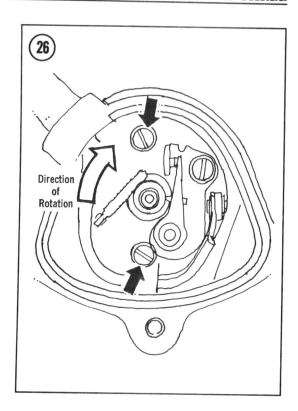

3. If the basic timing is correct, the timing light will light or the buzz box will sound. Rotate the crankshaft slightly in both directions past the mark. Each time the "S" passes the mark the lamp should light or the buzzer sound.

4. If the light does not flash each time the "S" passes the mark, loosen the two screws that hold the point plate (**Figure 26**) and turn the plate clockwise for retard or counterclockwise for advance. Then tighten the two screws.

5. Recheck the point gap and reset it if necessary, as described above. If the gap is incorrect, accurate timing may be impossible to achieve.

**Stroboscopic Timing**

Strobe timing lights are also commonly available. Beware of inexpensive ones because they usually are not bright enough.

1. Connect the timing light according to the instructions that are included with it. Connect cables (d) and (e) between the spark plug (a) and the high-tension lead (b). See **Figure 27**.

2. Start the engine and let it idle between 500 and 750 rpm.

3. Hold the timing light in front of the inspection hole (**Figure 28**) perpendicular to the rotational axis of the engine. At idle, the appropriate "S" mark should appear in line with the reference mark in the inspection hole (**Figure 29**). If the "S" appears below the reference mark, the timing is too retarded (**Figure 30**).

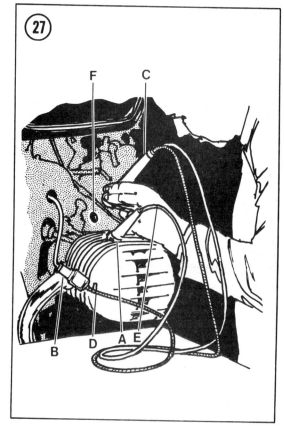

*NOTE*
*The top mark adjacent to the "S" is for R60 models. The middle mark is for R75 to R100/7 models. The bottom mark is for sport models.*

4. Increase engine speed to about 1,200 rpm. The "S" should disappear upward.

5. Increase engine speed to about 2,600 rpm. The "F" mark on the flywheel should appear in the inspection hole and line up with the reference mark. When this occurs, it indicates that ignition is in the fully advanced position.

*NOTE*
*When the ignition timing is correct, the strobe flash will move up and down as engine speed is increased and decreased. If this doesn't happen, the automatic advance unit may not be working. Check the advance mechanism for free movement of the governor weights and*

*for excessive side play of the mechanism on the shaft. If the side play is excessive, if the governor weights do not move freely or if the advance springs do not easily return the governor weights from the outer position, the advance mechanism should be replaced. The longitudinal play of the breaker cam should be between 0.2 and 0.6 mm (0.008 and 0.024 in.), and it should rotate easily.*

*Also, if the "S" mark lines up at idle but the "F" mark will not line up when the ignition is fully advanced, the advance unit is probably worn and should be replaced. If the condition cannot be corrected with a new unit or one that is known to be good, the timing should be adjusted in favor of the "F" mark.*

*If a split image appears (Figure 31), the cam lobes on the advance unit are not 180° apart or the cam is bent, although the latter is very rare. This condition can be corrected by honing away the most advanced lobe with a fine stone until it matches the other lobe.*

The timing difference between the cylinders must be within +/-2°. If it is not, check the cone seat of the advance mechanism for roughness. If roughness exists, it can be removed with pumice grinding paste. The maximum allowable out-of-round cone is 0.02 mm (0.0007 in.) as determined with an inside micrometer. If the tolerance is excessive, replace the advance mechanism.

## AIR CLEANER

A properly functioning air cleaner filter is essential to engine efficiency, long life and good gas mileage. The filter should be cleaned every 4,000 miles under normal conditions and more frequently if the motorcycle is operated under

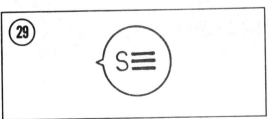

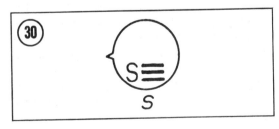

dusty conditions. The filter should be changed every 8,000 miles—more frequently under dusty conditions.

1. Loosen the three hose clamps on the left air intake tube (**Figure 32**), pull off the rubber hose and remove the tube.

2. Remove the screw from the housing (**Figure 33**), depress the kickstarter (if fitted) and tie it to the footrest. Remove the housing.

3. Remove the filter element (**Figure 34**). Tap it lightly and blow through it to dislodge dirt and dust.

> *CAUTION*
> *Do not use high-pressure compressed air to blow dust from the filter.*

4. Reinstall the filter in the housing, install the cover and reconnect the left carburetor tube and hoses.

## FUEL DELIVERY

The fuel tap that controls the flow of fuel to the carburetors is shown in **Figure 35**. It is important that the filter screen be periodically cleaned. The carburetor float bowls should also be inspected during this procedure.

1. Make sure there is gas in the tank, then turn off the fuel valve.

2. Disconnect the fuel lines at the carburetors and put the ends of the lines in a can to catch the fuel.

3. Turn the fuel tap on. Fuel should flow into the can.

4. Turn the tap to the RESERVE position. Fuel should flow.

5. Turn the tap to the OFF position. Fuel should cease to flow.

> *NOTE*
> *If fuel does not flow at ON or RESERVE positions, check the lines for kinks. If fuel flows with the tap in the OFF position, the valve packing is defective.*

6. Reattach the hoses to the carburetors. Make sure the fuel tap is OFF.

7. Hold the 24 mm nut at the top of the valve with a wrench and unscrew the 24 mm nut beneath the valve.

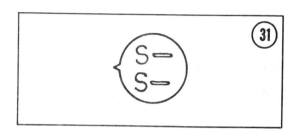

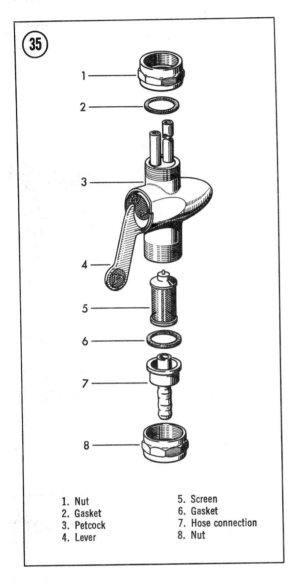

1. Nut
2. Gasket
3. Petcock
4. Lever
5. Screen
6. Gasket
7. Hose connection
8. Nut

Adjuster screw
Jamb nut

3

## CARBURETOR

To properly clean and service the carburetors they must be removed from the engine and disassembled. Refer to Chapter Six.

### Adjustment—Slide Carburetors

*CAUTION*
*Do not allow the engine to idle for extended periods of time during the adjustment. The lack of air flow over the engine may lead to engine overheating.*

1. Warm up the engine to normal operating temperature, then shut it off.
2. Turn the throttle grip to the idle position and check the free play in each throttle cable by pulling lightly on each outer cable. Each cable should have approximately 1 mm (1/32 in.) of free play. If free play is insufficient, loosen the jam nut (**Figure 36**) and rotate the adjuster screw until the required free play is achieved. Tighten the jam nut.

*CAUTION*
*In the next step, turn in the idle mixture screw carefully until it just bottoms. If the screw is tightened too much, the screw will be damaged and proper carburetor adjustment will be impossible.*

*CAUTION*
*The fuel tap threads into the top nut with a left-hand thread. Should you have need to remove the fuel tap from the tank, first make sure the tank is empty and then unscrew tap clockwise.*

8. Remove the filter and clean it thoroughly in gasoline. Also clean and inspect gasket. If it is damaged or excessively compressed, replace it.
9. Reinstall the strainer, gasket and lower T-fitting, and carefully tighten.
10. Reinstall the lower unit in the fuel tap and tighten carefully.
11. Reattach the carburetor hoses to the ends of the T-fitting.

3. Loosen the locknut (if so equipped) securing each idle mixture screw and turn each screw in until it just bottoms, then back it out 1 1/2 turns as a preliminary adjustment (A, **Figure 37**).

4. Start the engine and adjust each throttle stop screw (B, **Figure 37**) an equal amount until the engine idle speed is 1,000-1,200 rpm.

5. Each idle mixture screw must be adjusted individually with the engine running on only one cylinder. To determine the response to the adjustment, remove the spark plug lead from the cylinder *opposite* the carburetor being adjusted.

6. Remove the left-hand spark plug lead and start the engine. Rotate the idle mixture screw (A, **Figure 37**) on the right-hand carburetor clockwise until the engine begins to run roughly. Slowly back out the mixture screw (counterclockwise). The engine will run more smoothly. Contine backing the mixture screw out until the engine runs roughly again. Note the number of turns on the screw between each rough-running condition. The optimum adjustment point is approximately halfway between the rich and lean running conditions. For example, if the extremes occur two turns apart, turn the idle mixture screw one turn from either extreme. This procedure requires patience and close attention to the sound of the engine. Always allow a few seconds between each turn of the adjustment screw for the engine to respond properly. Stop the engine and carefully tighten the locknut securing the idle mixture screw, on models so equipped. Ensure that the screw is not allowed to turn once the proper adjustment is achieved.

7. Install the left-hand spark plug lead and remove the right-hand spark plug lead. Adjust the idle mixture screw on the left-hand carburetor as outlined in Step 6.

8. Stop the engine and install the right-hand spark plug lead. Start the engine and carefully adjust each throttle stop screw (B, **Figure 37**) an equal amount until an idle speed of 500-750 rpm is achieved.

9. Ensure that both spark plug leads are installed correctly and both idle mixture screw locknuts (if used) are tight.

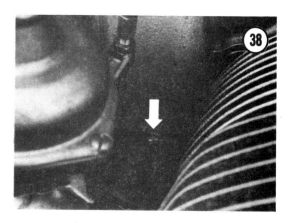

### Adjustment—Constant Vacuum Carburetors

1. Adjust the throttle cables so there is 4 mm (0.16 in.) free play of the cable sheath at the carburetor with the throttle grip closed. This preliminary setting ensures that the cable adjustment will not affect the idling adjustment of the carburetors.

2. Adjust the free play of the choke cables to 4 mm (0.16 in.).

3. Turn the butterfly stop screws in until they contact the butterflies. Then turn them in one additional turn. See **Figure 38**.

4. Turn the idle mixture screws in all the way and then turn them out one full turn. This is only a preliminary setting. Start the engine and warm it up to operating temperature.

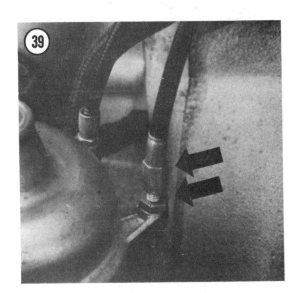

engine. Adjust the idle mixture screw on the *left* carburetor until the engine is running at 1,000 rpm.

7. Stop the engine and install the right-hand spark plug lead. Start the engine and carefully adjust each butterfly stop screw an equal amount until an idle speed of 600-800 rpm is achieved.

> *CAUTION*
> *Never allow the engine to idle for more than 10 minutes when cold or 1 minute when warm; it may overheat since there is no air flow for cooling.*

8. Adjust the choke cables so that when the choke arm is all the way down there is 0.5-1.0 mm (0.02-0.04 in.) free play in the cables. Adjust the throttle cables so there is 0.5-1.0 mm (0.02-0.04 in.) of free play (**Figure 39**).

9. When the idle has been correctly set and the cables adjusted, check the transition from idle to load by turning the throttle. Engine speed should increase proportionately. Check the cylinders individually by removing the opposite high-tension lead. Take care not to allow the disconnected lead to arc to the cylinder head and damage the finish. If the cylinders do not operate evenly, adjust the throttle cable on the slower cylinder for less free play.

> *NOTE*
> *When both carburetors have been adjusted, check your work by pulling and replacing one high-tension lead and then the other. The drop in idling speed should be the same for each cylinder. If it is not, readjust the cable adjuster on the slower cylinder until the speed of that cylinder corresponds to the other.*

## CLUTCH

If the clutch slips when engaged or if the motorcycle creeps forward when in gear, even with the clutch disengaged, the free play on the clutch control is out of adjustment.

1. To adjust, move the throw-out lever (located on the gearbox) forward by hand. See **Figure 40**. An increase in pressure should be felt when lever has moved about 2 mm (0.08 in). This is the clutch free play.

> *CAUTION*
> *Turn the screws in carefully and stop turning when you feel them seat. Turning the screws farther will bend them.*

5. Turn the idling mixture screws in or out evenly until the best engine idle speed is felt. This will be when the engine runs the fastest.

6. Remove the left-hand spark plug lead and start the engine. Rotate the butterfly stop screw on the *right* carburetor until the engine is running at 1,000 rpm. Stop the engine and install the left-hand spark plug lead. Remove the right-hand spark plug lead and start the

*NOTE*
*The clutch throw-out lever should be 90°*
*to the cable when the clutch is fully*
*engaged (Figure 41).*

2. If the free play is less than that specified above, loosen the knurled locknut at the handlever end of the cable and turn the cable adjuster in (clockwise) until the end play is correct. Retighten the knurled locknut.
3. If the free play is greater than that specified above, turn the cable adjuster out (counterclockwise) until the end play is correct and retighten the knurled locknut.

*NOTE*
*If correct free play cannot be obtained*
*with the above procedure, proceed as*
*follows:*

4. Turn the handlever adjuster all the way in.
5. Undo the locknut on the adjuster bolt in the end of the throw-out lever and screw the adjuster bolt in or out until the clearance at the handlever is approximately 2 mm (0.08 in.).
6. Tighten the locknut on the adjuster bolt.
7. Recheck the free play at the handlever and turn the adjuster screw out, if necessary, until it is correct. Then retighten the knurled locknut on the handlever.

## BATTERY

The battery is the heart of the electrical system. It should be checked and serviced regularly. The majority of electrical system troubles can be attributed to neglect of this vital component. Complete service, including charging, is presented in Chapter Seven.

*CAUTION*
*Do not spill battery electrolyte on*
*painted or polished surfaces. The liquid*
*is highly corrosive and will damage the*
*finish.*

Remove the inspection/fill plugs from the top of the battery and visually check the level of the electrolyte. It should be up to the bottom of the fill pipes. If the level is not correct, add distilled water.

*CAUTION*
*Add only distilled water; do not add*
*electrolyte.*

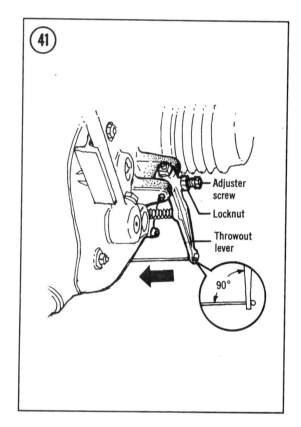

Inspect the battery terminals for condition and tightness. Flush off any oxidation with a solution of baking soda and water to neutralize the acid in the electrolyte. Lightly coat the terminals with Vaseline or a silicone grease to retard corrosion.

## FRONT FORKS

### Damping Oil

The damping oil in the front forks should be changed every 8,000 miles, at least once a year or at any time excessive bouncing of the front end indicates a low oil level. There is no practical way of checking and correcting the oil level; each fork leg must contain exactly 280 cc (0.6 pints) of damping oil if the front suspension is to operate correctly. The factory recommends the use of Shell 4000 shock absorber oil, BP Olex HL 2463 or a specially compounded 5W shock oil such as Belray.

If the front suspension continues to bounce or "hobby-horse" after the oil has been changed, major service may be required as described later in this manual.

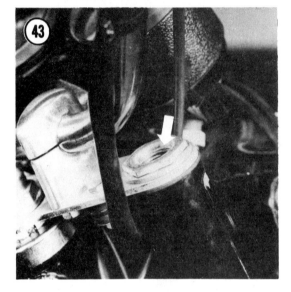

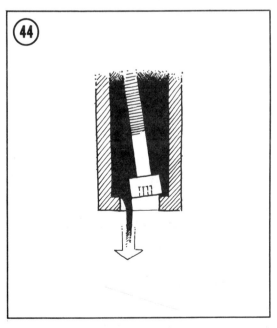

3

*NOTE*
*The filling capacity of the fork legs after*
*they have been disassembled is 280 cc.*
*For refilling the legs during oil change,*
*265 cc of oil should be poured into each*
*leg.*

1. Place the motorcycle on the centerstand to extend the fork legs. Remove the rubber cap from the bottom of each fork leg.
2. Place a drip pan beneath one of the fork legs. Hold the 4 mm Allen bolt to prevent it from turning and unscrew the 13 mm nut (**Figure 42**).
3. Unscrew the fill plug from the top of the fork leg with the pin wrench provided in the motorcycle tool kit (**Figure 43**). Push up on the Allen bolt and offset it so the oil will drain freely (**Figure 44**). Allow several minutes for the fork leg to drain and then drain the opposite leg in the same manner.
4. Reinstall the drain plugs and the rubber caps in the bottom of the fork legs.
5. Fill each fork leg with 265 cc of a recommended fork oil. Install the fill plugs and tighten them securely.

## FINAL DRIVE

The oil level in the final drive should be checked at each oil change. The oil level should be up to the bottom of the threads in the fill-plug opening with the motorcycle on the centerstand. See **Figure 45**.

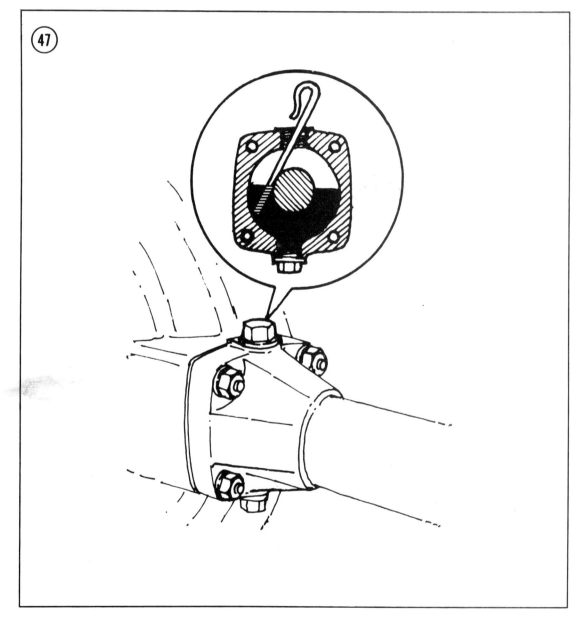

The final drive oil should be changed every 5,000 miles. Unscrew the drain plug (**Figure 46**) and allow at least 15 minutes for the oil to drain. Then screw in and tighten the plug and fill the final drive with 250 cc (0.44 Imp. pint or 0.53 US pint) of SAE 90 hypoid gear oil.

*NOTE*
*Before draining the final drive oil, ride the motorcycle for several miles to warm up the drive and oil so that it will drain freely.*

## DRIVE SHAFT

The drive shaft housing is a sealed unit. A locally fabricated dipstick can be used as shown in **Figure 47** to check if oil is present in the housing. However, to ensure an accurate quantity the oil should be changed. It is recommended that the gear oil be changed at least every 5,000 miles (8,000 km).

1. Drive the motorcycle until the gear oil is at normal operating temperature.

2. Place the motorcycle on the centerstand and position a drain pan beneath the final drive unit.

3. Remove the filler plug (**Figure 48**) and the drain plug (**Figure 49**). Allow several minutes for the oil to drain completely. Install and tighten the drain plug.

4. Add the specified amount of SAE 90 gear oil to the drive shaft housing (**Table 3**). Install and tighten the filler plug.

NOTE: If you own a 1979 or later model, first check the Supplement at the back of the book for any new service information.

# CHAPTER FOUR

# ENGINE

Upper end overhaul can be performed with the engine in the motorcycle, as can connecting rod bearing replacement. Camshaft and crankshaft service require removal of the engine. Upper end disassembly prior to engine removal makes removal easier in that overall weight of the engine is greatly reduced. Also, the motorcycle makes an excellent holding fixture for the engine during upper end disassembly and assembly.

## ENGINE REMOVAL

1. Drain the engine oil and remove the filter as described in Chapter Three.

2. Disconnect the ground lead from the battery. Remove the steering damper (**Figure 1**). Refer to Chapter Five and remove transmission.

3. Close the fuel taps and disconnect the lines.

4. Raise the seat and remove the 2 nuts from beneath the rear of the fuel tank (**Figure 2**). Pull the tank to the rear, lift up the front, and remove it.

5. Disconnect the plug-in terminals from the ignition coil, remove the high-tension leads, unscrew the mounting bolts, and remove the coils (**Figure 3**).

6. Unscrew the exhaust pipe nuts with BMW wrench No. 338/2 (**Figure 4**).

> ### CAUTION
> *The aluminum exhaust pipe nuts are easily damaged without the special tool. Do not try to improvise. The tool costs less than replacing the nuts.*

7. Remove the footrest nuts (**Figure 5**). On 1978 models, remove the gear selector linkage (**Figure 6**). Remove the bolts that attach the mufflers to the frame and loosen the pinch

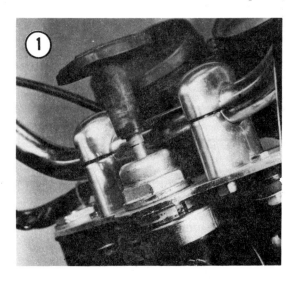

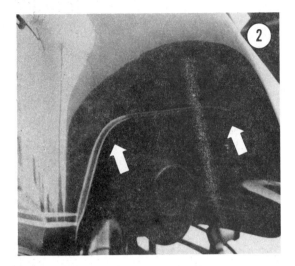

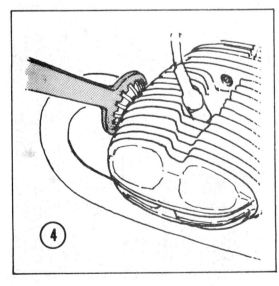

bolts that clamp the headpipes in the mufflers. Pull the mufflers off the head pipes and remove the head pipes and cross-over pipe as an assembly.

8. Disconnect the choke and throttle cables from the carburetors. Loosen the hose clamps on the air intake pipes and remove the pipes (**Figure 7**). Loosen the carburetor manifold clamp rings and remove the carburetors.

9. Remove the through bolt from the left side of the air filter housing **(Figure 8)**, remove the housing, and remove the filter.

10. Remove the bolts from the top engine cover and remove the cover **(Figure 9)**.

11. Disconnect the starter cable **(Figure 10)**.

12. Remove the front engine cover **(Figure 11)**.

13. Unplug the wires from the alternator **(Figure 12)**. Unscrew the tachometer drive lock bolt and disconnect the tachometer cable.

14. Disconnect the leads from the diode board **(Figure 13)**.

15. Disconnect the high-tension leads from the spark plugs and unplug the wire from the oil pressure sender **(Figure 14)**.

16. Disconnect the return springs from the center and side stands.

17. Remove the nuts located inboard of the larger fins on the heads **(Figure 15)**. Unscrew the cap nuts from the center of the rocker covers **(Figure 16)**. Place a drip pan beneath the rocker covers and remove them. Unscrew the spark plugs from the heads.

4

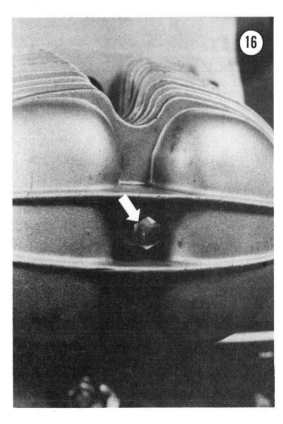

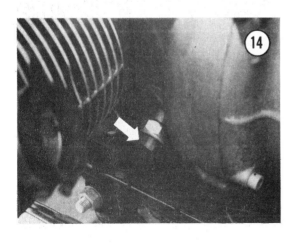

18. Unscrew the bolts from the rocker shaft supports (**Figure 17**). Remove the supports, the rockers, and the pushrods.

19. Remove the two 14mm nuts from each of the heads (**Figure 18**). Tap around the bottom fin of the head with a soft-face mallet and pull off the head.

CAUTION<br>*The fins are easily bent or broken. Be very careful.*

20. Tap around the base of each cylinder and pull them off, taking care not to allow the piston and rod assemblies to drop and hit the case.

21. Remove the snap rings from the pistons (**Figure 19**). Push out the pin with a pin extractor or a drift. It may be necessary to heat the pistons with a small torch to free the pins.

22. Hold the connecting rods in place with large rubber bands (**Figure 20**).

23. Unscrew the nuts from the front engine mounting through bolt (**Figure 21**). Tap out the rear through bolt. Tilt the engine forward and tape shop rags over the frame tubes to protect frame during engine removal and installation.

24. Tap out the front through bolt. With assistance, lift the engine, tilt it slightly to the left and down, and remove it to the left side.

NOTE: *If the engine is equipped with a large capacity sump, the sump must first be removed to provide working clearance.*

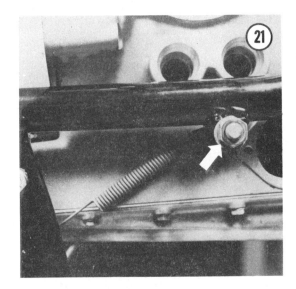

## ENGINE INSTALLATION

Engine installation should be accomplished by reversing the removal instructions. There are some additional points that will make installation easier.

1. Refer to **Figures 22 and 23** for the location of the spacers and spring hangers for the center and side stand return springs.

2. If the engine is equipped with an oversize sump, leave it off until the engine has been installed in the frame.

3. The long foot peg is on the right side.

4. When the engine has been installed, refer to *Cylinder/Piston Service* and *Cylinder Head Service* and assemble the upper end. Refer to Chapter Three and service and tune the engine.

## CYLINDER HEAD SERVICE

### Disassembly

Cylinder head service can be performed with the engine in the motorcycle. Refer to *Engine Removal* and carry out the following steps.

1. Disconnect the battery ground lead.

2. Remove the carburetors.

3. Remove the exhaust system.

4. Remove the cylinder heads.

5. Compress the valve springs and remove the valve keepers with a small magnet. Remove the top cap, springs, and the bottom cap. Remove the valves.

### Inspection

1. Check the cylinder head for cracks and for smoothness along the sealing surface. Clean carbon deposits from the combustion chamber with a soft wire brush. If possible, the combustion chamber should be bead blasted to remove carbon.

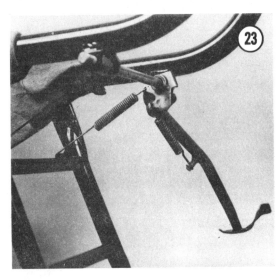

> CAUTION
> *Do not scrape carbon from the head. Hard, sharp-edge tools will scar the aluminum surfaces of the combustion chamber and create burrs which will cause hot spots during engine operation.*

2. In turn, install each valve in its guide and check the stem-to-guide clearance in two direc-

tions, 90 degrees apart (**Figure 24**). Attempt to rock the valve back and forth and observe the movement indicated by the dial. If the clearance is greater than specified in **Tables 1 and 2,** the valve and the guide should be replaced as a set. See *Valve Guide Replacement* following *Inspection.*

3. Measure the width of the contact surface on the valve head (**Figure 25**). If it is greater than the width specified in **Table 3,** replace the valve and the guide as a set.

4. Check the edge of the valve for burning and replace it if it is less than perfect.

5. Measure the vertical runout of the valve face with a dial indicator as shown in **Figure 26**. If the runout is greater than 0.0025mm (0.0001 in.), replace the valve.

6. Check to see if the valve is seating correctly in the head. Coat the contact surface of the valve and the seat with Prussian blue. Rotate the valve against the seat with moderate pressure, using a valve lapping stick. Remove the valve and inspect the seat and the valve. The contact pattern should be uniform on both the valve and the seat. If it is not, the head should

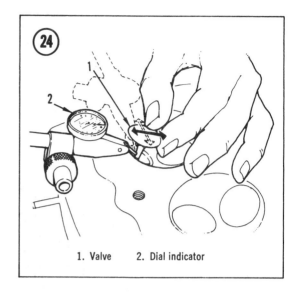

1. Valve        2. Dial indicator

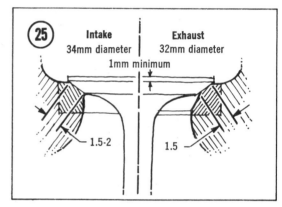

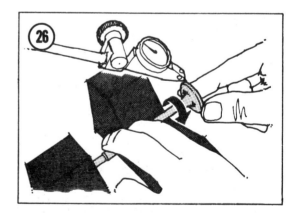

Table 1    STEM/GUIDE CLEARANCE

| Model | Clearance |
|---|---|
| R50/5 | |
| Intake | 0.10mm (0.004 in.) |
| Exhaust | 0.15mm (0.006 in.) |
| R60 | |
| Intake | 0.15mm (0.006 in.) |
| Exhaust | 0.2mm (0.008 in.) |
| R75, R90, R90S, R100 | |
| Intake | 0.15mm (0.006 in.) |
| Exhaust | 0.2mm (0.008 in.) |
| R60/7, R65/7, R75/7, R80/7, R100/7, R100S, R100RS | |
| Intake and exhaust | 0.15mm (0.006 in.) |

Table 2    VALVE GUIDE INTERNAL DIAMETER

| Model | Valve Size | Internal Diameter |
|---|---|---|
| All models | 8mm (Intake & exhaust) | 8.000 to 8.015mm (0.3152 to 0.3157 in.) |

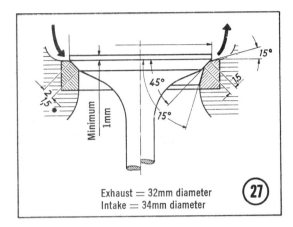

Exhaust = 32mm diameter
Intake = 34mm diameter
㉗

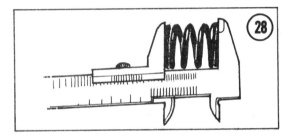

㉘

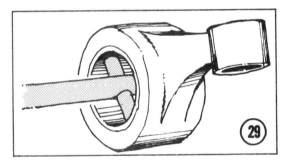

㉙

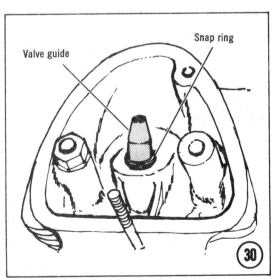

Valve guide

Snap ring

㉚

be entrusted to a dealer or automotive machine shop to have the seats ground and the valves lapped. The dimensions and angles are shown in **Figure 27** for reference.

7. Measure the free height of the valve springs with a vernier caliper (**Figure 28**). The correct free length is shown in **Table 4**. If there is doubt about the condition of the springs, have a dealer or automotive machine shop measure the installed spring force and compare it to the values shown in **Table 4**. Replace any springs that are not within specifications.

8. Measure the support area of the rocker arm shaft with an outside micrometer, and the diameter of the rocker arm bushing with an inside micrometer (**Figure 29**). If the clearance is greater than 0.047mm (0.0018 in.), the rocker and spindle should be replaced.

9. Check the rocker arms for cracks and inspect the contact surfaces for pits and galling. Replace any that are less than perfect.

**Valve Guide Replacement**

If there is excessive clearance between the valve stem and the guide, replace it as described below.

1. From the combustion chamber, tap the guide up into the head just far enough to permit removal of the snap ring (**Figure 30**).

2. Heat the cylinder head to about 400°F and tap the guide out of the head, into the combustion chamber (**Figure 31**).

CAUTION
*Do not drive out the guide through the top of the head. This will damage the valve guide bore.*

3. Install a snap ring on a new guide and press it into the head from the top while the head is still hot.

NOTE: *The guide must fit into the head with a tight interference fit — 0.023 to*

**Table 3    VALVE HEAD CONTACT SURFACE**

| Model | Contact Surface Width | |
|---|---|---|
| All models | | |
| Intake | 1.5mm | (0.0591 in.) |
| Exhaust | 2.0mm | (0.0787 in.) |

4

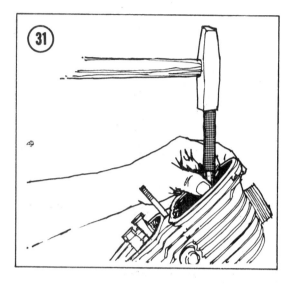

*0.061mm (0.0009 to 0.0024 in.). If this fit is not obtainable, use a 1mm oversize guide machined to the correct size.*

4. Allow the head and guide to cool, then ream the valve guide with an 8H7 reamer. The valve guide ID should be 8.000-8.015mm (0.315-0.316 in.).

**Assembly**

1. Reassemble the head in reverse order. **Figure 32** is provided for reference. After the valves, caps, springs, and keepers have been installed, rap sharply on the ends of the valve stems with a soft mallet to seat the keepers.

2. Install new head gaskets with the pushrod holes aligned **(Figure 33)**. Install the heads **(Figure 34)** and the pushrods **(Figure 35)**.

3. Install the rocker assemblies with the raised boss facing out **(Figure 36)**. Install flat washers,

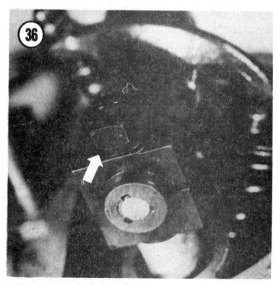

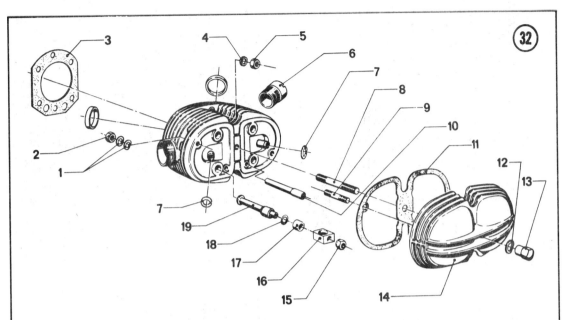

## CYLINDER AND CYLINDER HEAD — /5-6 MODELS

1. Lockwasher
2. Hex nut
3. Cylinder head gasket
4. Washer
5. Hex nut
6. Intake manifold
7. Lock ring
8. Stud
9. Stud
10. Protection tube
11. Gasket
12. Lockwasher for cap nut
13. Cap nut
14. Rocker box cover
15. Hex nut
16. Support for rocker arm shaft
17. Spacer sleeve
18. O-ring
19. Rocker arm support sleeve

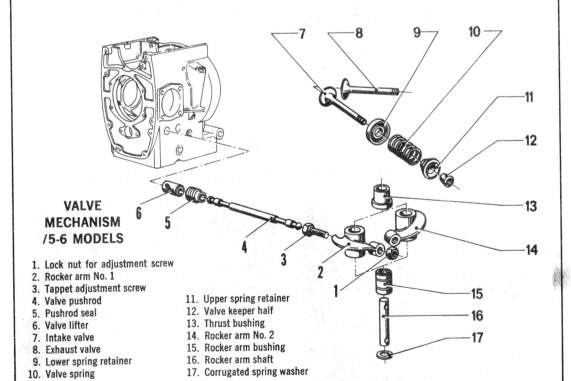

## VALVE MECHANISM /5-6 MODELS

1. Lock nut for adjustment screw
2. Rocker arm No. 1
3. Tappet adjustment screw
4. Valve pushrod
5. Pushrod seal
6. Valve lifter
7. Intake valve
8. Exhaust valve
9. Lower spring retainer
10. Valve spring
11. Upper spring retainer
12. Valve keeper half
13. Thrust bushing
14. Rocker arm No. 2
15. Rocker arm bushing
16. Rocker arm shaft
17. Corrugated spring washer

screw on the nuts, and tighten them to 10 ft.-lb. Remove all end play from the rockers and tighten the nuts to 28 ft.-lb. in a crisscross pattern. Check to make sure that the rockers contact the valve stems off-center. This is essential so that the rockers will rotate the valves.

> NOTE: *Early rocker supports can be updated by slotting them with a hacksaw (Figure 37).*

4. Screw on and tighten the top and bottom nuts (**Figure 38**).

5. Check the valve clearance. Correct valve clearance is specified in **Table 5**. First index the flywheel at OT with the cylinder being checked at TDC on the compression stroke (**Figure 39**). Loosen the locknut (**Figure 40**) and turn the adjuster screw until the clearance is correct. Then, rock the flywheel in each direction past OT and check to see if the gap increases. If it does, set the correct gap at the point where the gap is widest, without regard for the OT mark. When this is done, realign the OT mark and check the pushrod movement. It should be at least 0.025 mm (0.001 in.). In extremely cold climates the clearance should be at least 0.076 mm (0.003 in.). When adjustment is correct, rotate the crankshaft 360° to center the pushrods and recheck the clearance and correct it if necessary. Then, hold the adjuster bolt to prevent it from turning farther and tighten the locknut. Do this for all 4 rockers.

6. Continue assembly by completing the remaining disassembly steps in reverse.

## CYLINDER/PISTON SERVICE

### Disassembly

Cylinder/piston service can be performed with the engine in the motorcycle. Refer to *Engine Removal* and carry out the following steps.

1. Disconnect the battery ground lead.
2. Remove the carburetors.
3. Remove the exhaust system.
4. Remove the cylinder heads.
5. Remove the cylinders and pistons.
6. Carefully spread the ends of the piston rings and remove them from the pistons. Keep them

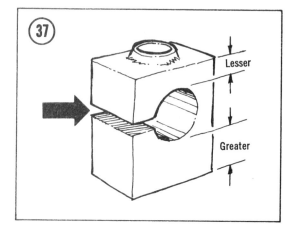

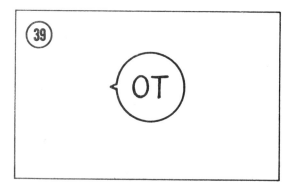

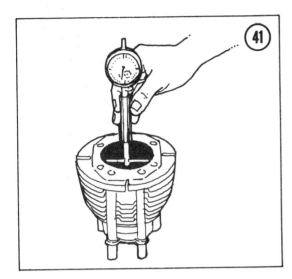

in order and do not mix rings from one piston with rings from the other.

### Inspection

1. With an inside micrometer, measure the cylinder bores at 3 points; at about 10mm (0.39 in.) from the top, at the middle, and near the bottom (**Figure 41**). Measure first in one axis, in line with the wrist pin, and then measure in a second axis, 90 degrees to the first. Two things are learned from this procedure — bore taper and out-of-roundness. If either taper or out-of-roundness exceed 0.01mm (0.0004 in.), the cylinders must be bored to the next oversize and new pistons fitted.

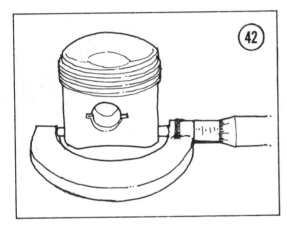

2. Measure the piston diameter at the bottom of the skirt, 90° from the wrist pin holes (**Figure 42**). Subtract the dimensions of the piston from the dimensions of the bore, at the cylinder flange. If the difference (total wear of piston and cylinder) is greater than 0.12 mm (0.0047 in.), the cylinder must be rebored to the next oversize and new pistons fitted. See **Table 6**.

NOTE: *If a rebore is called for, the new pistons must be obtained first. It's virtually impossible to manufacture all of a given size piston to the exact same dimensions. As a result, manufacturers grade their pistons to indicate size differences from normal. For example, the R50/5 engine has 3 piston sizes for just the first oversize — Grade A, 67.460mm; Grade B, 67.470mm; and Grade C, 67.480mm. If the cylinders were rebored to the normal first oversize (67.50mm) and afterward a set of Grade C first oversize pistons were purchased and installed, the clearance between the piston and the bore would be 0.02mm — noticeably less than the minimum allowable of 0.035mm.*

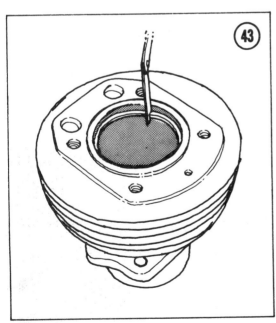

3. Carefully scrape or wire brush the carbon from the top of the piston and the ring grooves. If the grooves are damaged or worn, the piston should be replaced.

4. Measure the end gap of the rings by placing them in the cylinder, one at a time, and check them with a feeler gauge (**Figure 43**). For all engines except the R75, R90, and R100, the ring

Table 4    VALVE SPRING FREE HEIGHT

| Valve Spring | Free Length | Installed Length | Spring Force (Installed) |
|---|---|---|---|
| All models | 43.5mm (1.718 in.) | 37.6mm (1.48 in.) <br> *28.5mm (1.12 in.) | 64.0 lb. <br> 154.5 lb. |

*NOTE: For /5-6 models, spring load can also be measured at full compression.

Table 5    VALVE CLEARANCE

| | |
|---|---|
| Intake valves (rear valves) | |
| /7 models | 0.10 mm (0.004 in.) |
| All other models | 0.15 mm (0.006 in.) |
| Exhaust valves (front valves) | |
| /7 models | 0.15 mm (0.006 in.) |
| All other models | 0.20 mm (0.008 in.) |

end gap should be between 0.25 and 0.40mm (0.0098 and 0.0157 in.). End gap on the R75, R90, and R100 should be between 0.30 and 0.45mm (0.0118 and 0.0177 in.). Replace the rings as a set if the gap is greater than the maximum allowable.

5. Use a feeler gauge to measure the clearances between the rings and the ring lands (**Figure 44**). If the clearances are greater than the standard values (**Table 7**), replace the rings.

6. Measure the diameter of the piston pin, at the ends, with a micrometer. Then measure the pin bore in the piston with an inside micrometer.

The difference should be between 0.0 and 0.006mm (0.0 and 0.0002 in.). If it is not, the piston and pin should be replaced.

> NOTE: *Piston and pin sets are matched, and marked with either white or black dots. They should not be interchanged — a white pin should not be used with a black piston.*

**Reassembly**

Reassemble the piston and cylinder in reverse order of disassembly.

1. Before reinstalling the pistons on connecting rods, check to see that the piston pin is parallel to the cylinder seating surface on the crankcase. This check should be made with the engine on its side and the connecting rod in a true vertical position. Push the wrist pin into the connecting rod and place 2 equal height gauge blocks on the seating surface (**Figure 45**).

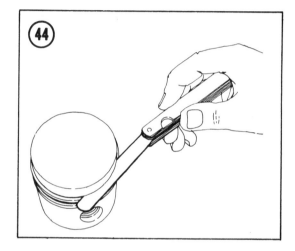

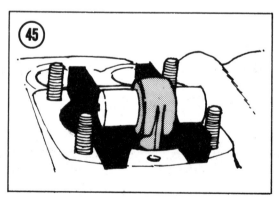

Rotate the crankshaft slowly until the wrist pin just touches the blocks. If the ends of the pins do not make contact at the same time, insert an arbor in the wrist pin hole and carefully bend the connecting rod in the direction of the high side.

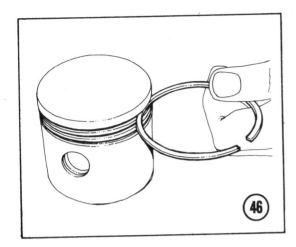

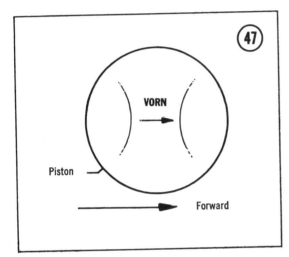

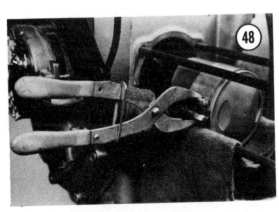

fully twist the rod in the direction opposite its present state.

3. Before installing the rings on the pistons, roll the rings in the grooves (**Figure 46**) to make sure there are no obstructions in the grooves, and that the clearances are correct.

4. Install the rings, preferably with a ring expander, making sure the manufacturer's marks are toward the top and the gaps are spaced 120 degrees apart.

5. Attach the pistons to the rods with the word VORN or the arrow pointing forward (**Figure 47**). This is important because all models have offset wrist pins.

6. Push the pins into the pistons, mating the piston to the connecting rod. It may be necessary to heat the pistons slightly.

7. Install new snap rings so that one end of the ring crosses the removal groove in the piston.

8. Before installing the cylinder, recheck to see that the ring gaps are offset by 120 degrees. Install a ring compressor (**Figure 48**) on the piston. Slip the barrel over the head of the piston and tap the barrel in place.

9. Reinstall the heads according to the instructions under *Cylinder Head Service*.

## CAMSHAFT AND CRANKSHAFT SERVICE

The camshaft and crankshaft are connected by an endless chain. As a consequence, they must be removed and installed together. The procedures that follow require a large torch — not a propane hobby torch — and several special tools. If a torch and the special tools are not available, do not attempt the job; entrust it to a dealer. The camshaft and crankshaft assemblies are shown in **Figures 49 and 50**.

### Disassembly

1. Refer to *Engine Removal* and remove the engine from the motorcycle.

2. Slowly rotate the crankshaft 360 degrees to push the tappets out of their bores (**Figure 51**) and remove them.

3. Disconnect the alternator leads (**Figure 52**). Lift the alternator brush springs, pull the brushes up in there holders, and jam them in

2. Check for twist in the connecting rod by inclining the rod to the side of the cylinder hole, and rotating the crank to bring the wrist pin in contact with the blocks. Again, if the ends of the pin do not make contact at the same time, insert an arbor in the wrist pin hole and care-

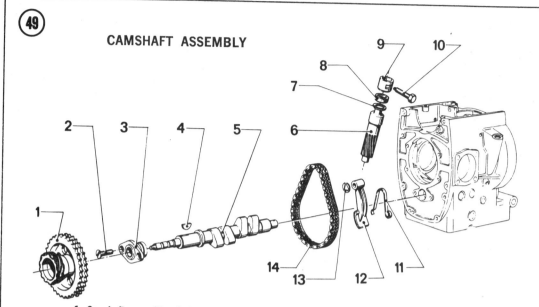

**CAMSHAFT ASSEMBLY**

1. Camshaft gear with spiral gear
   for tachometer
2. Flathead screw
3. Front camshaft bearing
4. Woodruff key
5. Camshaft with adjustable bearing
6. Drive gear for tachometer
7. Washer
8. Seal
9. Bushing for tachometer drive
10. Hex head bolt
11. Chain tension spring
12. Chain tensioner
13. Circlip
14. Timing chain

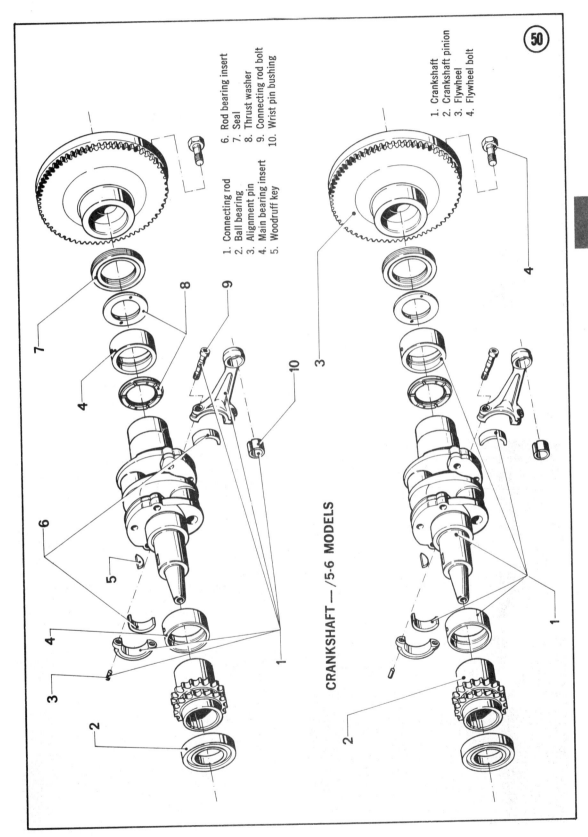

1. Connecting rod
2. Ball bearing
3. Alignment pin
4. Main bearing insert
5. Woodruff key
6. Rod bearing insert
7. Seal
8. Thrust washer
9. Connecting rod bolt
10. Wrist pin bushing

1. Crankshaft
2. Crankshaft pinion
3. Flywheel
4. Flywheel bolt

**CRANKSHAFT—/5-6 MODELS**

place with the springs. Unscrew the stator mounting bolts and remove the stator.

4. Unscrew the bolt from the center of the armature and press it off the shaft with a puller (**Figure 53**).

5. Unscrew the nut from the advance unit (**Figure 54**) and remove the unit. Unscrew the contact breaker screws (**Figure 55**) and remove the breaker assembly.

6. Unscrew the bolts from the timing cover (**Figure 56**) and remove the cover.

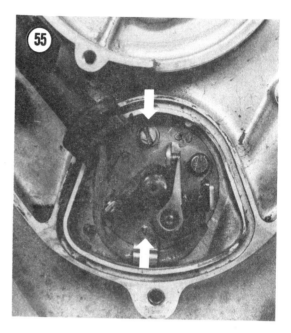

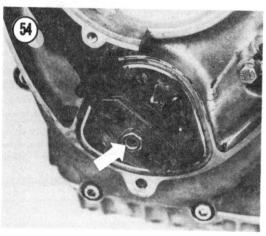

7. Remove the circlip from the cam chain tensioner pivot shaft (**Figure 57**) and remove the tensioner.

8. Unscrew the 2 camshaft bearing retainer screws located behind the camshaft (**Figure 58**).

9. Unscrew the 12-point socket-head bolts from the connecting rods (**Figure 59**) and remove the rods, caps, and bearings.

10. Install BMW puller No. 213 on the end of the crankshaft sprocket (**Figure 60**). The ears on the tool must slide over the sprocket. Tighten the puller bolt clockwise to pull off the sprocket, and at the same time pull the camshaft out of the engine.

**4**

CAUTION
*Take care not to allow the camshaft lobes to hit the case.*

NOTE: *If the crankshaft sprocket puller is not available, the chain can be broken and the camshaft and crankshaft removed individually. It is a good idea to routinely replace the chain and it is relatively inexpensive. Also, if the puller is used, it usually will damage the chain, requiring its replacement. The crankshaft sprocket can be pressed off; this is essential because the sprockets and chain must be installed together.*

11. Remove the clutch as described under *Clutch Removal/Installation.*

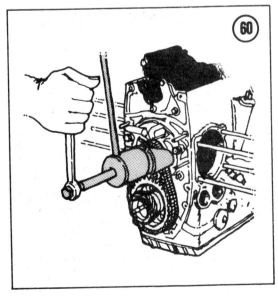

12. Install a holder like the one shown in **Figure 61** over one of the transmission mounting studs and bolt the other end to the flywheel with a clutch bolt. Unscrew the flywheel mounting bolts and remove the flywheel (**Figure 62**).

13. Unscrew the oil pump cover screws (**Figure 63**) and remove the cover. Remove the oil pump (**Figure 64**).

14. Unscrew the nuts from the front crankshaft bearing retainer (**Figure 65**). Install a puller (BMW tool No. 216) on the bearing retainer and crankshaft (**Figure 66**). Tighten the puller to remove the bearing retainer.

> NOTE: *It may be necessary to heat the case around the retainer. Take care not to heat the retainer.*

15. Rotate the crankshaft until the front counterweight is lined up with the recess at the top of the opening in the crankcase (**Figure 67**)

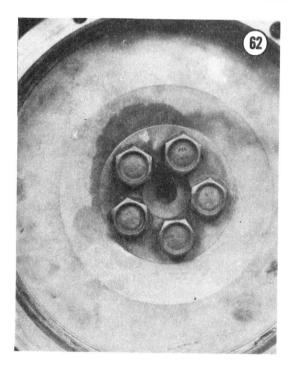

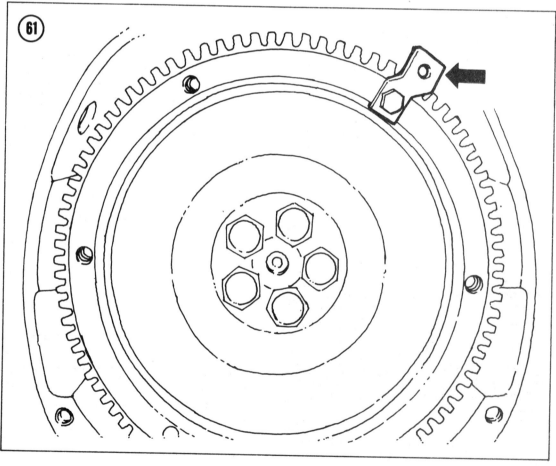

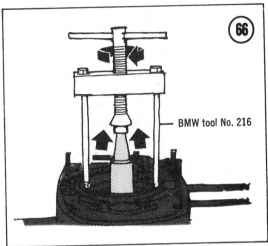

BMW tool No. 216

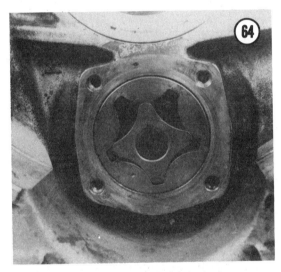

and pull out the crankshaft. On R75, R90, and R100 models turn the crankshaft until the blanking plugs in the counterweight face the starter, then tilt the front of the crankshaft down and pull it out of the crankcase (**Figure 68**).

16. Remove the thrust washers from the rear bearing bore (**Figure 69**).

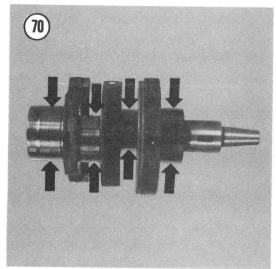

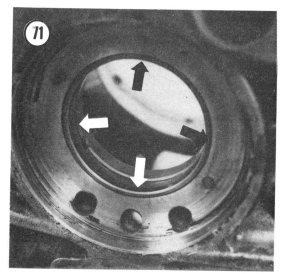

### Inspection

1. Measure the crankshaft main and connecting rod journals with a micrometer, on 2 axes, 90 degrees apart (**Figure 70**). Maximum allowable wear on the journals is 0.10mm (0.004 in.). Crankshaft journal sizes are identified by color coding. See **Table 8**.

> NOTE: *The maximum allowable runout of the front crank stub, measured with the crank supported at the main journals, is 0.02mm (0.0008 in.). If runout is greater than this value, the crank must be straightened in a press. This is a job for an expert. Also, if the wear of any or all journals exceeds the maximum al-*

*lowable of 0.10mm (0.004 in.), the crankshaft should be ground to the next undersize, and an appropriate set of new bearings installed.*

2. Measure the rear main bearing (**Figure 71**) on 2 axes, 90 degrees apart. The difference (clearance) between the journals and the bearings must be between 0.029 and 0.091mm (0.0011 and 0.0036 in.). If the clearance is not correct but the crankshaft journal is within specifications, replace bearing insert with an appropriately sized new bearing. See **Table 9**. If the journals are worn out of specification, the crankshaft must be reground to the next undersize and appropriate new bearing installed.

Table 6    OVERSIZE PISTON SIZES

| Cylinder Bore | R50/5 | R60/5 | R75/5 | | |
|---|---|---|---|---|---|
| Standard size | 67.00mm (2.638 in.) | 73.50mm (2.894 in.) | 82.00mm (3.228 in.) | | |
| First oversize | 67.50mm (2.657 in.) | 74.00mm (2.913 in.) | 82.50mm (3.248 in.) | | |
| Second oversize | 68.00mm (2.677 in.) | 74.50mm 2.933 in.) | 83.00mm (3.268 in.) | | |
| **Cylinder Bore** | **R60/6** | **R 75/6** | **R90/6, R90S** | | |
| Standard size Grade A | 73.460mm (2.892 in.) | 81.960mm (3.2268 in.) | 89.960mm (3.5417 in.) | | |
| Grade B | 73.470mm (2.893 in.) | 81.970mm 81.980mm | 89.970mm 89.980mm | | |
| | (2.893 in.) | 3.2276 in.) | 3.5425 in.) | | |
| First oversize Grade A | 73.960mm (2.912 in.) | 82.460mm (3.2465 in.) | 90.460mm 3.5614 in.) | | |
| Grade B | 73.970mm (2.9122 in.) | 82.470mm (3.2468 in.) | 90.470mm (3.5618 in.) | | |
| Grade C | 73.980mm (2.9126 in.) | 82.480mm (3.2472 in.) | 90.480mm (3.5622 in.) | | |
| Second oversize Grade A | 74.460mm (2.9315 in.) | 82.960mm (3.2661 in.) | 90.960mm (3.5811 in.) | | |
| Grade B | 74.470mm (2.9319 in.) | 82.970mm (3.2665 in.) | 90.970mm (3.5815 in.) | | |
| Grade C | 74.480mm (2.9323 in.) | 82.980mm (3.2669 in.) | 90.980 in. (3.5819 in.) | | |
| **Cylinder Bore** | **R60/7** | **R65/7** | **R75/7** | **R80/7** | **R100/7, S, RS** |
| Standard size Grade A | 73.470mm (2.893 in.) | 81.960mm (3.2268 in.) | 81.960mm (3.2268 in.) | 84.765mm (3.3372 in.) | 93.960mm (3.699 in.) |
| Grade B | 73.480mm (2.893 in.) | 81.970mm (3.2272 in.) | 81.970mm (3.2272 in.) | 84.775mm (3.3376 in.) | 93.970mm (3.6996 in.) |
| Grade C | 73.490mm (2.8933 in.) | 81.980mm (3.2276 in.) | 81.980mm (3.2276 in.) | 84.785mm (3.3380 in.) | 93.980mm (3.6970 in.) |
| First oversize Grade A | 73.970mm (2.9122 in.) | 82.210mm (3.2366 in.) | 82.460mm (3.2465 in.) | 85.015mm (3.3479 in.) | 94.210mm (3.7090 in.) |
| Grade B | 73.980mm (2.9126 in.) | 82.220mm (3.2370 in.) | 82.470mm (3.2468 in.) | 85.025mm (3.3474 in.) | 94.220mm (3.7094 in.) |
| Grade C | 73.990mm (2.9130 in.) | 82.230mm (3.2374 in.) | 82.490mm (3.2472 in.) | 85.035mm (3.3478 in.) | 94.230mm (3.7098 in.) |
| Second oversize Grade A | 74.470mm (2.9319 in.) | 82.460mm (3.2465 in.) | 82.960mm (3.2661 in.) | 85.265mm (3.3569 in.) | — |
| Grade B | 74.480mm (2.9323 in.) | 82.470mm (3.2468 in.) | 82.970mm (3.2665 in.) | 85.275mm (3.3573 in.) | — |
| Grade C | 74.490mm (2.9327 in.) | 82.490mm (3.2472 in.) | 82.980mm (3.2669 in.) | 85.285mm (3.3577 in.) | — |

4

Table 7    SIDE CLEARANCES

| Model | 1st Ring | 2nd Ring | 3rd Ring |
|---|---|---|---|
| /5, /6 Models | 0.06 to 0.07mm (0.0024 to 0.00276 in.) | 0.05 to 0.06mm (0.00197 to 0.00236 in.) | 0.03 to 0.04mm (0.0012 to 0.00157 in.) |
| /7 Models (all rings) | 0.04-0.07mm (0.0016-0.0028 in.) | | |

Table 9    MAIN BEARING MATERIAL THICKNESS

| Size | Thickness in Millimeters | | Thickness in Inches | |
|---|---|---|---|---|
| Standard | 2.5 | +0.003 −0.009 | 0.0984 | +0.0001 −0.0003 |
| First Undersize | 2.75 | +0.003 −0.009 | 0.1083 | +0.0001 −0.0003 |
| Second Undersize | 3.00 | +0.003 −0.009 | 0.1181 | +0.0001 −0.0003 |
| Third Undersize | 3.25 | +0.003 −0.009 | 0.1280 | +0.0001 −0.0003 |

3. Measure the connecting rod journals on 2 axes, 90 degrees apart. See **Table 10**.

4. Bolt the connecting rod caps to the rods, with the bearings installed, and measure the inside diameter on 2 axes, 90 degrees apart (**Figure 72**). The difference (clearance) between the journals and the bearings must be between 0.023 and 0.069mm (0.0009 and 0.0027 in.). If it is not correct, but the journal is within specifications, replace the bearing insert with an appropriately sized new one. If the journals are worn out of specification, they must be reground to the next undersize and new bearings installed. See **Table 11**.

5. Check the tightness of the wrist pin bushing in the connecting rod. It is an interference fit and the bushing should not move.

6. Check the clearance between the wrist pin bushing and the wrist pin by measuring the outside diameter of the pin and the inside diameter of the bushing (**Figure 73**). If the pin is coded white, the clearance should be between 0.015 and 0.023mm (0.0006 and 0.0009 in.). If it is

Table 8    MAIN BEARING JOURNAL DIAMETER

| /5, /6 and R90S | | | | |
|---|---|---|---|---|
| Journal | Code | Diameter in Millimeters | | Diameter in Inches |
| Standard | Red | 60.00 −0.010 / −0.020 | 2.362 | −0.00039 / −0.00078 |
| | Blue | 60.00 −0.020 / −0.029 | 2.362 | −0.00078 / −0.00114 |
| First Undersize | Red | 59.75 −0.010 / −0.020 | 2.352 | −0.00039 / −0.00078 |
| | Blue | 59.75 −0.020 / −0.029 | 2.352 | −0.00078 / −0.00114 |
| Second Undersize | Red | 59.50 −0.010 / −0.020 | 2.343 | −0.00039 / −0.00078 |
| | Blue | 59.50 −0.020 / −0.029 | 2.343 | −0.00078 / −0.00114 |
| Third Undersize | Red | 59.25 −0.010 / −0.020 | 59.25 | −0.00039 / −0.00078 |
| | Blue | 59.25 −0.020 / −0.029 | 2.333 | −0.00078 / −0.00114 |

| /7, R100S, and R100RS | | | | |
|---|---|---|---|---|
| Journal | Code | Diameter in Millimeters | | Diameter in Inches |
| Standard | Red | 60.00 −0.030 / −0.040 | 2.362 | −0.0012 / −0.0016 |
| | Blue | 60.00 −0.040 / −0.049 | 2.362 | −0.0016 / −0.0019 |
| First Undersize | Red | 59.75 −0.030 / −0.040 | 2.352 | −0.0012 / −0.0016 |
| | Blue | 59.75 −0.040 / −0.049 | 2.352 | −0.0016 / −0.0019 |
| Second Undersize | Red | 59.50 −0.030 / −0.040 | 2.343 | −0.0012 / −0.0016 |
| | Blue | 59.50 −0.040 / −0.049 | 2.343 | −0.0016 / −0.0019 |
| Third Undersize | Red | 59.25 −0.030 / −0.040 | 2.333 | −0.0012 / −0.0016 |
| | Blue | 59.25 −0.040 / −0.049 | 2.333 | −0.0016 / −0.0019 |

4

coded black, the clearance should be between 0.018 and 0.026mm (0.0007 and 0.0010 in.). If the clearance is greater than specified, the bushing must be replaced. This is a job for a skilled machinist; the old bushing must be pressed out, and a new one pressed in and machined to the correct diameter for the specified clearance.

> NOTE: *The fit of the pin to the bushing is correct when the pin can be pushed through the bushing with light thumb pressure.*

7. Install the oil pump and check the clearance between the pump cavity and the outer rotor (**Figure 74**). The clearance should be between 0.1 and 0.17 (0.0039 and 0.0067 in.).

8. With a straightedge, check the clearance between the rotors and the cover. The clearance should be 0.05mm (0.0020 in.).

9. Check clearance between inner and outer rotors (**Figure 75**). The clearance should be between 0.12 and 0.30mm (0.0047 and 0.0118 in.).

10. Check the rotors for galling or pitting. If either condition exists, or if the clearances are not to specifications, replace the rotor set.

## Replacing Main Bearings

1. Heat the engine to 180°-200°F. Install the bearing mandrel (BMW tool No. 205), making sure the 2 holes in the mandrel line up with the washer locating pins (**Figure 76**), and press out the bearing.

2. With the engine still warm, place the aluminum block of the bearing mandrel on the removal sleeve. Place the engine over the fixture so that the 2 locating pins fit into the holes in the aluminum block. Place the new bearing into the bore, with bearing joint positioned 90 degrees to the right of top center. The holes in the bearing should be exactly vertical.

3. Put the fiber-bushed installation mandrel into the bearing, making sure the recesses in the mandrel are lined up with the locating pins (**Figure 77**), and press the bearing into the bore.

4. Drive out the front bearing locating pin, from the inside, with a drift (**Figure 78**).

5. Heat the bearing retainer (180°-200°F), place it on the fixture, and press it out with the removal mandrel.

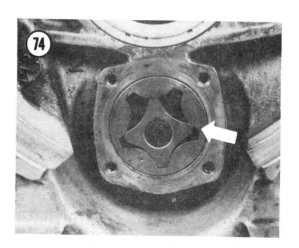

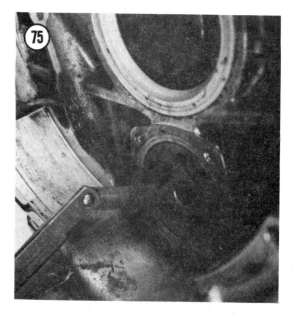

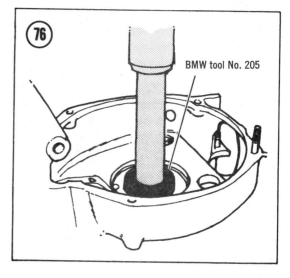

BMW tool No. 205

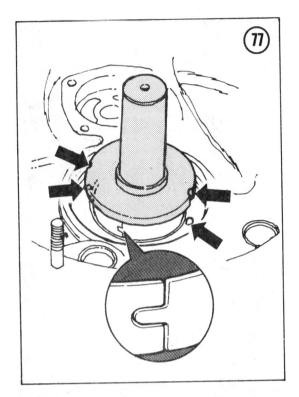

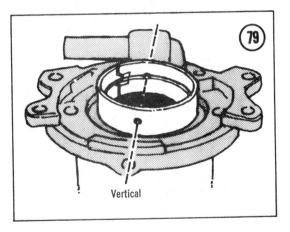

Vertical

6. With the retainer still warm, start the new bearing into the bore, with the joint positioned 26 degrees to the left of the top center, and with the oil holes positioned exactly vertical (**Figure 79**). Press the bearing into the retainer.

7. Clamp the bearing retainer in a vise, using jaw protectors, and drill two 3.15mm (0.124 in.) holes in the bearing, through the passages in the retainer. Carefully deburr the holes in the bearing.

8. Through the pin locating boss on the smaller flange of the retainer (**Figure 80**), very carefully begin to drill a hole in the bearing with a 3.825mm (0.156 in.) drill. *Do not drill completely through.* Finish the hole with a 3.750mm (0.148 in.) drill.

9. Ream the hole with a hand reamer (No. 4H8), but do not ream it completely through; this provides a blind hole for the locating pin which prevents it from going all the way through the bearing and coming in contact with the crank journal.

10. Clamp the bearing installation mandrel in the vise, slide the bearing retainer onto the mandrel, and tap the locating pin into the hole until it is 0.5 to 1.0mm (0.0197 to 0.0394 in.) below the surface of the pin boss. Then, stake the edge of the pin boss hole with a centerpunch to prevent the pin from backing out (**Figure 81**). Carefully deburr the hole in the bearing.

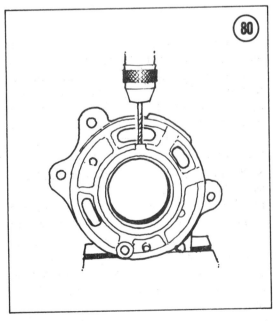

**Reassembly**

1. Install a green thrust washer on the locating pins, inside against the rear main bearing (**Figure 82**). Install a red thrust washer on the outside of the bearing. The locating pins should protrude the same distance on both sides. If they do not, heat the engine and move the pins with a drift.

2. Coat the main bearing shells with Molykote Paste G. Heat the engine housing to 180°F, turn it vertically with the front end up, and carefully install the crankshaft (**Figure 83**).

3. Install the front bearing retainer. Then install the flywheel and torque the 5 retaining bolts to 5.8 to 6.2 mkg (34.7 to 37.6 ft.-lb.).

4. Turn the engine horizontal and install a dial indicator on the clutch housing (**Figure 84**). Measure the end play of the crank by moving it forward and back. The crankshaft end play should be between 0.08 and 0.15mm (0.0031 and 0.0059 in.). If it is not, it can be corrected with a little arithmetic and the selection of a proper thrust washer (**Table 12**).

5. First remove the flywheel and measure the rear thrust washer with a micrometer.

*Example:*

| | |
|---|---|
| Actual end play | 0.18mm (0.0071 in.) |
| Desired end play | ± 0.12mm (0.0047 in.) |
| Difference | 0.06mm (0.0024 in.) |
| Add thickness of washer removed | + 2.48mm (0.0977 in.) |
| Thrust washer should be | 2.54mm (0.1000 in.) |

6. Select a thrust washer that is as close to the desired size as possible. It shouldn't be more than 0.03mm (0.0012 in.) or less than 0.04mm (0.0016 in.) of the desired thickness. Install the washer on the locating pins.

7. Install a new crankshaft rear seal. Tap it all the way home and oil it lightly.

8. Install the cam sprocket key in the crankshaft. Assemble the sprockets and chain with the reference marks on the sprockets aligned (**Figure 85**). Coat the inside bore of the crankshaft sprocket with anti-sieze lube. Set the camshaft partway into the crankcase and at the same time start the crankshaft sprocket over the

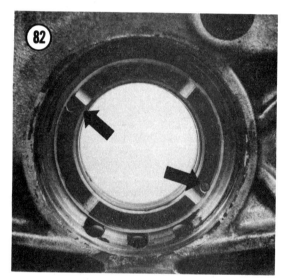

crankshaft. If necessary, rotate the crankshaft to line up the key with the keyway in the sprocket — don't disturb the relationship of the sprockets. Carefully guide the rear camshaft journal into its bore in the case. Tap the crankshaft sprocket down into place until it bottoms on the crankshaft shoulder.

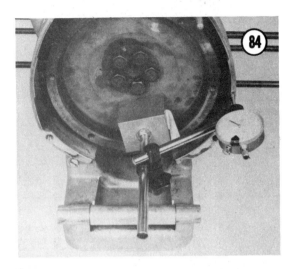

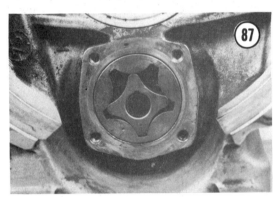

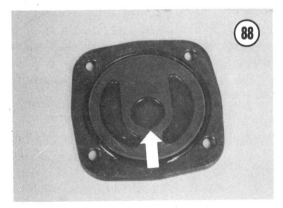

9. Heat the front bearing and install it on the crankshaft. Install the chain tensioner. Make sure the circlip is correctly seated (**Figure 86**).

10. Install the oil pump rotor Woodruff key in the end of the camshaft. Install the inner and outer rotors (**Figure 87**) with marks out.

11. Install the oil pump cover with a new O-ring. The recess in the cover (**Figure 88**) engages the shaft. This must be located at the bottom. Lightly coat the sealing surface of the cover with gasket cement. Apply a thread locking compound to the screws and screw them in and tighten them in a crisscross pattern.

Table 10    CONNECTING ROD BEARING JOURNAL DIAMETER

| Size | Diameter in Millimeters | | Diameter in Inches | |
|---|---|---|---|---|
| Standard | 48.00 | −0.009 −0.025 | 1.89 | −0.0003 −0.0009 |
| First Undersize | 47.75 | −0.009 −0.025 | 1.88 | −0.0003 −0.0009 |
| Second Undersize | 47.50 | −0.009 −0.025 | 1.87 | −0.0003 −0.0009 |
| Third Undersize | 47.25 | −0.009 −0.025 | 1.86 | −0.0003 −0.0009 |

Table 11    CONNECTING ROD BEARING MATERIAL THICKNESS

| Size | Thickness | |
|---|---|---|
| | Millimeters | Inches |
| Standard | 1.983 to 1.993 | 0.0781 to 0.0785 |
| Select-fit undersize | 1.995 to 2.005 | 0.0786 to 0.0789 |
| First undersize | 2.108 to 2.118 | 0.0830 to 0.0834 |
| Second undersize | 2.233 to 2.243 | 0.0879 to 0.0883 |
| Third undersize | 2.358 to 2.368 | 0.0928 to 0.0932 |

12. Set the crank journals at TDC. They are at TDC when they are in a horizontal plane and lined up with their respective cylinder spigot holes. The forward journal will line up with the left hole and the rear journal with the right. Line up the OT mark on the flywheel with the timing hole. If necessary, rotate the crank slightly to line up the bolt holes in the crank with those in the flywheel. Push the flywheel on. Attach the holder (**Figure 89**), screw in the bolts, and tighten them in a crisscross pattern to the value shown in **Table 13**.

CAUTION
*Take care not to push the crankshaft forward when installing the flywheel. If this occurs, the interior thrust washer is likely to drop down and out of alignment with the crankshaft. Double check to make sure the thrust washer is correctly in place.*

13. Install the clutch as described under *Clutch Removal/Installation.*

14. Install the connecting rod bearing inserts in the rods and caps so the tabs lock in the recesses in the rods and caps (**Figure 90**).

15. Coat the connecting rod bearing inserts with Molykote Paste G or preassembly lubricant. Do not use oil. Install the rods and caps with the locating pins toward the front of the engine (**Figure 91**). Tighten the bolts progressively until they are snug. Then, tighten them to 4.8-5.2 mkg (35-37 ft.-lb). After tightening the bolts, raise each rod and allow it to fall slowly under its own weight. Do this several times to ensure that the assembly lube is not interferring with the movement of the rods. If the rods will not move as indicated, disassemble them and check for burrs. Position the rods with rubber bands to prevent them from hitting the edges of the holes (**Figure 92**).

16. Install the oil pickup with a new gasket located between the pickup and the pipe. Screw in and tighten the bolts (**Figure 93**). Install the filter screen and retaining clip (**Figure 94**).

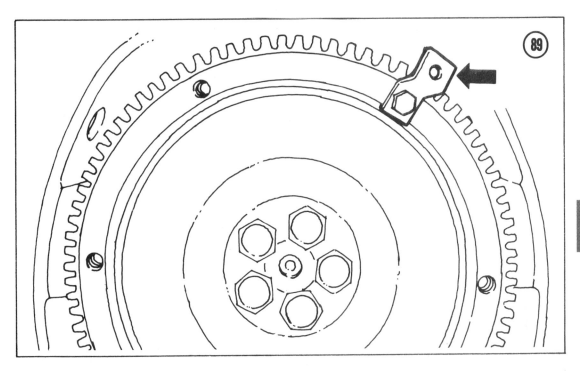

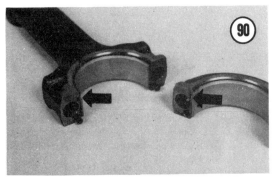

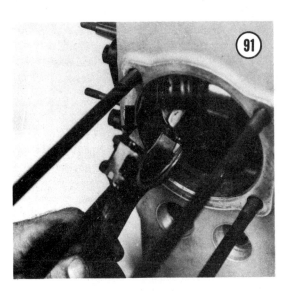

17. Coat the mating surfaces of the crankcase and oil sump with gasket cement. Install the gasket on the pan and install the pan with the drain plug at the back. Screw in and tighten the bolts in the pattern shown (**Figure 95**).

> NOTE: *If the engine is equipped with an oversize sump, do not install it until the engine has been installed in the motorcycle.*

18. Coat the sealing surface on the front of the crankcase with gasket cement. Install a new gasket and carefully line it up with the holes so the bolts will go in without having to be forced by the gasket (**Figure 96**).

19. Coat the 2 holes at the top of the case with gasket cement and install the small fiber washers (**Figure 97**). If your gasket set does not have these washers, make washers from the old gasket. They are essential for correct spacing of the front cover. Don't omit them.

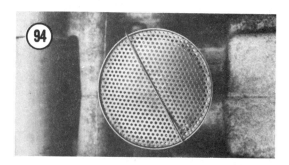

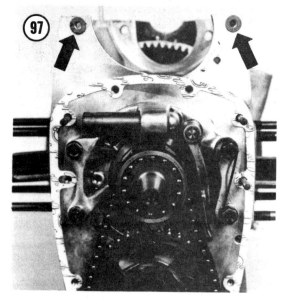

20. Install a new seal in the camshaft bore in the timing cover (**Figure 98**). Install the crankshaft seal.

21. Heat the bearing bore in the timing case so it will slide over the bearing.

22. Set the cover in place and tap it on evenly. Screw in and tighten the Allen bolts in the pattern shown (**Figure 99**). Screw on and tighten the 3 nuts.

23. Install the contact breaker plate and feed the lead through the rubber breather tube (**Figure 100**).

24. Connect the condenser leads (**Figure 101**).

25. Install the centrifugal advance assembly with the flat in the hole engaging the flat on the shaft. Screw on and tighten the nut (**Figure 102**).

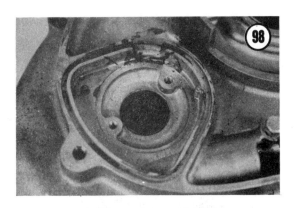

26. Install the alternator rotor. Install the flywheel holding strap and screw on and tighten the rotor bolt (**Figure 103**).

27. Install the stator, and screw in and tighten the 3 bolts (**Figure 104**). Connect the electrical leads as shown. The large plug must be installed with the ribbed face facing out. Pull the springs away from the brushes, push the brushes down and into contact with the slip rings, and release the springs.

28. Check the battery and relay terminal nuts on the starter to make sure they are tight. Connect the leads and route the primary lead under the front of the starter (**Figure 105**). Set the starter in place. Make sure the dust cover clip (**Figure 106**) is in place before installing the rear bolts. Start all bolts into their threads before tightening them. Install the dust cover.

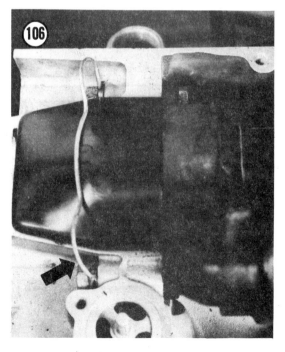

29. Install the engine breather plate (**Figure 107**), washer (**Figure 108**), spring (**Figure 109**), and circlip (**Figure 110**). Install the circlip in the appropriate groove of the post. Coat the sealing surface of the engine breather cover with non-hardening gasket cement. Install the cover with the breather pipe to the rear, and screw in and tighten the screws (**Figure 111**).

30. Refer to *Engine Installation* and install the engine in the motorcycle.

**4**

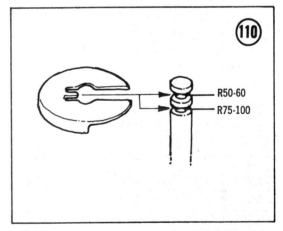

R50-60
R75-100

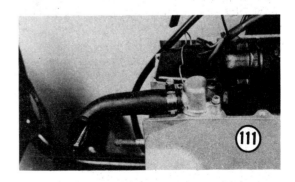

## CLUTCH AND FLYWHEEL

**Disassembly**

The clutch and flywheel can be removed with
the engine installed in the motorcycle. The
transmission must be removed as described in
Chapter Five.

1. Progressively unscrew the clutch retaining
bolts one turn at a time until the tension on the
clutch spring and pressure plate is relaxed.
Then unscrew them completely.

2. Remove the pressure ring and shims (if fitted), the disc, pressure plate, and diaphragm
spring (**Figure 112**).

> NOTE: *A simple strap holding fixture
> can be fabricated from sheet stock to
> prevent the flywheel from turning when
> the clutch bolts and flywheel bolts are
> loosened and tightened (**Figure 113**).*

3. Lock the flywheel to prevent it from turning
and unscrew the flywheel mounting bolts
(**Figure 114**). Remove the flywheel by carefully
prying on one side and then the other with
screwdrivers or tire irons inserted behind the
flywheel. Pad the bell housing with shop rags at
the pry points to prevent damage to the casting.

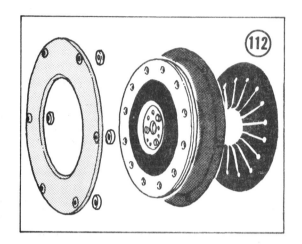

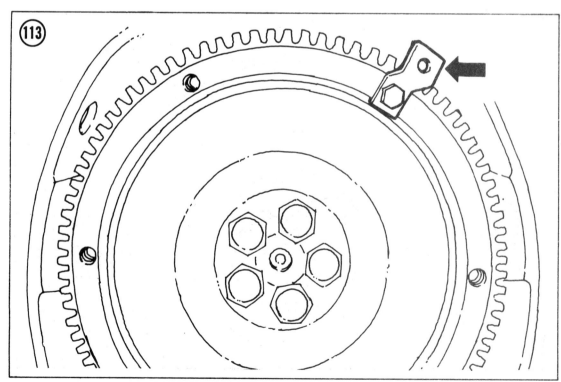

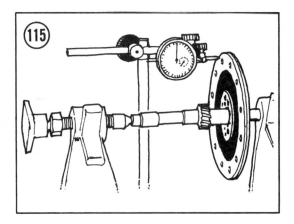

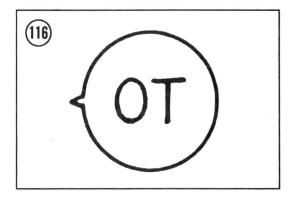

## Inspection

1. Check the thickness of the clutch lining with a micrometer. The combined thickness should be 4.5mm (0.177 in.) or greater. If not, replace the clutch disc.

2. If the lining is satisfactory on the disc, check the runout of the disc with a dial indicator (**Figure 115**). The maximum allowable runout is 0.15mm (0.006 in.). It's difficult to satisfactorily straighten the plate; instead, it should be replaced.

3. Use a straightedge to check the pressure plate for warping. If it is noticeably warped, it should be replaced.

## Assembly

1. Rotate the crankshaft to bring the pistons to TDC. Line up the OT mark on the flywheel with the fixed timing mark in the case (**Figure 116**) and install the flywheel.

2. Screw in the flywheel bolts and run them down finger-tight. Install the flywheel holding strap (**Figure 117**). Tighten the bolts in a crisscross pattern to the value shown in **Table 13**.

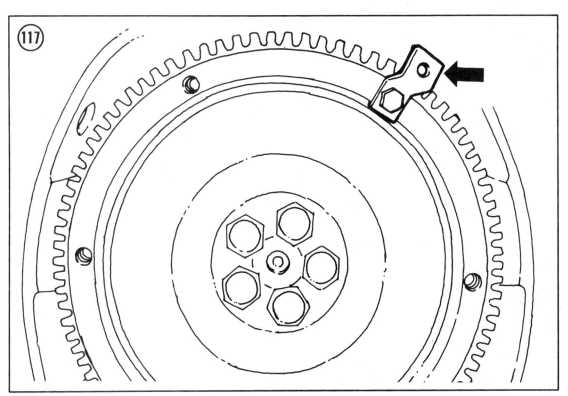

3. Check the flywheel runout, on the clutch mounting surface, with a dial indicator (**Figure 118**). Rotate the flywheel 360 degrees and observe the gauge. If the runout is greater than 0.10mm (0.0039 in.) and the flywheel is correctly seated on the crankshaft, it should be removed and turned down or straightened by a machine shop.

> NOTE: *If runout is checked with the engine in the motorcycle and the crankshaft horizontal, press forward on the crankshaft as it is rotated to take up the normal end play.*

4. Reinstall the clutch in the reverse order of disassembly, using the centering arbor (BMW tool No. 529). Tighten the clutch mounting bolts to the value shown in **Table 14**.

5. Install the transmission as described in Chapter Five and adjust the clutch as described in Chapter Three.

**Table 13     FLYWHEEL MOUNTING BOLT TORQUE**

| Model | Torque |
|---|---|
| R50/5, R60/5, R 75/5 | 5.8-6.2 mkg (42-45 ft.-lb.) |
| R60/6, R75/6 | 6.0-6.5 mkg (43-47 ft.-lb.) |
| R90/6, R90 S[1] | 7.0-7.5 mkg (51-54 ft.-lb.) |
| R60/7, R75/7, R80/7, R100/7, S, RS[2] | 1.0-1.1 mkg (72-76 ft.-lb.) |

1. Bolt head unmarked
2. Bolt head marked "K x 12.9"

**Table 14     CLUTCH MOUNTING SCREW TORQUE**

| Model | Torque |
|---|---|
| /5 Models | 1.5-2.0 mkg (11-14.5 ft.-lb.) |
| /6, /7 Models | 2.3 mkg (17 ft.-lb.) |

**Table 12     THRUST WASHER SIZES**

| Color | Millimeters | Inches |
|---|---|---|
| Red | 2.483 to 2.530 | 0.0978 to 0.0996 |
| Blue | 2.530 to 2.578 | 0.0996 to 0.1015 |
| Green | 2.578 to 2.626 | 0.1015 to 0.1034 |
| Yellow | 2.626 to 2.673 | 0.1034 to 0.1052 |

**NOTE:** If you own a 1979 or later model, first check the Supplement at the back of the book for any new service information.

# CHAPTER FIVE

# TRANSMISSION

The transmission in /5 models is a 4-speed, constant-mesh unit. The transmission in /6 and /7 models is a 5-speed, constant-mesh type. Because of differences between the two types, disassembly, inspection and assembly are covered separately under the headings *$/5$ Transmission* and *$/6$ and $/7$ Transmission*. The removal/installation procedure is the same for both types.

All of the transmission repair procedures in this chapter are within the capability of a skilled hobbyist mechanic. However, there are several special tools that are essential to any work other than removal of the transmission. These tools — the output flange holding fixture, output flange puller, and rear cover puller — will run more than $100, and it's unlikely that you would ever have use for them more than once.

As an alternative, it is suggested that rebuilding the transmission be entrusted to your dealer. Brown Motor Works in Pomona, California is accustomed to doing rebuilds by mail order and has a substantial parts inventory that ensures a quick turn-around time (usually within 48 hours from the time the transmission is received). For convenience and assurance that the transmission will be safe in shipment, plans for a simple but strong shipping frame are shown in **Figure 1**. The mailing address for Brown Motor Works is

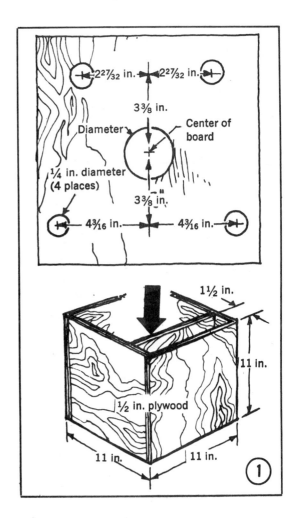

included in the suppliers list at the end of
Chapter Eleven.

## TRANSMISSION REMOVAL

1. Put the motorcycle on its center stand and
place a block beneath the frame, immediately
behind the stand, for additional support. Drain
the transmission.

2. Remove the air cleaner as described in
Chapter Three. Disconnect the choke cables at
the carburetors and hang the left half of the air
filter cover, with the choke cable attached, out
of the way. Remove the right-hand carburetor.
Unscrew the front mounting bolt from the right
half of the air filter cover. Remove the right-
hand cover half.

3. Lift the dust cover on the speedometer
cable, unscrew the retainer bolt, disconnect the
battery ground cable, and pull the speedometer
cable out of the transmission (**Figure 2**).

4. Remove the battery.

5. On 1978 models, remove the gear selector
and linkage (**Figure 3**).

6. Remove the clamp from the dust boot over
the universal joint. Place a drip pan beneath the
universal joint and push the boot back as far as
it will go. Lock the rear wheel with the brake
and unscrew the 4 bolts which attach the drive
shaft to the output flange (**Figure 4**).

> NOTE: *Use a 10mm 12-point box
> wrench for these bolts.*

7. Remove the protective caps from the swing
arm pivots, loosen the locknuts, and unscrew
the pivot bolts (**Figure 5**).

> NOTE: *The special tool provided with
> the bike to loosen the locknut is not
> strong enough. Instead, machine the
> outside of a 27mm socket so that it will
> fit inside the frame opening (**Figure 6**).*

8. Unscrew the locknut from the brake pedal
pivot bolt, then remove the pivot bolt (**Figure 7**). Disconnect the cable from the clutch
operating arm and remove the arm from the
transmission. Disconnect the lead from the
neutral indicator switch.

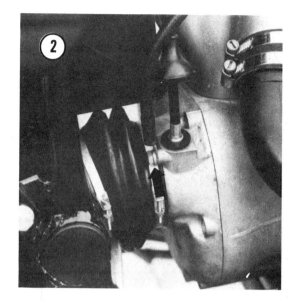

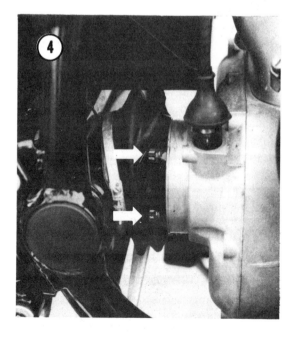

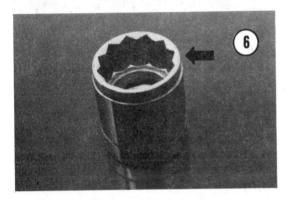

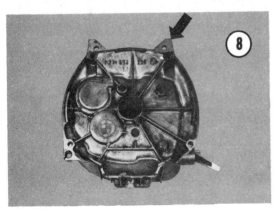

9. Unscrew the 3 remaining transmission mounting bolts (top and bottom left, bottom right). See **Figure 8**. Note the tab on the top left bolt for reference during installation.

10. Insert a wooden wedge (¾ in. square, 15 in. long) between the tire and the frame and move the swing arm back as far as it will go.

11. Carefully pull back on the transmission and remove it to the left side.

### TRANSMISSION INSTALLATION

Follow the removal steps in reverse order to install the transmission. Refer to Chapter Nine, *Final Drive Reassembly*, and reinstall the swing arm. Preload and tighten the swing arm pivot pins as described there and tighten locknut with modified socket described in the NOTE above.

Fill the transmission and drive shaft housing as described in Chapter Three. Adjust the clutch free play as described in Chapter Three.

> CAUTION
> *Do not tighten the 4 transmission mounting bolts until assembly and installation are complete. Then, start the engine and allow it to idle. Pull in on the clutch lever to align the engine, transmission, and clutch, then tighten the transmission mounting bolts in a crisscross pattern. Readjust the clutch free play as described in Chapter Three.*

### OUTPUT FLANGE SEAL REPLACEMENT

It is not necessary to completely disassemble the transmission to replace the output flange seal. Refer to *Transmission Disassembly* and carry out Steps 1 through 7. Then, proceed as follows:

1. Remove the shims from the cover and note their locations so they may be correctly installed.

2. Knock out the old seal and clean the seal bore to remove dirt, grease, and seal particles.

3. Carefully drive a new seal into the bore with the open side of the seal facing out.

4. Clean the taper on the output shaft and inside the flange with a non-petroleum-base cleaner.

5

5. Lightly grease the outer faces of the shims and install them in the cover (**Figure 9**).

6. Install the cover and tighten the screws in a crisscross pattern to 0.8-0.9 mkg (6-6.5 ft.-lb.).

7. Recheck the output shaft and flange tapers to make sure they are clean and dry. Install the flange and the flange holder (No. 234). Tighten the 24mm flange nut to 22-24 mkg (160-170 ft.-lb.).

8. Refer to *Transmission Installation* and install the transmission. Refer to Chapter Three and adjust the clutch and fill the transmission with oil.

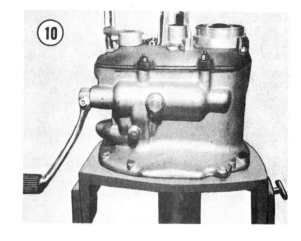

## /5 TRANSMISSION

### Disassembly

1. Mount the transmission in a workstand (BMW tool No. 6000) with an adapter (BMW tool No. 6005/1). See **Figure 10**.

> NOTE: *If a workstand and adapter are not available, have an assistant hold the transmission on 2 blocks of wood so the input shaft does not contact the workbench (Figure 11).*

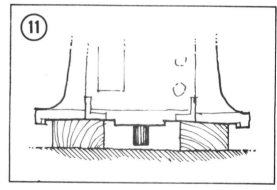

CAUTION
*Do not clamp the input shaft in a vise to hold the transmission.*

WARNING
*Some of the operations require that the transmission be heated. Use asbestos gloves or oven mitts to prevent burns.*

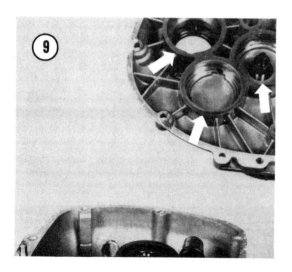

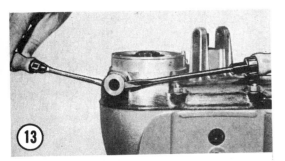

2. Drain the transmission oil.

3. Refer to **Figure 12** and remove the clutch thrust rod and felt seal. Discard the seal. Use a new seal when assembling the transmission.

4. Unscrew the speedometer cable bolt and remove the drive bushing (**Figure 13**).

5. Install the output flange holder (BMW tool No. 234) and tighten the 4 fixture bolts evenly and snugly (**Figure 14**). If they are run down finger-tight there is a chance the flange fingers will be bent. Hold the fixture with a bar and unscrew the 24mm output flange nut. This holder is essential for work on the output flange.

CAUTION
*Do not rest the bar against the clutch pivot arms on the rear cover (**Figure 15**). The arms are not intended to withstand the force exerted when the flange nut is loosened and tightened, and could easily break off.*

6. Install the puller on the output flange (BMW tool No. 232) and tighten the bolts securely. Hold the puller with a bar and tighten the puller bolt to remove the flange (**Figure 16**).

7. Remove the speedometer drive gear (**Figure 17**).

**5**

8. Unscrew the seven 6mm nuts from the rear of the transmission (**Figure 18**).

9. Install the cover puller (BMW tool No. 233). See **Figure 19**. Heat the transmission cover in the area of the bearings to about 200°F. Tap around the cover and at the same time tighten the extractor bolt to remove the cover.

10. Remove the spacers and seal from the cover (**Figure 20**).

11. Mark the shifting forks and their respective eccentric bushings for position.

12. Refer to **Figure 21** and unscrew the two 6mm Allen bolts which hold the shifting forks (**Figure 22**). Remove the retaining plate.

13. With the housing still warm, remove the 3 transmission shafts and the shifting forks as a unit (**Figure 23**). It may be necessary to tap on the housing with a soft-face mallet to free the shafts from their bearings. Make sure the shifting forks clear the opening in the case. Remove the oil baffle from the output shaft bearing seat in the housing.

**Inspection**

1. Check all gears, bearings, bushings, shafts, and spacers for wear, galling, pitting, and chipped and broken teeth and splines. Replace those pieces that are not in good condition.

2. Check the play between the gears and the bushings. Measure the gear bores with an inside micrometer, and the bushings with an outside micrometer. Subtract the bushing dimension from the gear dimension to determine the play. If the clearances exceed the specifications (**Table 1**), replace the bushings.

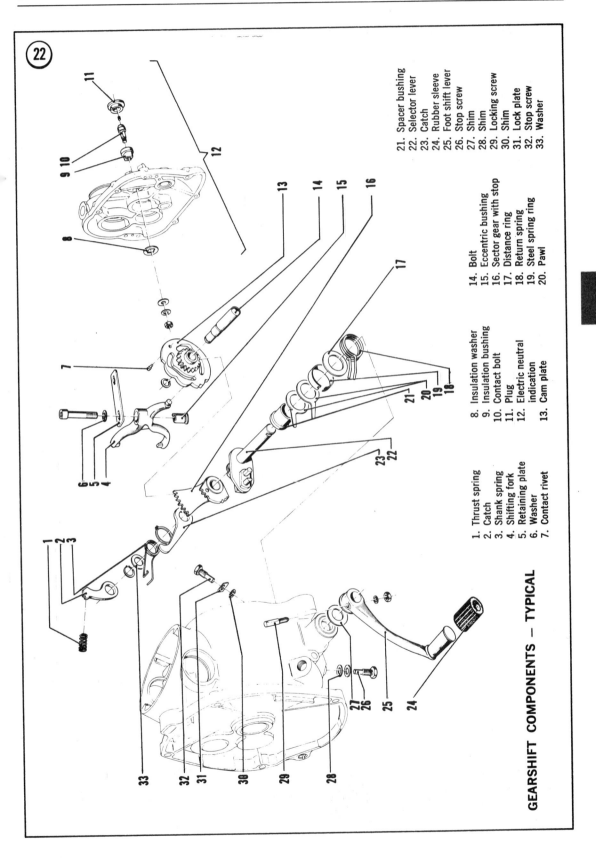

**GEARSHIFT COMPONENTS — TYPICAL**

1. Thrust spring
2. Catch
3. Shank spring
4. Shifting fork
5. Retaining plate
6. Washer
7. Contact rivet
8. Insulation washer
9. Insulation bushing
10. Contact bolt
11. Plug
12. Electric neutral indication
13. Cam plate
14. Bolt
15. Eccentric bushing
16. Sector gear with stop
17. Distance ring
18. Return spring
19. Steel spring ring
20. Pawl
21. Spacer bushing
22. Selector lever
23. Catch
24. Rubber sleeve
25. Foot shift lever
26. Stop screw
27. Shim
28. Shim
29. Locking screw
30. Shim
31. Lock plate
32. Stop screw
33. Washer

5

Table 1    GEAR TO BUSHING CLEARANCES

| Model | Clearance |
|---|---|
| /5 Series | |
| 1st and 4th | 0.040 to 0.085mm (0.0016 to 0.0033 in.) |
| 2nd and 3rd | 0.025 to 0.075mm (0.0009 to 0.0030 in.) |

Table 2    SHAFT TO BUSHING CLEARANCES

| Model | Clearance |
|---|---|
| /5 Series | |
| 1st | 0.005-0.035mm (0.0002-0.0014 in.) |
| 2nd and 3rd* | — |
| 4th | 0.005-0.047mm (0.0002-0.0019 in.) |
| *2nd and 3rd gear bushings and shafts are prefitted and must be replaced together. | |

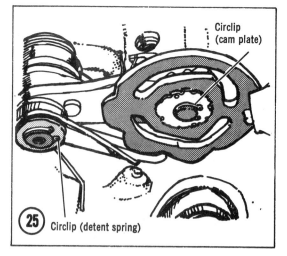

3. Check the play between the bushings and the shafts, with inside and outside micrometers. If the clearances exceed specifications (**Table 2**), replace the bushings.

4. Inspect the taper on the output end of the main shaft for galling and scoring. This type of damage indicates that the output flange has spun on the shaft. If this has occurred, the main shaft must be replaced. See *Main Shaft Disassembly/Assembly*.

5. Inspect the drive splines on the input shaft for signs of wear. The shaft shown in **Figure 24** is severely worn, caused by misalignment of the engine and transmission. It had to be replaced. See *Input Shaft Disassembly/Assembly*.

6. Inspect the shifting dogs for chips and wear, and replace any gears that are affected.

7. Refer to **Figure 25** and remove the circlip from the selector detent spring shaft. Routinely replace the spring and the circlip with new parts.

8. Refer to **Figure 26** and inspect the pawls, teeth, and guide paths in the gear selector mechanism for wear and damage. Replace any pieces that are less than satisfactory. See *Selector Mechanism Removal/Installation*.

9. Inspect the teeth on the kickstarter assembly for wear and damage and replace any pieces that are less than satisfactory. Check the spring tension by pulling the kickstarter pedal down. The spring should feel firm and should hold the pedal against the stop.

If the starter assembly must be disassembled for repair, refer to *Kickstarter Removal/ Installation*.

## Assembly

1. Refer to *Selector Mechanism Disassembly/ Assembly* and install the selector in the case if it was removed.

2. Refer to *Kickstarter Removal/Installation* and install the kickstarter in the cover if it was removed.

3. Refer to *Main Shaft Disassembly/Assembly* and assemble the main shaft if it was disassembled.

4. Refer to *Input Shaft Disassembly/Assembly* and assemble the input shaft if it was disassembled.

5. If the output shaft, the couplings, or the forks have been replaced with new ones, the forks must be readjusted. Heat the transmission housing to 180° to 210°F and install the fixture (BMW tool No. 504). See **Figure 27**.

6. Install the shifting forks into the sliding couplings and into the shift cam plate. Then, secure the forks with the 2 Allen bolts.

NOTE: *The bolts can be installed easily if the cam plate is placed in the fourth gear position for installation of the bolt on the third/fourth gear fork, and in the second gear position for installation of the bolt in the first/second gear fork.*

7. Move the cam to neutral. Adjust the forks by rotating the eccentric bushings until the sliding couplings are centered exactly between their respective gears. Use an inspection mirror for this.

8. Make sure the ears on the forks are fully engaged in the couplings, and the couplings are not pressed against the the gears.

9. Mark the position of each eccentric bushing on its shifting fork (**Figure 28**) and remove the output shaft and forks from the transmission.

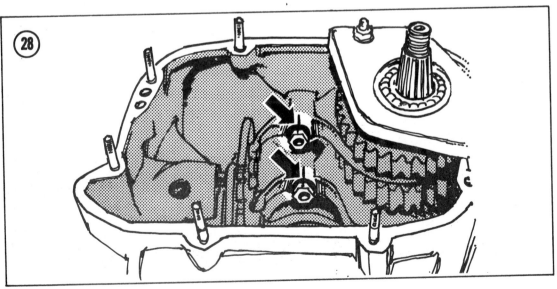

10. If necessary, reheat the transmission housing to 180° to 210°F.

11. Place the oil guide for the output shaft into the bearing bore.

12. Insert the output shaft, the cluster gear, and the shift forks as a unit into the transmission. Make sure the shift forks do not bind on the edges of the case opening.

13. Place a new gasket on the transmission housing and then install the fixture (BMW tool No. 504) to the support end of the output shaft (**Figure 29**). Measure the distance from the upper edge of the ball bearing to the surface of gasket.

14. Measure the distance from the mating surface of the cover to the bottom of the bearing bore (**Figure 30**). Subtract the previous dimension from this one to determine the actual end play. Shim the difference to 0.1mm (0.0039 in.) end play. Prior to installing the cover, hold the shims in place with a small bit of grease.

15. Measure the end play of the cluster shaft in exactly the same manner. Its end play also should be 0.1mm (0.0039 in.).

16. Place a 20mm (0.787 in.) bushing (BMW tool No. 5061) on the end of the input shaft and measure the distance from the top surface of the bushing to the mating surface of the transmission housing (**Figure 31**). Subtract 20mm (0.787 in.) — the thickness of the bushing — from the measurement.

17. Next, measure the distance from the mating surface of the cover to the shoulder of the bushing, installed in the bearing (**Figure 32**). Subtract the result from the previous measurement and shim the difference to 0.1mm (0.0030 in.) with a shim/oil retainer.

18. Remove the bushing from the bearing (**Figure 33**) and place the correct retainer on the bearing, with its raised outer edge facing the transmission. Then, reinstall the bushing.

19. Check the position of the neutral indicator contact with a gauge (BMW tool No. 5097,

**Figure 34**). If necessary, bend or file the contact carefully until it just touches the gauge.

> NOTE: *Stick the cupped spacer (14, Figure 35) to the input shaft bearing in the rear cover with stiff grease. The edges of the spacer should stick up and the center should be flush with the inside bore of the bearing.*

20. Heat the cover to 180° to 210°F, start it onto the shaft, and depress the kickstarter partway (**Figure 36**). Slowly push the cover into place and at the same time carefully move the starter lever up and down until its engagement with the starter gear can be felt. Then, tap the cover all the way down and install the nuts, tightening them in a crosswise pattern.

21. Double check the operation of the neutral indicator by attaching the negative terminal of the battery to the transmission and connecting a continuity light between the positive battery terminal and the neutral indicator connector on the transmission. With the transmission in neutral the light should be on and when it is shifted into first or second gear the light should go out.

**Main Shaft Disassembly/Assembly**

1. Place the output shaft in a press tube, with first gear supported by split plates (**Figure 37**). Press off the gear, the thrust washer, and the ball bearing.

2. Refer to **Figure 38** and remove the floating bushing, the second washer, and the sliding coupling for first and second gear. Remove the circlip and splined washer, and then second and third gear.

3. Remove the circlip from the forward end of the output shaft and place 2 bars between fourth gear and the sliding coupling. Set the

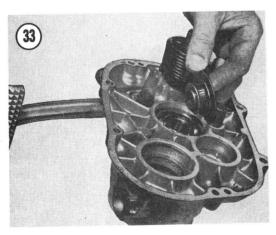

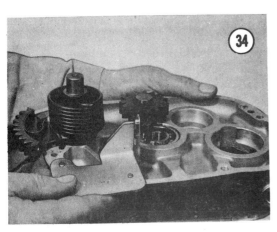

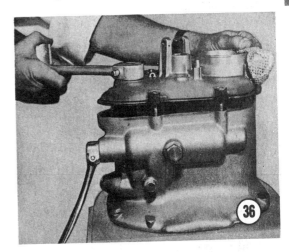

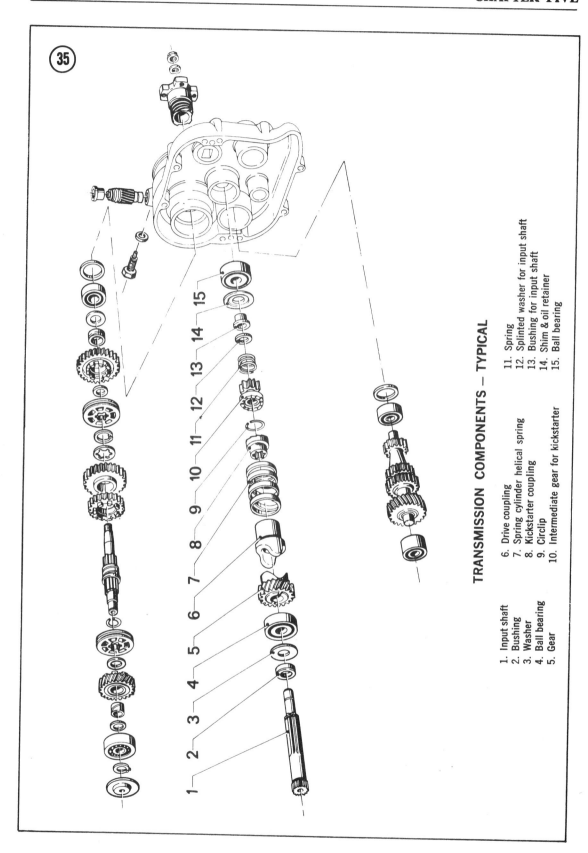

TRANSMISSION COMPONENTS – TYPICAL

1. Input shaft
2. Bushing
3. Washer
4. Ball bearing
5. Gear
6. Drive coupling
7. Spring cylinder helical spring
8. Kickstarter coupling
9. Circlip
10. Intermediate gear for kickstarter
11. Spring
12. Splinted washer for input shaft
13. Bushing for input shaft
14. Shim & oil retainer
15. Ball bearing

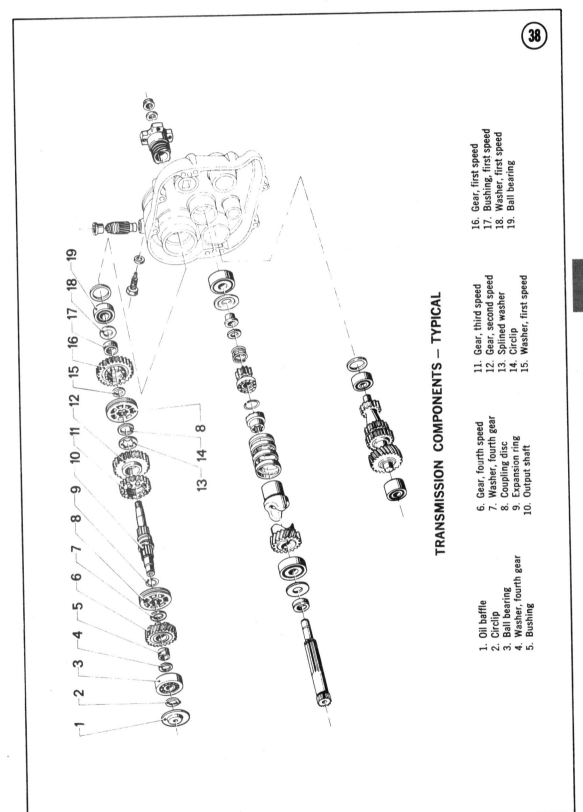

**TRANSMISSION COMPONENTS — TYPICAL**

1. Oil baffle
2. Circlip
3. Ball bearing
4. Washer, fourth gear
5. Bushing

6. Gear, fourth speed
7. Washer, fourth gear
8. Coupling disc
9. Expansion ring
10. Output shaft

11. Gear, third speed
12. Gear, second speed
13. Splined washer
14. Circlip
15. Washer, first speed

16. Gear, first speed
17. Bushing, first speed
18. Washer, first speed
19. Ball bearing

shaft in a press tube (**Figure 39**) and press off the bearing. Then, remove the float bushing, the washers, and sliding coupling.

4. Reverse the above to assemble the main shaft. Oil all contact surfaces with assembly lube. Make certain the circlips are firmly seated. Check to see that the dogs on the sliding gears will fully engage with the slots in the gear coupling discs.

### Input Shaft Disassembly/Assembly

1. Remove the thrust washer, spring, and kickstarter gear (**Figure 40**).

2. Compress the shock absorber spring and remove the circlip (**Figure 41**). If BMW tool No. 319/1 (shown) is not available, very carefully compress the shock absorber spring in a vise. When the circlip has been removed, very carefully release the pressure on the spring and then disassemble the shaft.

WARNING
*The shock absorber spring is very strong. Inadvertent release of the spring*

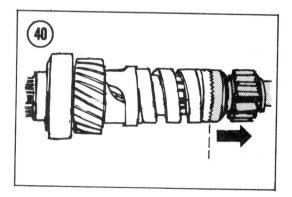

*could propel the kickstarter ratchet with sufficient force to cause serious injury. As a precaution, make certain there is no one in front of the shaft during this operation.*

3. If the shaft is being replaced, heat the forward bearing bushing and remove it from the shaft. Install it on the new shaft while it is still hot, with the collar forward (**Figure 42**).

4. Refer to **Figure 43** and assemble the remaining components, using a liberal amount of assembly lube. Compress the assembly and install a new circlip to retain the shock absorber spring. Make certain the circlip is correctly seated before releasing the pressure — then release it very carefully.

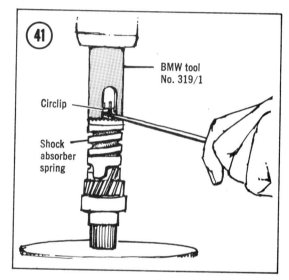

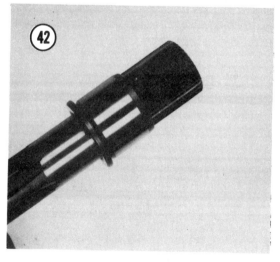

5. Install the kickstarter gear, spring, washer, bushing, and oil slinger with the raised outer lip facing away from the end of the shaft. Press on the bearing.

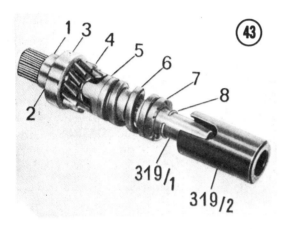

1. Seal sleeve
2. Washer
3. Ball bearing
4. Input shaft
5. Drive coupling
6. Kickstarter spring
7. Kickstarter ratchet
8. Circlip
319/1 BMW tool
319/2 BMW tool

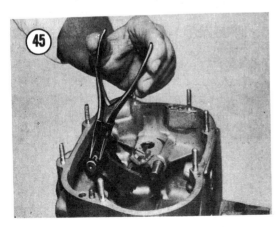

**Selector Mechanism Removal/Installation**

1. Remove the circlip and shift cam plate (**Figure 44**). Then remove the second circlip and washer and detent spring.

2. Remove the circlip, pawl, and shift segment (**Figure 45**).

3. Remove the nut and bolt from the gear selector (**Figure 46**), and remove the selector and spacer.

4. Remove the shift selector assembly from the case.

5. Reverse the above steps to install the selector mechanism. The shoulder on the selector bushing must face the inner lever (**Figure 47**).

6. Insert the positioners in the circular leaf spring and slide the assembly over the bushing, with one positioner on each side of the shorter pin (**Figure 48**).

**5**

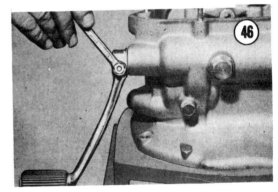

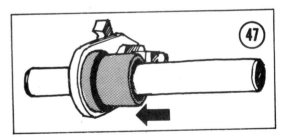

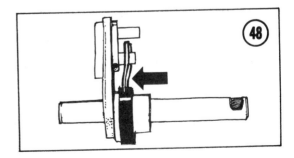

7. Install the washer and then the return spring (**Figure 49**), with the curved ends of the spring toward the lever.

8. Install the complete assembly into the transmission housing. The return spring ends must straddle the pin in the housing.

9. Replace the shim on selector shaft and reinstall selector lever and wedge bolt. Check end play of shaft. It should be 0.2mm (0.0078 in.). If it is not, correct it with another shim of different thickness.

10. Slide the segment and selector gear onto the shaft. The engagement notches in the selector lever must be equal distance from the selecting teeth on both sides of the segment. It may be necessary to bend the return spring to correctly position the selector lever (**Figure 50**).

11. Install the pawl on the segment and secure it with a circlip. Install the detent spring and washer and secure them with the other circlip.

12. Install the shift cam plate. The second tooth on segment must mesh with the marked tooth on the cam plate (**Figure 51**). Install the circlip.

13. Check the overshift between the pawl and detent notches (**Figure 52**). The overshift should be 1mm (0.039 in.). If it is not, correct it with a shim on the selector limiting bolt.

## /6 AND /7 TRANSMISSION

### Disassembly

1. Remove the clutch thrust pushrod (**Figure 53**). Remove the felt seal from the pushrod and discard it.

NOTE: *Use a new seal when the transmission is assembled.*

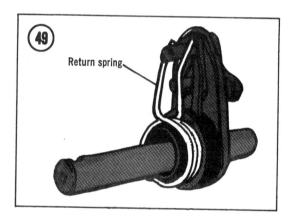

49

Return spring

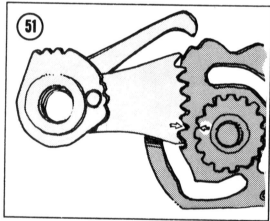

51

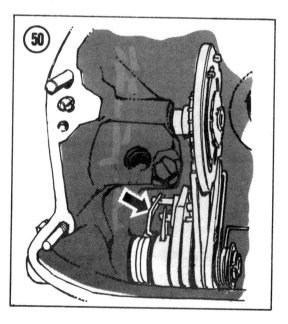

50

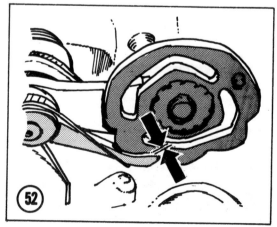

52

2. Unscrew the bolt that holds the speedometer drive and remove the drive (**Figure 54**).

3. Install the output flange holder (BMW tool No. 234) and tighten the 4 fixture bolts evenly and snugly (**Figure 55**). If they are run down just finger-tight, there is a chance that the flange fingers may be bent. Hold the fixture with a bar and unscrew the 24mm output flange nut. This holder is essential for work on the output flange.

#### CAUTION
*Do not rest the bar against the clutch pivot arms on the rear cover (**Figure 56**). The arms are not intended to withstand the force exerted when the flange nut is loosened and tightened, and could easily break off.*

4. Remove the holding fixture and install the output flange puller (BMW tool No. 232). See **Figure 57**. As with the flange holding fixture,

tighten the bolts down evenly and snugly with a wrench. Hold the puller with a bar and tighten the puller bolt to draw the flange off the output shaft. Remove the flange from the puller and remove the speedometer drive gear from the cover (**Figure 58**).

5. Unscrew the screws that attach the cover to the rear of the transmission (**Figure 59**). Collect the spring washers from behind the screws.

6. Install the extractor (BMW tool No. 231). See **Figure 60**.

7. Heat the cover in the area of the bearings (**Figure 61**). Tap around the cover and at the same time tighten the extractor bolt to remove the cover.

8. Remove the shims from the bearings and seat them in their respective bores in the outer cover (**Figure 62**). It may not be necessary to

reshim the shafts when the transmission is assembled, so it is essential that the original shims be correctly located. Also remove the oil baffle from the lay shaft and place it in its bore in the outer cover.

9. Remove the gear selector lever (**Figure 63**).

10. Pull the selector shaft out of the case

(**Figure 64**). If the shaft will not come out easily, it is likely that the end of it is burred over. In such case, carefully remove any burrs from the end of the shaft with a fine file before attempting to remove it; if it is drawn out forcibly, burred, it will damage the bushing in the case.

11. Unscrew the 2 bolts from the front of the gearbox (**Figure 65**) to release the shift mechanism. Pull out the shifter (**Figure 66**).

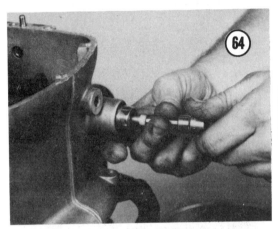

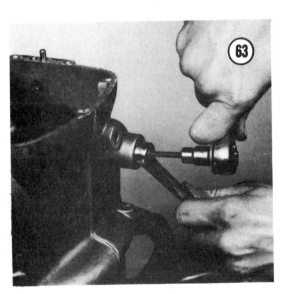

12. Remove the shifting forks. Note that the 1st/2nd fork has a flat on the boss (**Figure 67**). Install the forks on the shaft for reference during assembly.

13. Remove the input shaft (**Figure 68**).

14. Heat the front of the case to release the lay shaft and main shaft bearings (**Figure 69**).

15. Lift out the shafts (**Figure 70**) as an assembly.

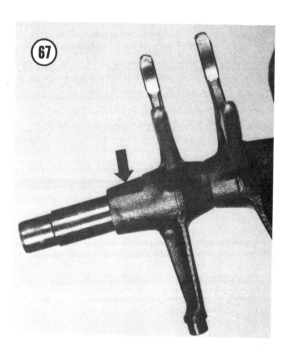

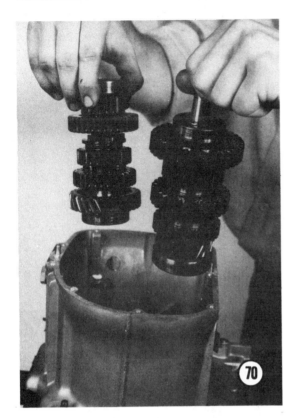

16. Remove the oil baffles from the bearing bores (**Figure 71**).

17. Heat the case and remove the roller bearing for the input shaft (**Figure 72**). Remove the input shaft bearing seal and discard it.

**Main Shaft Disassembly/Assembly**

1. Support the main shaft 1st gear with press plates and press off the gear, thrust washer, and rear bearing assembly (**Figure 73**).

2. Refer to **Figure 74** and remove the bushing, shim, and 4th gear.

3. Remove the circlip, thrust washer, 2nd gear, and the washer behind it.

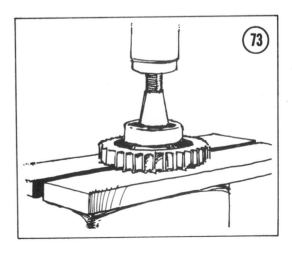

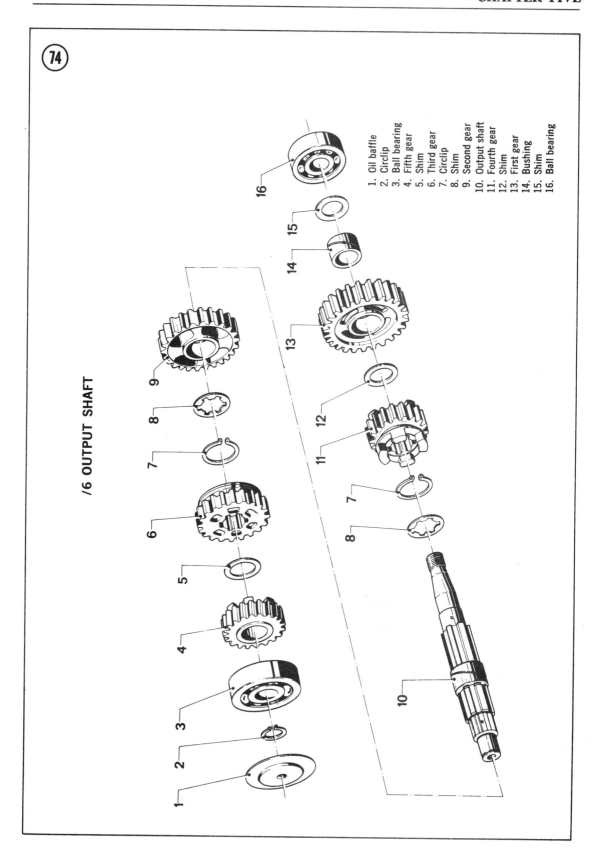

74

1. Oil baffle
2. Circlip
3. Ball bearing
4. Fifth gear
5. Shim
6. Third gear
7. Circlip
8. Shim
9. Second gear
10. Output shaft
11. Fourth gear
12. Shim
13. First gear
14. Bushing
15. Shim
16. Ball bearing

/6 OUTPUT SHAFT

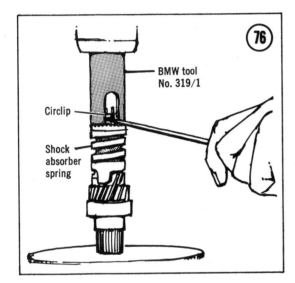

BMW tool
No. 319/1

Circlip

Shock
absorber
spring

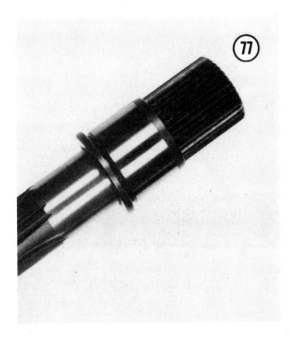

4. Remove the circlip from the forward end of the shaft. Support the main shaft 5th gear with press plates and press off the forward bearing. Remove the washer, 3rd gear, and the circlip.

5. Reverse the above steps to assemble the main shaft and gears. Make certain the circlips are correctly seated in their grooves. Use a liberal amount of assembly lube on all of the contact surfaces. When assembly is complete, check to make sure that the engagement dogs and slots completely engage on all sliding gears.

### Input Shaft Disassembly/Assembly

1. Remove the input shaft bearings (**Figure 75**) with a press so the oil slingers won't be damaged.

2. Very carefully compress the shock absorber spring in a vise and remove the snap ring (**Figure 76**). Slowly release the pressure on the spring and then disassemble the shaft.

> WARNING
> *The shock absorber spring is very strong. Inadvertent release of the spring could propel the kickstarter ratchet (if fitted) or collar with sufficient force to cause serious injury. As a precaution, make certain there is no one in front of the shaft during this operation.*

3. Heat the forward bearing inner race and slide it on the shaft with the collar up (**Figure 77**).

4. Refer to **Figure 76** and assemble the remaining components, using a liberal amount of assembly lube. Compress the assembly and install a new circlip to retain the shock absorber spring. Make certain that the circlip is correctly seated before releasing the pressure — and then release it very carefully.

5. Install the rear oil slinger and then the rear bearing with the raised outer lip of the slinger facing away from the bearing (**Figure 78**).

### Shift Mechanism Disassembly/Assembly

With the exception of the routine replacement of the detent spring described under *Inspection*, there is no need to disassemble the shift mechanism if the camplates, pawls, and segments are in satisfactory condition.

If disassembly is required to replace one or more parts, refer to **Figure 79** for the relationship of the parts. When installing the selector discs, make sure that the first teeth on both discs mesh (**Figure 80**). Pay particular attention to the positions of the stop rollers and spring tangs during disassembly so that the parts may be correctly assembled. Make sure all of the circlips are correctly seated. Liberally coat all of the contact surfaces with assembly lube.

**Inspection**

1. Check all gears, bearings, bushings, shafts, and shims for wear, galling, pitting, and chipped and broken teeth and splines. Replace those pieces that are not in good condition.

2. Inspect the taper on the output end of the main shaft for galling and scoring. This type of damage indicates that the output flange has spun on the shaft. If this has occurred, the main shaft must be replaced.

3. Inspect the drive splines on the input shaft for signs of wear. The shaft shown in **Figure 81** is severly worn, caused by misalignment of engine and transmission. It had to be replaced. (See *Input Shaft Disassembly/Assembly*.)

4. Inspect the shifting dogs between 2nd and 4th gear on the intermediate shaft (**Figure 82**). If the dogs are chipped or broken, the entire intermediate shaft must be replaced as an assembly.

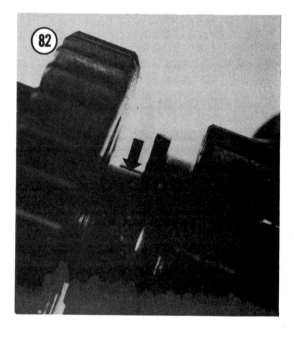

## /6 SHIFT MECHANISM

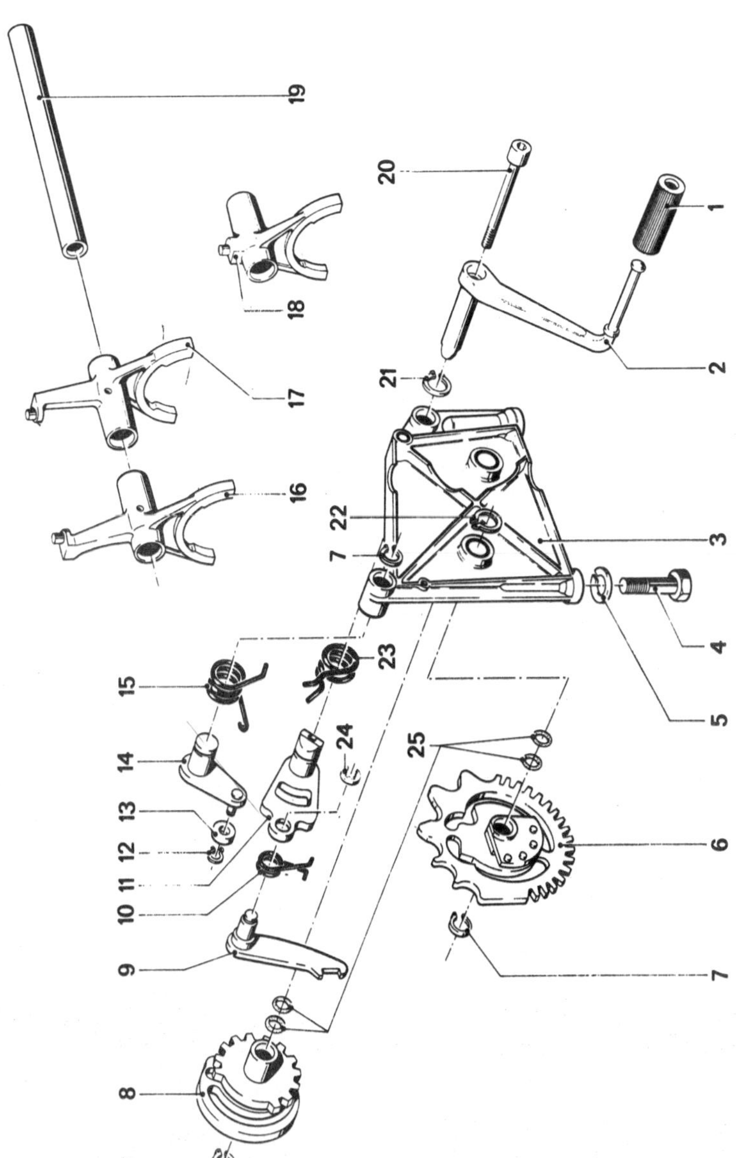

1. Sleeve
2. Foot shift lever
3. Bearing bracket
4. Spacer screw
5. Lockwasher
6. Cam plate
7. Circlip
8. Cam plate
9. Pawl
10. Detent spring
11. Segment
12. Circlip
13. Roller
14. Lever
15. Detent spring
16. First and second gear shift fork
17. Fifth gear shift fork
18. Third and fourth gear shift fork
19. First, second and fifth gear axle
20. Cylinder head screw
21. Circlip
22. Lockwasher
23. Detent spring
24. Lockwasher
25. Gasket

5. Check the air cleaner clip bolt (**Figure 83**) and tighten it, if necessary, using a thread-locking compound. If this bolt is loose, oil will seep up around the bolt.

6. Remove the circlip from the selector detent spring shaft (**Figure 84**) and routinely replace the spring and circlip.

7. Check the play between the gears and the bushings. Measure the gear bores with an inside micrometer, and the bushings with an outside micrometer. Subtract the bushing dimension from the gear dimension to determine the play. If the clearances exceed the specifications shown in **Table 3**, replace the bushings.

**Table 3    GEAR TO BUSHING CLEARANCES**

| Model | 1st and 2nd |
|---|---|
| All Models | 0.040 to 0.085mm (0.0016 to 0.0034 in.) |

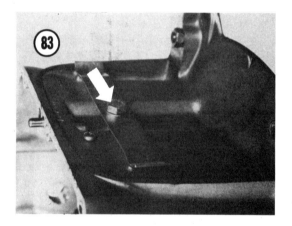

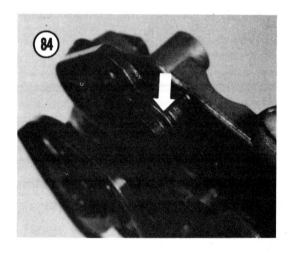

8. Check the play between the bushings and the shafts, with inside and outside micrometers. If the clearances exceed the specifications shown in **Table 3**, replace the bushings.

9. Refer to **Figure 85** and inspect the pawls, teeth, and guide paths in the gear selector mechanism for wear and damage. Replace any pieces that are less than satisfactory. When installing the selector discs, make sure the first teeth on both discs mesh (**Figure 86**). Pay particular attention to the positions of the stop rollers and spring tangs when disassembling the selector mechanism so the parts may be correctly assembled.

10. Inspect the teeth on the kickstarter assembly (if fitted) for wear and damage and replace any pieces that are less than satisfac-

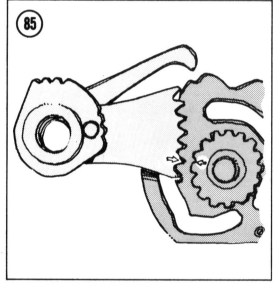

tory. Check the spring tension by pulling the kickstarter pedal down. The spring should feel firm and should hold the pedal against the stop.

If the starter assembly must be disassembled for repair, refer to **Figure 87** and remove the pedal from the shaft. Remove the circlip that holds the shackle in place and remove the shackle from the shaft. Note the locations of the spring tangs and carefully pull the starter shaft out of the cover. Reassemble the kickstarter assembly by reversing these steps.

**Assembly**

1. Install the oil slingers in the bearing cavities in the case (**Figure 88**). Install the forward input shaft bearing and seal.

2. The main shaft and intermediate shaft must be installed together. First, install the intermediate shaft selector fork on the shaft

5

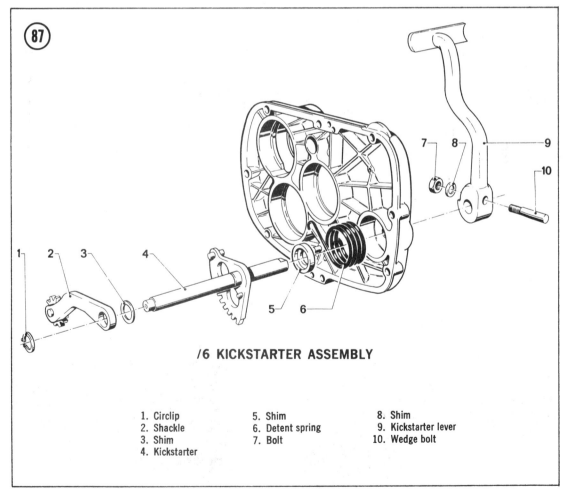

**/6 KICKSTARTER ASSEMBLY**

1. Circlip
2. Shackle
3. Shim
4. Kickstarter
5. Shim
6. Detent spring
7. Bolt
8. Shim
9. Kickstarter lever
10. Wedge bolt

(**Figure 89**) with the long boss down. This fork must fit over the stationary spindle in the case (**Figure 90**).

3. Assemble the 2 gearsets along with their shifting forks and spindles. Note the orientation of the machined flat on the 1st/2nd fork. This fork must be on top and the long bosses should face away from each other (**Figure 91**).

4. Install the gearsets, forks, and spindles in the case as an assembly (**Figure 92**).

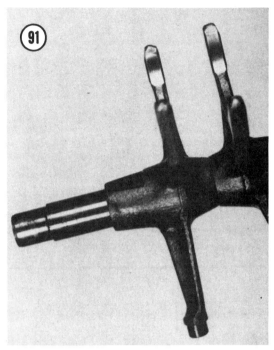

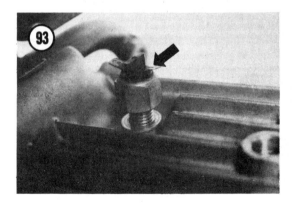

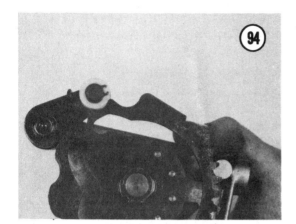

5. Unscrew the neutral indicator switch far enough so its plunger is flush with the inside of the case (**Figure 93**). This will keep it from being damaged when the selector is installed.

6. Shift the selector mechanism to neutral (**Figure 94**). Install selector and screw in and tighten bolts in the front of case (**Figure 95**).

7. Install the selector shaft and pedal. Shift the selector through all 5 gears and neutral to ensure there is no binding.

8. Install the input shaft (**Figure 96**). Install the oil slinger with the raised lip down, then install the bearing assembly on the end of the shaft (**Figure 97**).

5

9. Coat the sealing surface of the case with gasket cement and install a new gasket **(Figure 98)**.

10. With a parallel bar and a depth gauge, measure the distance between the top of each of the 3 shaft bearings and the mating surface of the case with the gasket installed **(Figure 99)**. Take several readings around each bearing; lateral movement of the shafts will provide different readings, so be patient and make sure the read distance is accurate.

11. Measure the distance between the top and the bottom of each of the 3 bearing bores in the end cover. Subtract the first measurements from the second to determine the actual end-float. The required end-float is 0.0-0.1mm (0.0-0.004 in.). Select appropriate shims to achieve the required end-float.

NOTE: *Install the shims between the bearings and the oil slingers, not between the oil slinger and the cover.*

12. Install the cover and tighten the screws in a crisscross pattern to 0.8-0.9 mkg (6-6.5 ft.-lb.).

13. Refer to *Output Flange Seal Replacement* and install the seal and flange.

14. Install the clutch throwout bearing **(Figure 100)**.

15. Install the clutch pushrod with a new felt seal **(Figure 101)**.

16. Refer to *Transmission Installation* and install the transmission in the motorcycle. Refer to Chapter Three and fill the transmission with oil and adjust the clutch.

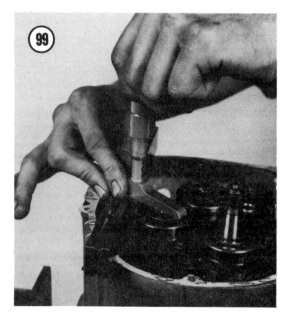

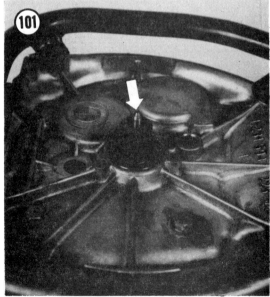

NOTE: If you own a 1979 or later model, first check the Supplement at the back of the book for any new service information.

# CHAPTER SIX

# FUEL SYSTEM

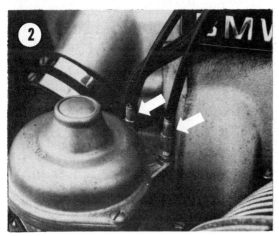

There are three carburetors with which BMW motorcycles are equipped; slide-type Bing; slide-type Dell'Orto; and constant-vacuum diaphragm-type Bing. Adjustment procedures are presented in Chapter Three. Removal, disassembly, inspection, and assembly are covered in this chapter.

## CARBURETORS

### Removal

1. Turn the fuel taps off. Place a small container beneath each of the carburetors in turn and drain the float bowls. On Bing carburetors, release the spring clip that holds the bowl and remove the bowl (**Figure 1**). On Dell'Orto carburetors, unscrew the drain plug from the bottom of the bowl. During installation, be careful not to damage the float.

2. Disconnect the cables. On slide-type Bing carburetors, unscrew the ring nuts from the top of the carburetors and remove the slide assembly along with the cable. On Dell'Orto carburetors, unscrew the screws that attach the top cap and remove the slide assembly along with the cables. On constant-vacuum carburetors, disconnect the cables from the levers (**Figure 2**) after the adjusters have been loosened.

3. Loosen the clamps on the carburetor breather tubes and the manifold (**Figure 3**) and disconnect the carburetors from the cylinders.

### Installation

Reverse the removal procedure to install the carburetors. Refer to Chapter Three and adjust the idle speed and cable free play. With the engine running, check for air leaks around the manifolds by squirting the joints with WD-40. If the idle speed changes, an air leak is present. It can most likely be corrected by further tightening of the clamps. If this does not work, remove the carburetor and check for foreign matter on the sealing surfaces or breaks and cracks in the manifold tubes.

### Disassembly

1. Refer to the appropriate exploded views and disassemble the carburetors (**Figures 4 and 5**, slide-type Bing; **Figures 6 and 7**, constant-vacuum Bing; and **Figure 8**, Dell'Orto).

2. Remove the jets and place them in individually labeled envelopes. Do not mix the parts of one carburetor with those of the other.

### Inspection and Adjustment

1. Clean all of the metal parts with carburetor cleaner and blow them dry with compressed air. Carburetor cleaner can be purchased in a small dip tank equipped with a basket (**Figure 9**). If the tank is kept sealed when not is use, it will last for many cleanings.

2. Clean each jet with compressed air. Do not use wire to clean the jets; it can cause burrs in the soft brass jets and alter their flow rates. If air will not remove obstructions, use a broom-straw.

3. Check gaskets and sealing washers to see if they are damaged or excessively compressed, and replace them if necessary. Replace any O-rings that are damaged or deteriorated. Replace the diaphragms in constant-vacuum carburetors if they are torn or deteriorated.

### Assembly

1. Refer to the appropriate exploded views and assemble the carburetors. Take care not to overtighten jets; the threads in the carburetor bodies can be easily stripped.

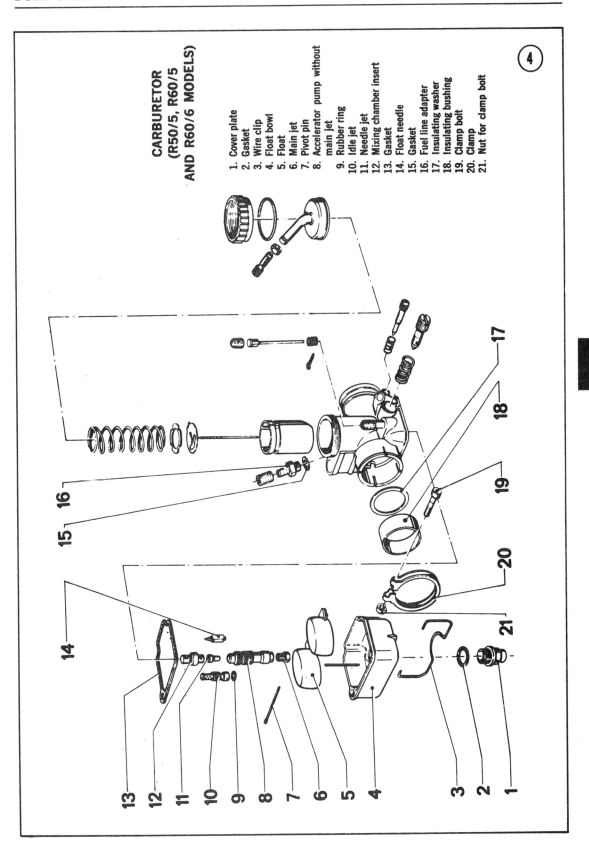

**CARBURETOR (R50/5, R60/5 AND R60/6 MODELS)**

1. Cover plate
2. Gasket
3. Wire clip
4. Float bowl
5. Float
6. Main jet
7. Pivot pin
8. Accelerator pump without main jet
9. Rubber ring
10. Idle jet
11. Needle jet
12. Mixing chamber insert
13. Gasket
14. Float needle
15. Gasket
16. Fuel line adapter
17. Insulating washer
18. Insulating bushing
19. Clamp bolt
20. Clamp
21. Nut for clamp bolt

6

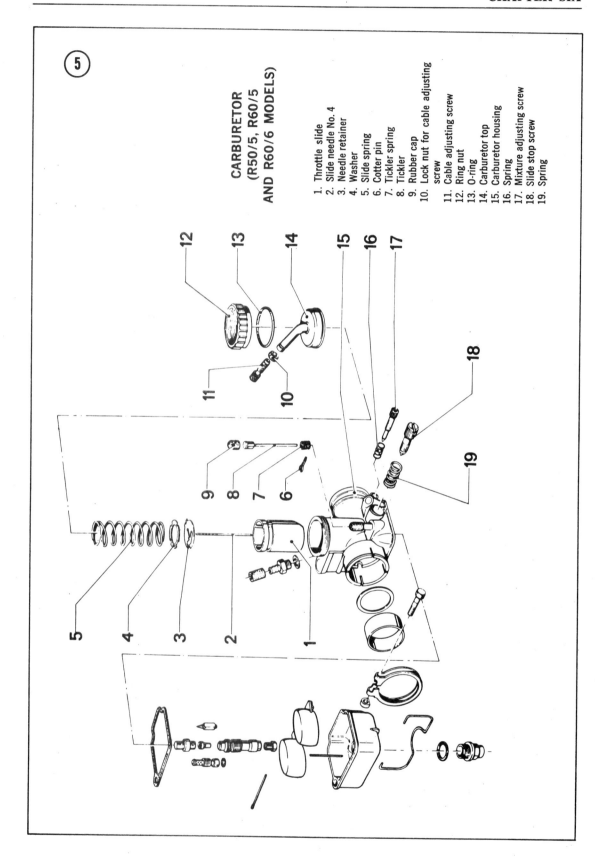

CARBURETOR
(R50/5, R60/5
AND R60/6 MODELS)

1. Throttle slide
2. Slide needle No. 4
3. Needle retainer
4. Washer
5. Slide spring
6. Cotter pin
7. Tickler spring
8. Tickler
9. Rubber cap
10. Lock nut for cable adjusting screw
11. Cable adjusting screw
12. Ring nut
13. O-ring
14. Carburetor top
15. Carburetor housing
16. Spring
17. Mixture adjusting screw
18. Slide stop screw
19. Spring

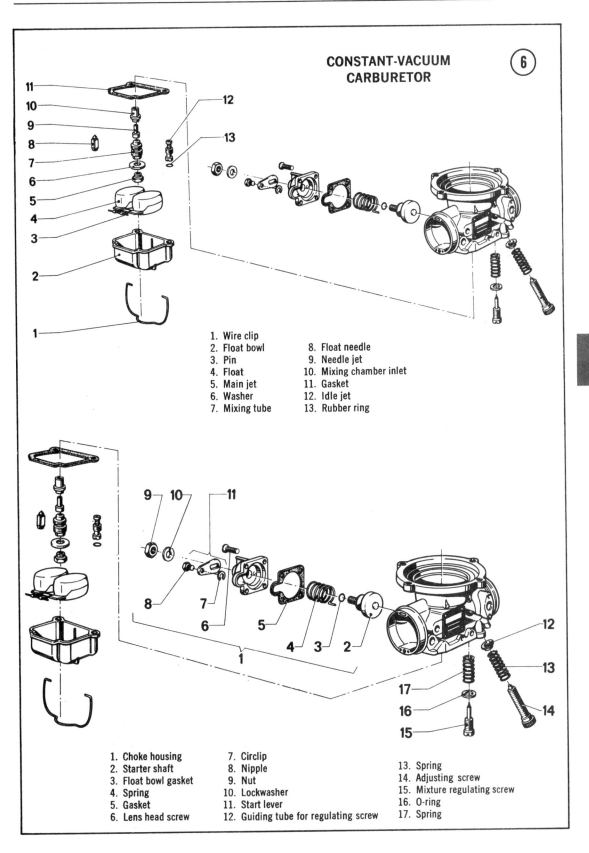

CONSTANT-VACUUM
CARBURETOR

6

1. Wire clip
2. Float bowl
3. Pin
4. Float
5. Main jet
6. Washer
7. Mixing tube
8. Float needle
9. Needle jet
10. Mixing chamber inlet
11. Gasket
12. Idle jet
13. Rubber ring

1. Choke housing
2. Starter shaft
3. Float bowl gasket
4. Spring
5. Gasket
6. Lens head screw
7. Circlip
8. Nipple
9. Nut
10. Lockwasher
11. Start lever
12. Guiding tube for regulating screw
13. Spring
14. Adjusting screw
15. Mixture regulating screw
16. O-ring
17. Spring

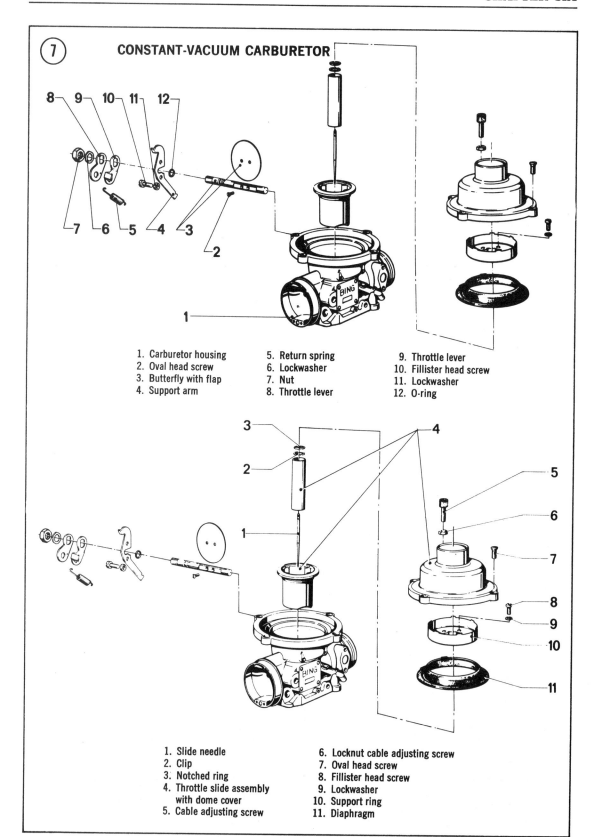

**CONSTANT-VACUUM CARBURETOR**

1. Carburetor housing
2. Oval head screw
3. Butterfly with flap
4. Support arm
5. Return spring
6. Lockwasher
7. Nut
8. Throttle lever
9. Throttle lever
10. Fillister head screw
11. Lockwasher
12. O-ring

1. Slide needle
2. Clip
3. Notched ring
4. Throttle slide assembly with dome cover
5. Cable adjusting screw
6. Locknut cable adjusting screw
7. Oval head screw
8. Fillister head screw
9. Lockwasher
10. Support ring
11. Diaphragm

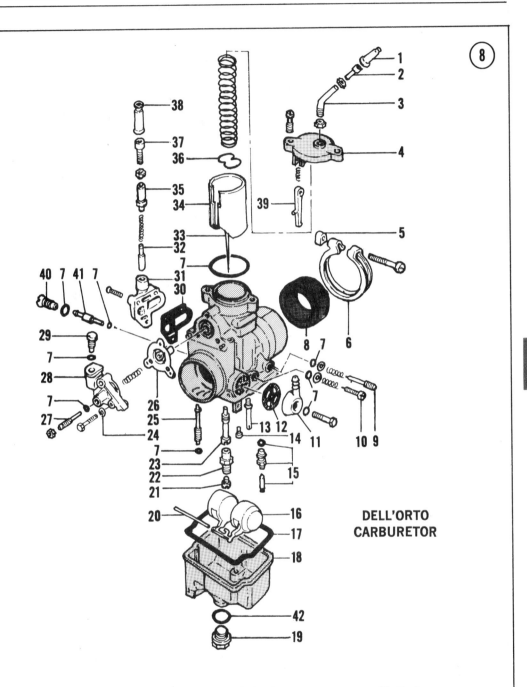

**DELL'ORTO CARBURETOR**

1. Adjuster cover
2. Adjuster
3. Cable guide
4. Carburetor top
5. Nut, clamp screw
6. Clamp
7. O-ring seal
8. Insulating bushing
9. Idling mixture screw
10. Pilot air screw
11. Filter cover
12. Filter screen
13. Accelerator pump jet
14. Pilot jet
15. Float needle assembly
16. Float
17. Float bowl seal
18. Float bowl
19. Bowl drain
20. Float pivot pin
21. Main jet
22. Main jet holder
23. Atomizer
24. Washer
25. Starting jet
26. Accelerator pump diaphragm
27. Regulating screw, accelerator pump
28. Accelerator pump body
29. Accelerator pump valve
30. Choke body gasket
31. Choke body
32. Choke slide
33. Needle
34. Throttle slide
35. Choke cap
36. Needle clip
37. Cable adjuster
38. Adjuster cover
39. Accelerator pump cover
40. Jet cover, accelerator pump
41. Clamp screw
42. Gasket

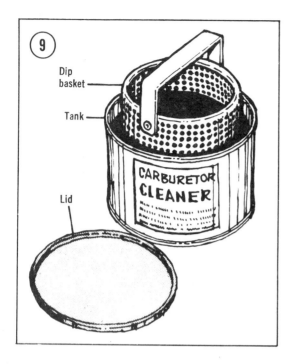

Dip basket

Tank

Lid

CARBURETOR CLEANER

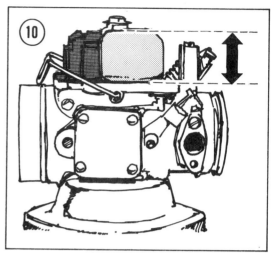

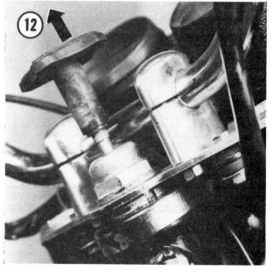

2. When installing the diaphragms on constant-vacuum carburetors, make sure the tab on the diaphragm engages the slot in the carburetor body; this is important in that it controls the relationship of the slide to the venturi.

3. Install the carburetors as described and refer to Chapter Three and adjust the cable free play and the idle speed.

**Float Level**

The float valve maintains a constant fuel level in the float bowl on the side of the carburetor to supply the demands of the engine at all engine speeds. As the chamber fills with fuel, the float rises, thereby pushing the valve needle into the valve to shut off the incoming fuel. As the fuel level drops, so does the needle, permitting fuel to flow into the bowl and replenish the supply.

1. Remove the carburetors. Leave all cables connected. Unsnap the float bowl retainer clip and remove the float bowl.

2. Turn the carburetor upside down and hold the float parallel to the float bowl sealing surface (**Figure 10**). The brass tab on the float should just touch the ball in the end of the float needle but not compress it. If necessary, care-

fully bend the tab to correct the position of the float.

3. Reinstall the float bowls, making sure the bowls and gaskets are correctly seated. Reinstall the carburetors on the engine and adjust them as outlined in Chapter Three.

**FUEL TANK AND FUEL VALVES**

Fuel tanks and fuel valves are shown in exploded view in **Figure 11**.

**Disassembly**

1. Disconnect the battery ground lead and remove the steering damper knob (**Figure 12**) if fitted.

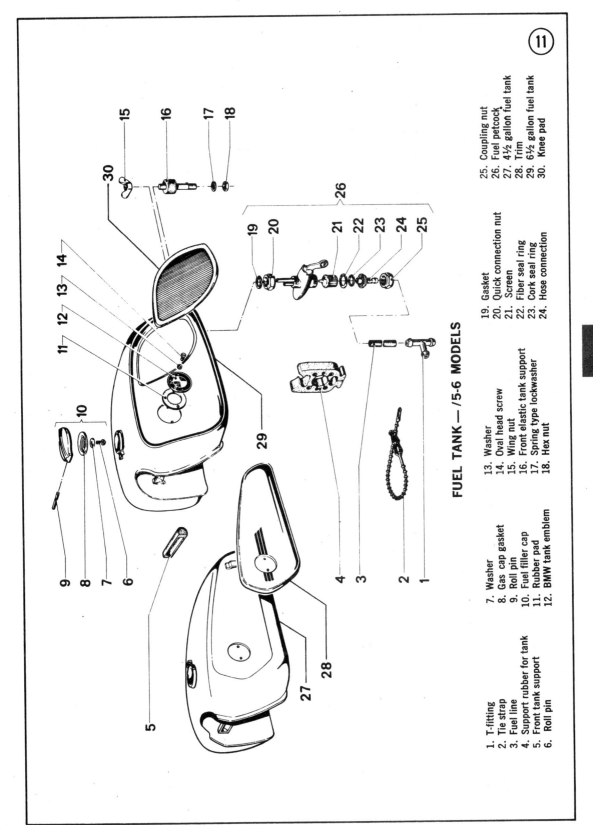

**FUEL TANK — /5-6 MODELS**

1. T-fitting
2. Tie strap
3. Fuel line
4. Support rubber for tank
5. Front tank support
6. Roll pin
7. Washer
8. Gas cap gasket
9. Roll pin
10. Fuel filler cap
11. Rubber pad
12. BMW tank emblem
13. Washer
14. Oval head screw
15. Wing nut
16. Front elastic tank support
17. Spring type lockwasher
18. Hex nut
19. Gasket
20. Quick connection nut
21. Screen
22. Fiber seal ring
23. Cork seal ring
24. Hose connection
25. Coupling nut
26. Fuel petcock
27. 4½ gallon fuel tank
28. Trim
29. 6½ gallon fuel tank
30. Knee pad

6

2. Turn both fuel valves off and pull off the fuel lines (**Figure 13**).

3. Lift the seat and remove the 2 hold nuts beneath the fuel tank (**Figure 14**). Pull the tank back, lift up the front, and remove it.

4. Empty the tank and remove the fuel valves by unscrewing the top union nuts.

> NOTE: *The tank should not remain empty for long periods; otherwise, the sealing gaskets will dry out and leak.*

5. Disassemble the valves (**Figure 15**).

> NOTE: *The narrow shoulder ends of the 2 unions on each valve have left-hand threads.*

**Inspection**

1. Check the tank for leaks. Make sure the vent hole is clear.

2. Check the rubber mounts and bushings for deterioration and replace them if necessary.

3. Clean the fuel valves and the filter screens.

4. Check the fuel lines for leaks and cracks and replace them if there is the slightest doubt about their condition.

**Assembly**

1. Assemble the fuel valves and install them in the tank.

2. Coat the rubber mounts and bushings with rubber lube or WD-40 to make installation and future removal easier.

3. Install the tank, taking care not to crimp any of the electrical wiring along the top frame tube.

4. Connect the fuel lines.

5. Fill the tank with fresh gasoline, open the fuel valves, and check for leaks.

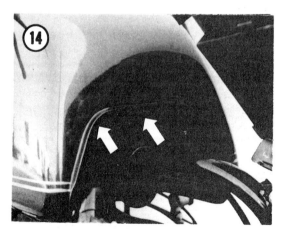

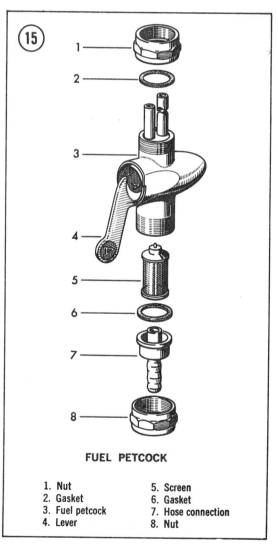

**FUEL PETCOCK**

1. Nut
2. Gasket
3. Fuel petcock
4. Lever
5. Screen
6. Gasket
7. Hose connection
8. Nut

NOTE: If you own a 1979 or later model, first check the Supplement at the back of the book for any new service information.

# CHAPTER SEVEN

# ELECTRICAL SYSTEM

Ignition systems, charging systems, batteries, starting system, lighting equipment, horn, control switches, wiring harness, and instruments are presented in this chapter. Routine adjustments for the ignition systems are cover in Chapter Three.

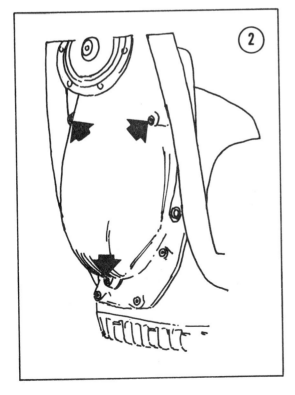

## IGNITION

BMW /5, /6, and /7 models are equipped with battery-coil type ignition, with automatic (centrifugal) spark advance control (**Figure 1**). Primary electrical power is supplied to the ignition through the battery and charging circuits. The advance mechanism and breaker cam are driven directly off the end of the camshaft.

**7**

### Disassembly

1. Disconnect the battery ground at transmission. Remove the front engine cover (**Figure 2**).

2. Unscrew the nut on the end of the camshaft and remove the advance mechanism (**Figure 3**).

3. Unplug the condenser wire, remove the screw from the point plate, and remove the contact breaker assembly (**Figure 4**).

4. Remove the fuel tank and disconnect the ground lead on the battery.

5. Disconnect the high-tension lead and the wires to terminals "1" and "15" on the coil (**Figure 5**).

6. Unscrew the Allen bolts (**Figure 6**) and remove the coil.

### Inspection

Inspection procedures, reassembly steps, and adjustment are covered in Chapter Three.

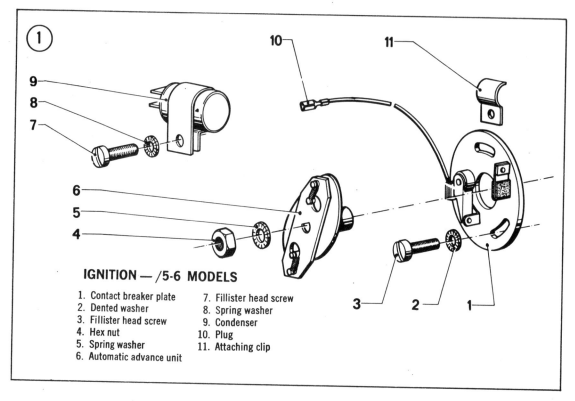

**IGNITION — /5-6 MODELS**

1. Contact breaker plate
2. Dented washer
3. Fillister head screw
4. Hex nut
5. Spring washer
6. Automatic advance unit
7. Fillister head screw
8. Spring washer
9. Condenser
10. Plug
11. Attaching clip

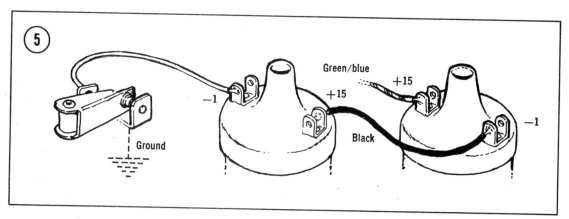

## Coil Testing

The ignition coils should be tested with an electrical bench tester. If you have such a tester, follow the instructions included with it and check the spark length. At start (300 sparks per minute) the spark length should be 8mm (0.3120 in.). At engine operating speeds (3,600 sparks per minute) spark length should be 13.5mm (0.532 in.).

If you do not have access to a bench tester, have the coil checked by an automotive or motorcycle electrical service specialist.

## Reassembly

1. Remount the coils with the Allen bolts. Be sure the ground wire is connected to the front bolt on the left coil. Reconnect the input wires and the high-tension leads (**Figure 5**).

2. Install the fuel tank. Be careful not to crimp or smash the electrical leads.

## Contact Breakers and Advance Mechanisms

Disassembly, inspection, service, and replacement of contact breakers, condensers, and advance mechanisms are covered in Chapter Three.

## CHARGING SYSTEM

This charging system consists of a 3-phase alternator, a diode-type rectifier, and a mechanical voltage regulator (**Figure 7**). The alternator is driven off the end of the crankshaft.

The rotor is an electromagnet, rather than a permanent magnet, and is energized by a demand signal from the regulator through contact brushes and slip rings.

### Testing Charging Circuit

1. Check the battery and make sure it is charged to its normal range.

2. Start the engine and bring its speed up to about 1,000 rpm.

3. Disconnect the battery ground lead and connect a voltmeter between the indicator light terminal D+ (blue lead) on the regulator and ground.

4. Increase the engine speed to about 2,000 rpm and check the reading on the voltmeter. It should be between 13.5 and 14.2 volts.

5. Turn on the main light switch and turn the headlight to high beam. Again, check the voltmeter. It should read between 13.9 and 14.8 volts.

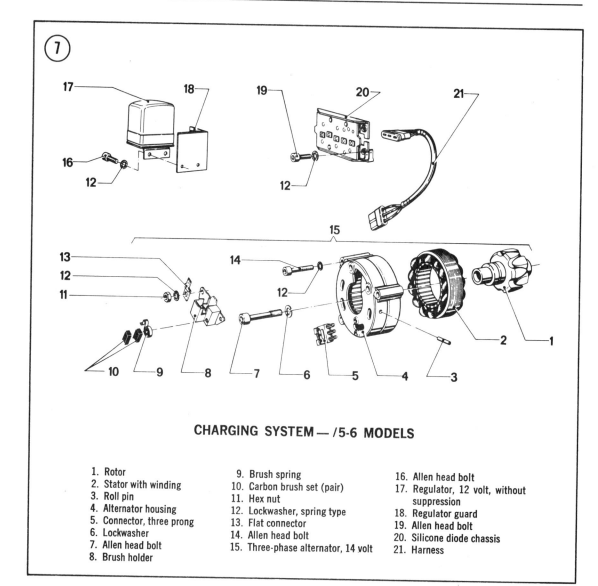

## CHARGING SYSTEM — /5-6 MODELS

1. Rotor
2. Stator with winding
3. Roll pin
4. Alternator housing
5. Connector, three prong
6. Lockwasher
7. Allen head bolt
8. Brush holder
9. Brush spring
10. Carbon brush set (pair)
11. Hex nut
12. Lockwasher, spring type
13. Flat connector
14. Allen head bolt
15. Three-phase alternator, 14 volt
16. Allen head bolt
17. Regulator, 12 volt, without suppression
18. Regulator guard
19. Allen head bolt
20. Silicone diode chassis
21. Harness

## Alternator Preliminary Test

If the charge indicator light remains lit when the engine is running and the battery is known to be in good condition, a simple test can be made to determine if the trouble is in the regulator or the alternator.

1. Unplug the electrical connector from the voltage regulator and bridge the D+ (blue) contact and the DF (black) contact with a short piece of insulated wire (**Figure 8**).

2. Start the engine and run it at 1,000-2,000 rpm. If the charge indicator light goes off, the trouble is in the regulator. If the light remains on, the trouble is in the alternator.

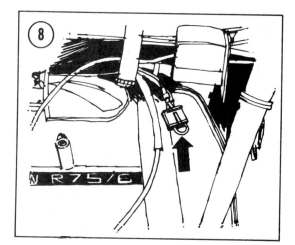

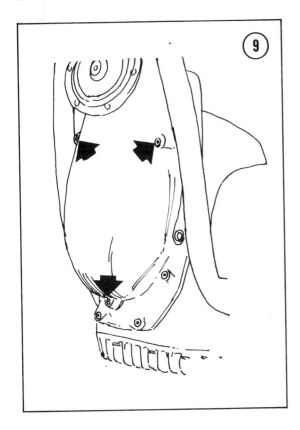

## Alternator Disassembly

1. Disconnect the battery. Remove the front engine cover (**Figure 9**).

2. Pull the 3-prong plug from the stator. Lift exciter brushes part way out of their holders and jam them in place with their springs. See **Figure 10**.

3. Unscrew the Allen bolts from the stator housing and remove the housing (**Figure 11**).

4. Unscrew the bolt from the center of the armature and press it off the shaft with a puller.

5. Remove the two 8mm hex nuts from the inside of the stator housing and remove the brush holder and brushes.

## Alternator Inspection

1. Check the armature slip rings for scoring. If necessary, have them turned in a lathe to a high finish. This is a job for an expert. Maximum diameter of the slip rings is 26.8mm (1.055 in.). Maximum permissible out-of-round of the slip ring is 0.06mm (0.0024 in.).

2. Check the conditions of the brushes. They should slide easily in their holders, and the

holddown springs should hold them firmly against the slip rings.

### Alternator Reassembly

1. If the brushes are replaced, make sure that solder does not run down into the wires.

2. Place the insulator bushing on the stud on the brush holder (**Figure 12**), install the insulator washers, and then reassemble the brush holder and the stator housing.

3. Reassemble the rotor and stator in reverse order of disassembly.

### Rectifier Disassembly

Silicon diodes are used to rectify the AC produced by the alternator to DC for storage in the battery and for operation of the components of the electrical system. A rectifier is a biased electrical device. It permits current to flow in only one direction. The rectifier performs its function by allowing the alternating current to flow in only one direction, cancelling the reverse pulse and thus rectifying the current to DC.

Because of the rectifier's bias, care must be taken during testing to hook up the test leads and the test battery in correct polarity. Failure to do this will result in a damaged rectifier.

1. Unscrew the 4 mounting screws and remove the diode rectifier chassis (**Figure 13**).

2. Withdraw the plug from the rectifier.

### Rectifier Testing

Use a service tester to check the continuity of the rectifier. Do not use a megger because the diodes may be damaged by the instrument's high voltage.

1. Test the rectifier for continuity in both directions.

2. Continuity in one direction indicates the rectifier is in good condition. Continuity in both directions, or in neither direction, indicates the rectifier is defective.

### Rectifier Reassembly

1. Insert the plug into the rectifier chassis.

2. Hold the rectifier in place on the timing case and reinstall the 4 screws.

### Voltage Regulator

The voltage regulator (**Figure 14**) is not adjustable. If a test of the charging circuit indicates the regulator may be defective, it should be removed and replaced or inspected and serviced by an authorized Bosch service center.

## BATTERY

The electrolyte level of the battery should be checked regularly, as described in Chapter Three.

### Removal

1. Remove the side covers and left air cleaner cover, and raise the seat.

2. On /5 models, remove the rubber hold-down strap. On /6 and /7 models, unscrew the nuts from the hold-down frame and remove the frame (**Figure 15**). Disconnect the leads from the battery — first the negative (ground) and then the positive.

3. Lift the battery forward and out the left side. Be careful not to spill the corrosive electrolyte.

### Inspection

1. Clean the terminals and clamps with a solution of baking soda and water.

2. Check the level of the electrolyte. It should be about 6mm (¼ in.) above the top of the plates. Top up any cells that are low, using only distilled water.

3. Measure the specific gravity of the electrolyte with a hydrometer, reading it as shown in **Figure 16**. Generally, the specific gravity

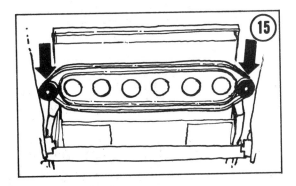

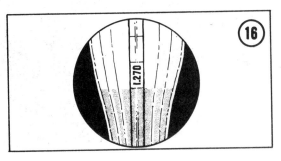

should be between 1.26 and 1.28. If it is less than 1.189 at 68°F (20°C), the battery should be charged. Specific gravity varies with ambient temperature.

### Battery Charging

A trickle charger is recommended for restoring a low-voltage battery. Most inexpensive automotive type chargers have a charging rate between 2 and 5 amperes.

A "quick charge" should never be applied to a fully discharged battery and only seldom to one that is partially discharged; the heat resulting from a quick charge is harmful to the battery.

> **WARNING**
> *During charging, highly explosive hydrogen gas is released from the battery. The battery should be charged only in a well-ventilated area, and sparks and open flames should be kept away. Never check the charge of a battery by arcing across the terminals; the resulting spark can ignite the hydrogen gas.*

1. Connect the positive charger lead to the positive battery terminal, and the negative lead to the negative terminal. Reversing the leads can result in damage to both the charger and the battery.

2. Remove the vent caps from the battery, select 12 volts on the charger, and switch it on. The battery should remain on the charger for about 10 hours, and not less than 8, if it is to receive a full charge. If the output of the charger is adjustable, it is best to select a low setting — about 1½ to 2 amps.

3. After a suitable charging period (8 to 10 hours), switch off the charger, disconnect the battery, and check the specific gravity. It should be within 1.26 to 1.28. If it is, and if after an hour's time the reading is the same, the battery is charged.

### Installation

1. Make sure the battery terminals, cable clamps, and case are free of corrosion. Check the rubber pad in the battery case and replace it if it is excessively compressed or rotted.

2. Install the battery in reverse order of removal. Be careful to route the vent tube so

7

that it is not crimped. Connect the positive terminal first, then the negative terminal. Don't over-tighten the clamp bolts, but make them snug enough so the clamps can't be rotated on the terminals.

3. Coat the terminals with a silicone spray, or Vaseline, to retard decomposition of the lead.

### STARTING SYSTEM

The electric starting system is shown schematically in **Figure 17**.

This section discusses servicing the starter motor, the solenoid, and the engagement mechanism. The kickstarter is covered in the transmission section of this handbook.

The starting system is shown in **Figures 18 and 19**.

### STARTER

#### Disassembly

1. Remove the fuel tank.

2. Remove the left half of the air filter housing and the air filter.

3. Loosen the hex nut **(Figure 20)** which holds the right housing in place, and remove housing.

4. Remove the right air intake tube **(Figure 21)**.

5. Unscrew the 2 Allen bolts **(Figure 22)** and remove the upper engine cover.

6. Disconnect ground lead from battery.

7. Disconnect the 2 starter cables **(Figure 23)**.

8. Remove 2 rear mounting bolts **(Figure 24)**.

9. Loosen the top horn mounting bolt. Unscrew the 3 Allen bolts from the front cover and remove it.

10. Use a socket wrench and remove the bolt inside the timing case **(Figure 25)**.

11. Pull the starter to the rear and lift it out.

#### Inspection

Overhaul of the starter motor should be entrusted to an expert.

1. Check the commutator brushes for wear. The springs should hold them firmly against the commutator. They should move freely in their holders. If the pressure is insufficient, replace the brushes.

2. Check the commutator for wear and burning. If the wear is excessive, or if burned spots are present (indicating arcing), have the commutator turned down and replace the brushes.

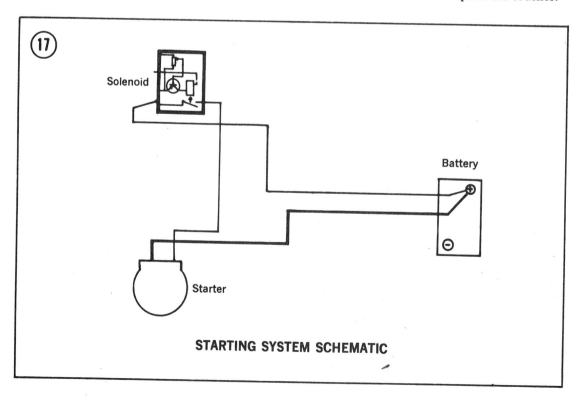

**STARTING SYSTEM SCHEMATIC**

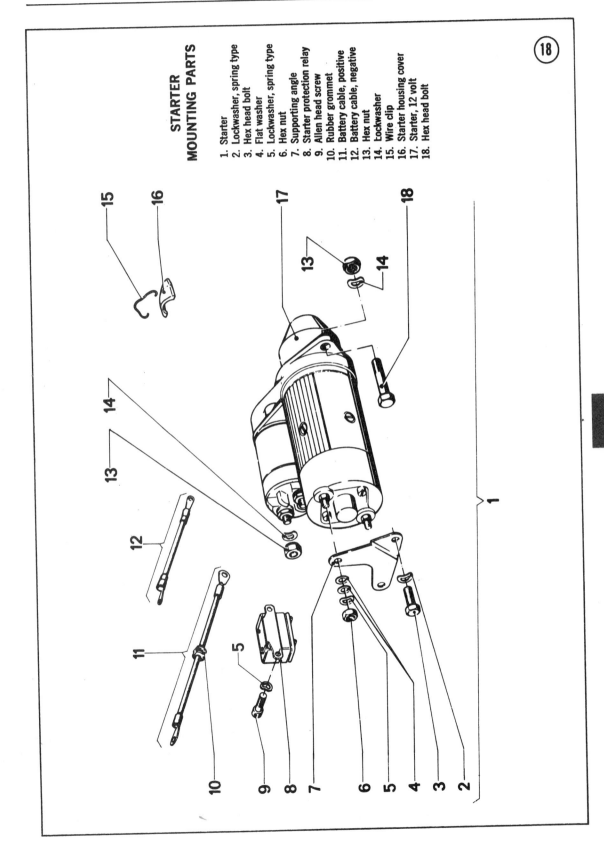

**STARTER MOUNTING PARTS**

1. Starter
2. Lockwasher, spring type
3. Hex head bolt
4. Flat washer
5. Lockwasher, spring type
6. Hex nut
7. Supporting angle
8. Starter protection relay
9. Allen head screw
10. Rubber grommet
11. Battery cable, positive
12. Battery cable, negative
13. Hex nut
14. Lockwasher
15. Wire clip
16. Starter housing cover
17. Starter, 12 volt
18. Hex head bolt

7

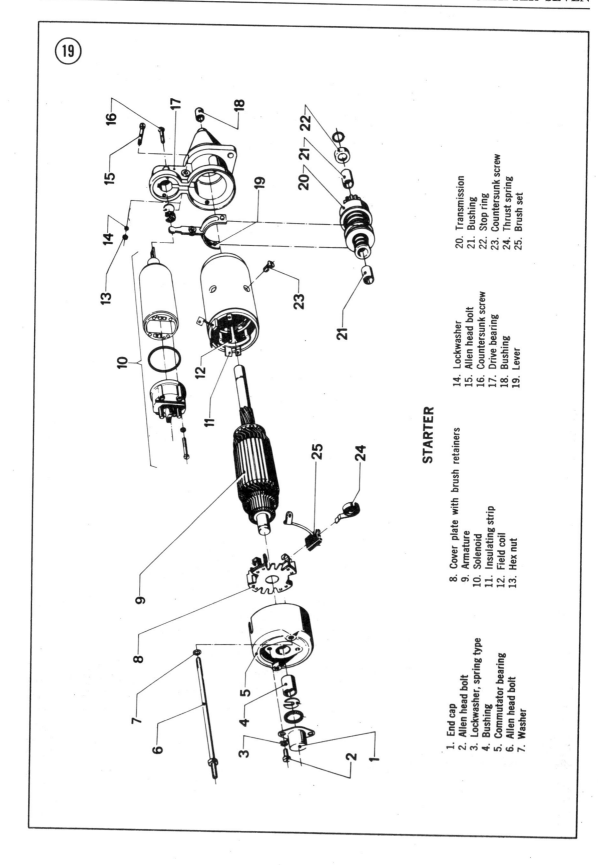

**STARTER**

1. End cap
2. Allen head bolt
3. Lockwasher, spring type
4. Bushing
5. Commutator bearing
6. Allen head bolt
7. Washer
8. Cover plate with brush retainers
9. Armature
10. Solenoid
11. Insulating strip
12. Field coil
13. Hex nut
14. Lockwasher
15. Allen head bolt
16. Countersunk screw
17. Drive bearing
18. Bushing
19. Lever
20. Transmission
21. Bushing
22. Stop ring
23. Countersunk screw
24. Thrust spring
25. Brush set

7

3. Check the electrical continuity of the armature and the shaft. If a short is present, the armature must be replaced.

4. Check the pinion gear on the engagement mechanism. Replace the pinion if the teeth are excessively worn or broken.

5. With the solenoid removed from the starter, reconnect the starter switch leads and depress the starter button. It should emit a loud click, and the actuating arm should be drawn into the solenoid body. If this does not occur, the solenoid should be replaced.

### Reassembly

Reassemble the starter and reinstall it in reverse order of the disassembly.

NOTE: *When reinstalling the front engine cover, make sure the condenser lead tube is correctly routed through its notch in the cover (Figure 26).*

### STARTER PROTECTION RELAY (/5 ONLY)

If starter can be engaged with engine running faster than idle, starter protection relay is malfunctioning and should be replaced or checked and serviced by an authorized Bosch service center.

To remove the relay, first remove the fuel tank. Then, disconnect the ground cable at the battery. Remove the 2 bolts and lockwashers (**Figure 27**) and unplug the 5 leads (**Figure 28**).

When reconnecting the leads, note which color wire goes on each terminal as follows:

No. 87      black
No. 15      green
No. 30      red (three)
No. 31b     brown/black
No. D +     blue (two)

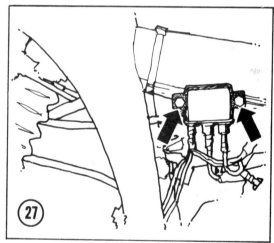

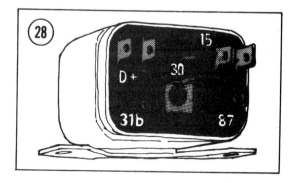

## LIGHTING, WIRING, AND INSTRUMENTS

Covered in this section are lighting equipment, horn, control switches, wiring harnesses, and instruments. Unless otherwise noted, reassembly is in reverse order of disassembly.

## HEADLIGHT

Refer to **Figure 29** (/5 models) and **Figure 30** (/6 and /7 models) for construction of the headlight.

### Disassembly

1. Carefully pry off the rim with a screwdriver and remove the rim, lens, and reflector.

2. Remove the bulb holder from the reflector **(Figure 31)**.

3. Remove the bulb from the holder by pushing in, turning it counterclockwise, and pulling out.

### Inspection

1. Visually check the bulb for broken filaments and replace it if necessary. If the filament is intact but the bulb won't light, connect it directly to the battery with jumper wires; it may have a gas leak which is not visually apparent.

2. Check the wiring for frayed insulation and corrosion of the plugs and terminals.

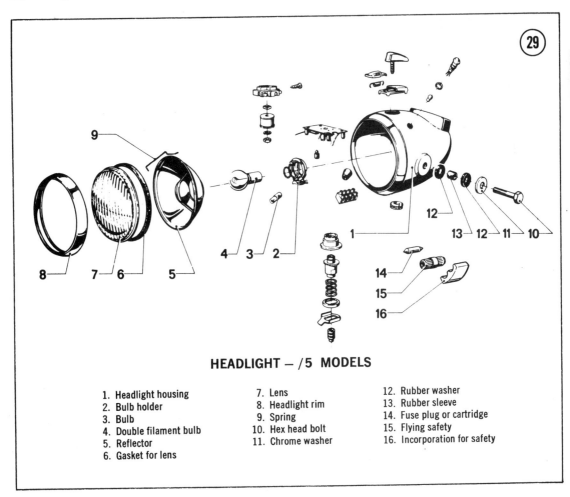

**HEADLIGHT — /5 MODELS**

| | | |
|---|---|---|
| 1. Headlight housing | 7. Lens | 12. Rubber washer |
| 2. Bulb holder | 8. Headlight rim | 13. Rubber sleeve |
| 3. Bulb | 9. Spring | 14. Fuse plug or cartridge |
| 4. Double filament bulb | 10. Hex head bolt | 15. Flying safety |
| 5. Reflector | 11. Chrome washer | 16. Incorporation for safety |
| 6. Gasket for lens | | |

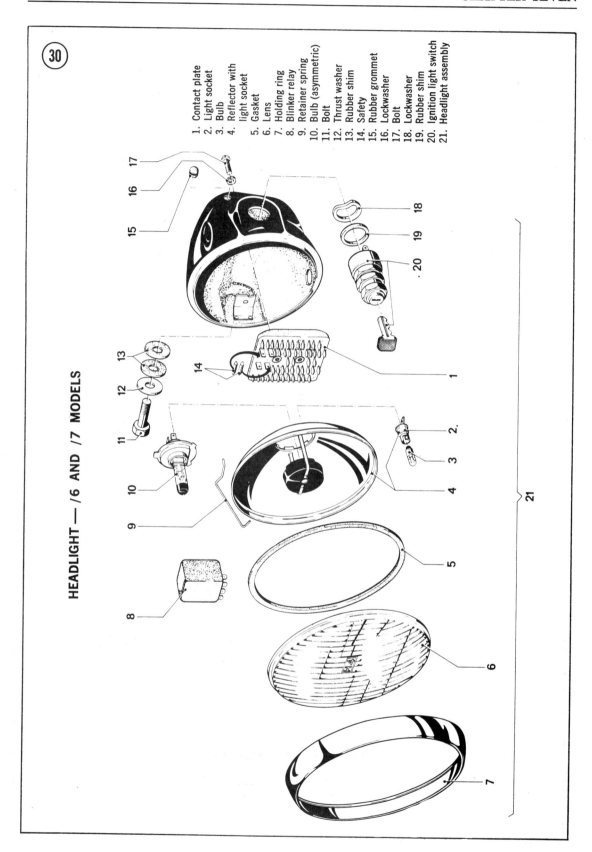

**HEADLIGHT — /6 AND /7 MODELS**

30

1. Contact plate
2. Light socket
3. Bulb
4. Reflector with light socket
5. Gasket
6. Lens
7. Holding ring
8. Blinker relay
9. Retainer spring
10. Bulb (asymmetric)
11. Bolt
12. Thrust washer
13. Rubber shim
14. Safety
15. Rubber grommet
16. Lockwasher
17. Bolt
18. Lockwasher
19. Rubber shim
20. Ignition light switch
21. Headlight assembly

## Adjustment

Refer to **Figure 32**.

1. Check the tire pressure for solo operation and adjust it if necessary (Chapter Ten).

2. Set the adjusters on the rear spring/shock absorbers in the SOLO position.

3. Place the motorcycle perpendicular to a light-colored wall, at a distance of 16.5 feet (5 meters), measured from the wall to the headlight lens.

4. Slightly loosen the mounting bolts on either side of the headlight body.

5. With the motorcycle on its wheels, mount it and have someone measure the distance from the center of the headlight lens to the ground.

6. Mark a cross on the wall at the same distance from the ground.

7. Switch on the headlight and select high beam. Align the headlight so that the cross is in the center of the illuminated area.

8. Select low beam. The upper edge of the illuminated area should be 2 inches (5 cm) below the cross, rising to the left where, at its apex, it meets the horizontal line of the cross.

9. When the adjustment is correct, tighten the headlight mounting bolts.

## TAIL/STOPLIGHT REPLACEMENT

Refer to **Figure 33** for this procedure.

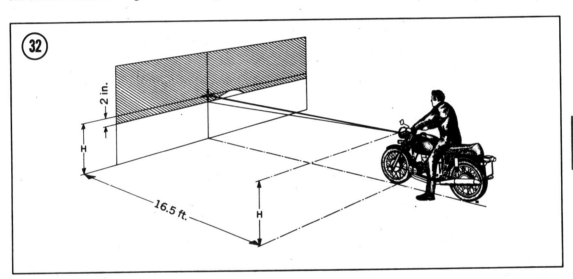

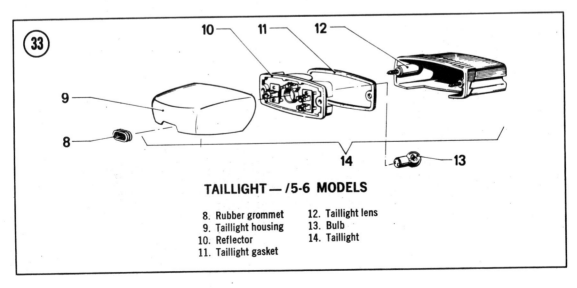

**TAILLIGHT — /5-6 MODELS**

8. Rubber grommet
9. Taillight housing
10. Reflector
11. Taillight gasket
12. Taillight lens
13. Bulb
14. Taillight

1. Remove the Phillips head screws from either side of the lens and pull it off (**Figure 34**).

2. Remove the bulbs from their sockets by pushing in, turning counterclockwise, and pulling out.

3. Install new bulb and install lens.

> CAUTION
> *When installing the taillight lens, don't overtighten the screws or the lens may crack.*

## TURN SIGNAL LAMP REPLACEMENT

Refer to **Figure 35** for this procedure.

1. Remove the 2 screws from the lens and remove the lens.

2. Remove the bulb from its socket by pushing in, turning counterclockwise, and pulling out.

3. Install new bulb and install lens.

> CAUTION
> *When installing lens, don't overtighten the screws or the lens may crack.*

## FLASHER RELAY

The relay is located inside the headlight body. See **Figure 36**.

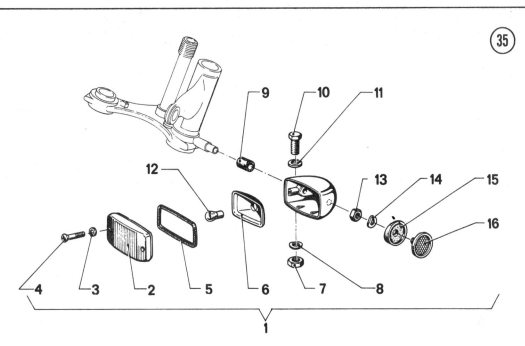

## FRONT TURN SIGNALS — /5-6 MODELS

1. Blinker light turn signal, front
2. Amber signal lens
3. Gasket
4. Oval head screw
5. Gasket
6. Reflector
7. Hex nut
8. Lockwasher, spring type
9. Rubber plug
10. Hex head bolt
11. Flat washer
12. Bulb
13. Hex nut
14. Lockwasher
15. Spacer
16. Turn signal reflector

7

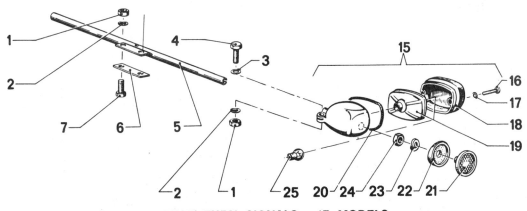

## REAR TURN SIGNALS — /5 MODELS

1. Hex nut
2. Lockwasher, spring type
3. Flat washer
4. Hex head bolt
5. Turn signal holder
6. Spacer
7. Hex head bolt
15. Blinker light turn signal rear
16. Oval head screw
17. Gasket
18. Turn signal lens
19. Reflector
20. Gasket
21. Red reflector for turn signal
22. Spacer
23. Lockwasher, spring type
24. Hex nut
25. Bulb

## Replacement

1. Remove the headlight lens and reflector as described earlier.

2. Pull the relay out of its socket (**Figure 37**).

3. Install new relay in socket and install headlight.

## Inspection

1. Flasher rate should be between 65 and 90 times per minute. If the rate is abnormal, check the ratings on the signal bulbs; the flashing rate is affected by the resistance of the bulbs.

2. Check for frayed wiring insulation and corroded terminals.

3. If the wiring and connections are sound and if the bulb ratings are correct and the flasher still does not operate normally, replace it.

## IGNITION SWITCH

Refer to **Figure 38** (/5 models) and **Figure 39** (/6 and /7 models) for construction of the ignition switch.

### Disassembly

1. Remove the headlight lens and reflector as described earlier.

2. Disconnect the battery ground lead.

3. Note the positions of the leads and remove the switch from the headlight body.

### Inspection

1. Check the switch terminals for tightness and corrosion. Check wiring for frayed insulation.

2. Refer to the wiring diagrams at the end of the chapter. Check the continuity of the switch, in each of the 3 operating positions (**Figure 40**), with a bench tester. If the test lamp lights, the circuit is good. If it does not, the circuit is open and the switch must be repaired or replaced.

## SWITCHES

Service on dimmer, turn signal, horn, and starter switches is limited to continuity checks in the appropriate circuits.

1. Check the terminals of the switch being tested for tightness and for corrosion of the contacts. Check wiring for frayed insulation.

2. Refer to wiring diagrams at the end of the chapter. Check the continuity of each switch, in its operating position, with a bench tester. If the test lamp lights, the circuit is good. If it does not, the circuit is open and the switch must be repaired or replaced.

## HORN

Service on the horn is limited to checking continuity (see above), increasing or decreasing the volume, and cleaning the contacts inside the horn.

1. To adjust the volume of the horn, loosen the locknut in the center of the horn face and turn

## HEADLIGHT AND
## IGNITION SWITCH — /5 MODELS

1. Contact bushing
2. Contact plate
3. Bakelite spacer
4. Spring
5. Ignition lock
6. Cover
7. Connector
8. Rubber grommet
9. Clamp bolt
10. Hex nut
11. Lockwasher
12. Elastic mount
13. Square nut
14. Push-button plug
15. Sheet metal screw
16. Switchplate with wires
17. Chrome switch cover
18. Spring
19. Plastic slide
20. Ignition key
21. Turn signal indicator lamp, green
22. Rubber O-ring for indicator light
23. Bulb
24. Rubber grommet

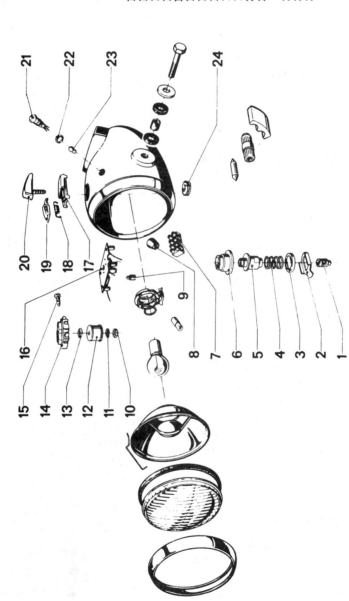

7

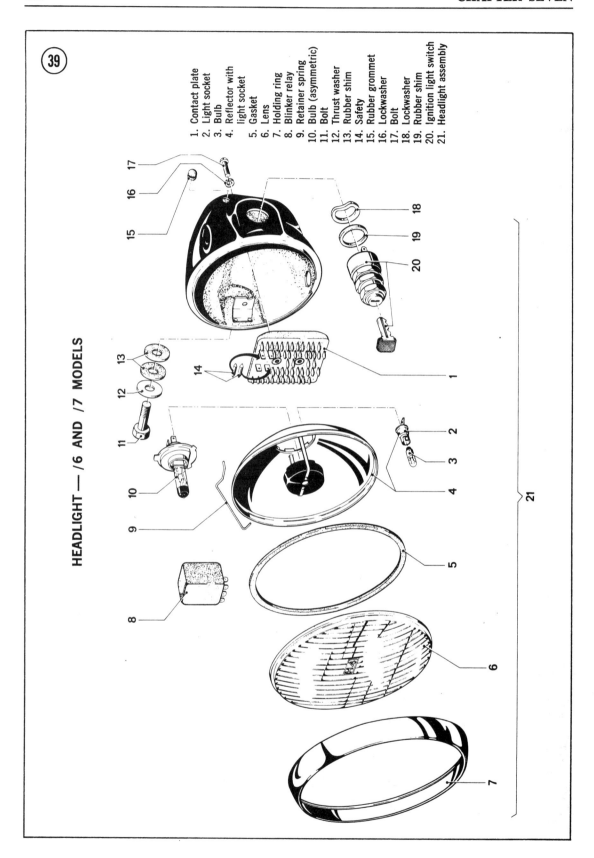

**39**

HEADLIGHT — /6 AND /7 MODELS

1. Contact plate
2. Light socket
3. Bulb
4. Reflector with light socket
5. Gasket
6. Lens
7. Holding ring
8. Blinker relay
9. Retainer spring
10. Bulb (asymmetric)
11. Bolt
12. Thrust washer
13. Rubber shim
14. Safety
15. Rubber grommet
16. Lockwasher
17. Bolt
18. Lockwasher
19. Rubber shim
20. Ignition light switch
21. Headlight assembly

1. Black    2. Green (two)

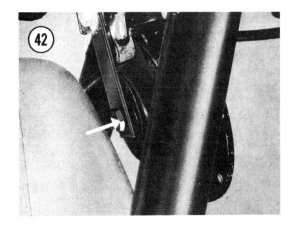

the adjuster screw in to increase it or out to decrease it. Retighten the locknut.

2. If switch and wiring continuity are good and the horn won't sound, disconnect the leads (**Figure 41**), unscrew the bolt (**Figure 42**), and remove the horn.

3. Unscrew the screws from the horn face and remove it.

4. Dress the contacts with a point file or flexstone, reassemble horn, and adjust its volume.

### FRONT BRAKE LIGHT SWITCH

1. Check the continuity of the switch and inspect the wiring for frayed insulation and corroded contacts.

2. With the brake lever free play correctly adjusted (**Figure 43**), rotate the switch adjuster located behind the cable adjuster. The brake lamp should light when about one-half of the free play is taken up.

### REAR BRAKE LIGHT SWITCH

1. Check the continuity of the switch and inspect the wiring for frayed insulation and corroded contacts.

2. With the brake pedal adjusted in accordance with the instructions in Chapter Ten, loosen the locknut on the adjuster bolt (**Figure 44**). Rotate the adjuster so that the brake lamp lights when about one-half of the free play is taken up. Retighten the locknut.

### OIL PRESSURE SWITCH

The oil pressure sensing switch is located on the left side of the engine, at the bottom of the

kg/cm² (28 psi) or rises above 5 kg/cm² (71 psi). If continuity of the switch circuit is good and the warning light remains on during normal engine operation, replace the switch. If the light continues to remain on, have the engine checked by a BMW service specialist for malfunction of the lubrication system or excessively worn crankshaft bearings.

## NEUTRAL SWITCH

Servicing of the neutral indicator switch is covered in Chapter Five, *Transmission Assembly*.

## INDICATOR LIGHTS

Indicator and warning lights have bayonet-type bases. Their service is limited to continuity checks, visual inspection for broken filaments, and replacement. The turn signal indicator light is mounted in the headlight body, and the neutral indicator, high beam indicator, and oil pressure light are mounted in the speedometer/tachometer body.

## INSTRUMENTS

The speedometer and tachometer are cable driven. Repairs should be made only by an ex-pert. The instruments are shown in **Figure 45** (/5 models) and **Figure 46** (/6 and /7 models). An electronic tachometer is fitted to 1978 /7 models.

### Disassembly

1. Remove the headlight ring, lens, and reflector as outlined earlier.

2. Disconnect the cables from the rear of the instrument.

3. Remove clamping brace and lift speedometer/tachometer out of the headlight body.

## WIRING HARNESS

The wiring harness is color coded in accordance with the wiring diagrams at the end of the book. Continuity checks can be conducted with the harness installed; it should be removed and replaced only if insulation is frayed or burned. To remove harness, first remove fuel tank, seat, and light lenses. Unscrew and unplug harness leads from electrical components, unfasten harness straps, and remove harness. Reinstall new harness in reverse order of disassembly.

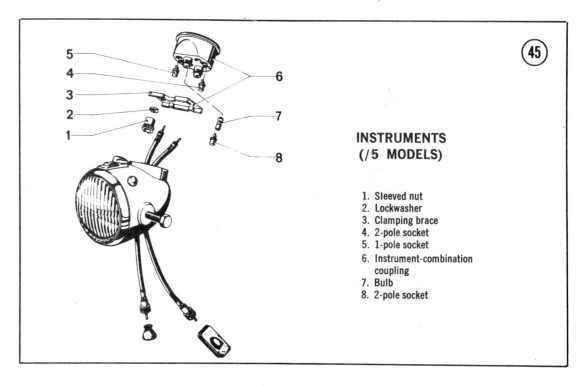

(45)

**INSTRUMENTS (/5 MODELS)**

1. Sleeved nut
2. Lockwasher
3. Clamping brace
4. 2-pole socket
5. 1-pole socket
6. Instrument-combination coupling
7. Bulb
8. 2-pole socket

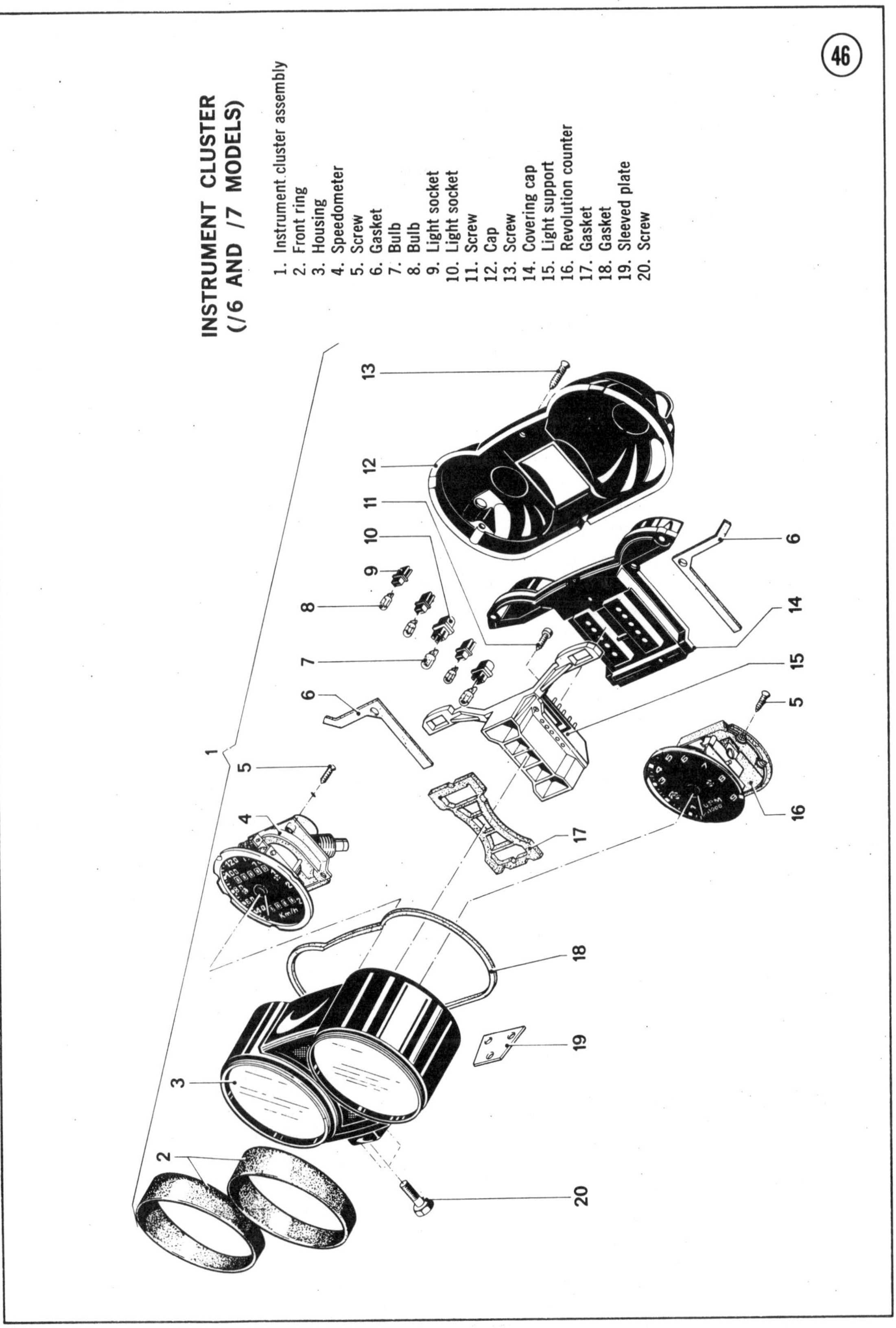

## INSTRUMENT CLUSTER (/6 AND /7 MODELS)

1. Instrument cluster assembly
2. Front ring
3. Housing
4. Speedometer
5. Screw
6. Gasket
7. Bulb
8. Bulb
9. Light socket
10. Light socket
11. Screw
12. Cap
13. Screw
14. Covering cap
15. Light support
16. Revolution counter
17. Gasket
18. Gasket
19. Sleeved plate
20. Screw

46

7

# FRONT SUSPENSION, STEERING, AND FRAME

The front suspension is shown in **Figures 1 through 3**. Refer to these exploded views when disassembling and assembling the front suspension and steering.

## DAMPING OIL

The damping oil in the front forks should be changed every 8,000 miles or once a year, or at anytime excessive bouncing of the front end indicates a low oil level. Changing of the damping oil is described in Chapter Three.

## STEERING DAMPER—FRICTION TYPE (/5)

### Disassembly

1. Remove the circlip from the bottom of the damper rod and unscrew the damper knob (**Figure 4**).

2. Remove the knob, spring washer, pressure plate, and rubber guide ring inside the center tube.

3. Unscrew the Allen bolt from the frame and remove the damper plate (**Figure 5**).

### Inspection and Reassembly

Check the contact surfaces of the damper plate and replace the unit if they are excessively

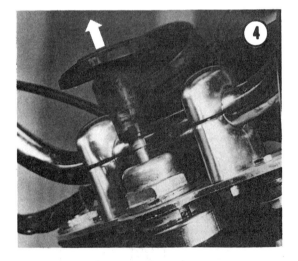

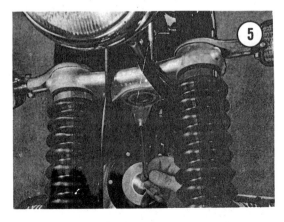

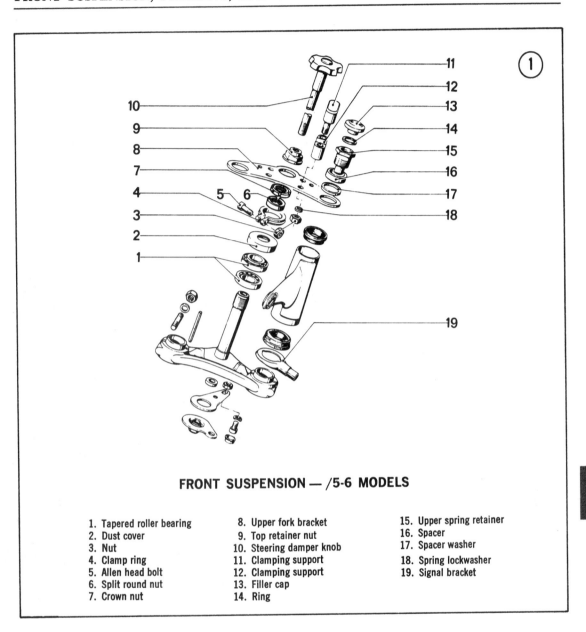

**FRONT SUSPENSION — /5-6 MODELS**

1. Tapered roller bearing
2. Dust cover
3. Nut
4. Clamp ring
5. Allen head bolt
6. Split round nut
7. Crown nut
8. Upper fork bracket
9. Top retainer nut
10. Steering damper knob
11. Clamping support
12. Clamping support
13. Filler cap
14. Ring
15. Upper spring retainer
16. Spacer
17. Spacer washer
18. Spring lockwasher
19. Signal bracket

worn, pitted, or galled. Reassemble the damper in reverse order of disassembly.

### STEERING DAMPER— HYDRAULIC (/6 and /7)

The hydraulic steering damper on /6 and /7 models (**Figure 6**) can be adjusted with the knob at the top of the steering head to suit different riding and load conditions. The assembly is self-locating during installation and requires no preliminary adjustment.

**Removal/Installation**

1. Rotate the damper knob so the "O" points straight ahead. Unscrew the screw from the center of the knob and pull the knob straight up and off the control shaft (**Figure 7**).

2. Remove the clips from the damper ball-joints and pull the joints off the balls (**Figure 8**).

3. From beneath the bottom fork clamp, unscrew the Allen bolts and remove the damper adjuster assembly (**Figure 9**). Be careful not to

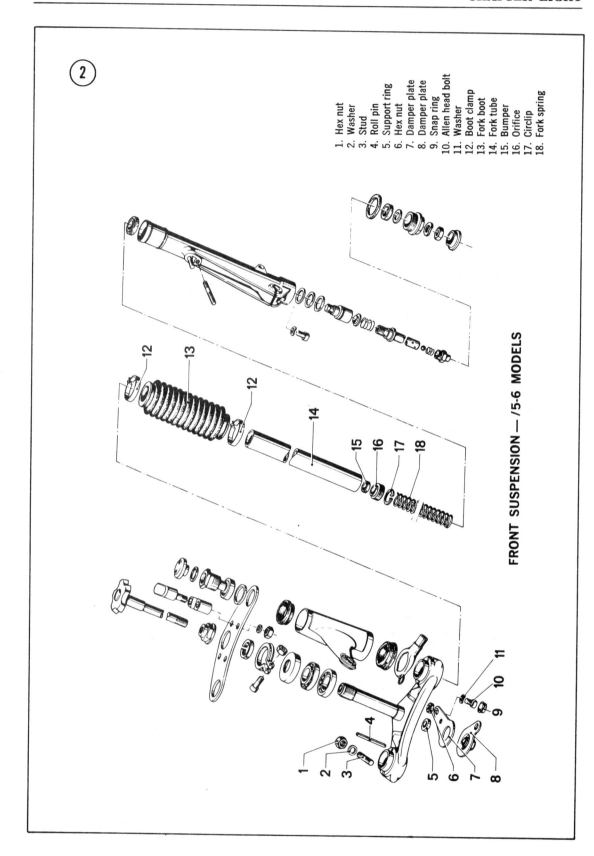

1. Hex nut
2. Washer
3. Stud
4. Roll pin
5. Support ring
6. Hex nut
7. Damper plate
8. Damper plate
9. Snap ring
10. Allen head bolt
11. Washer
12. Boot clamp
13. Fork boot
14. Fork tube
15. Bumper
16. Orifice
17. Circlip
18. Fork spring

FRONT SUSPENSION — /5-6 MODELS

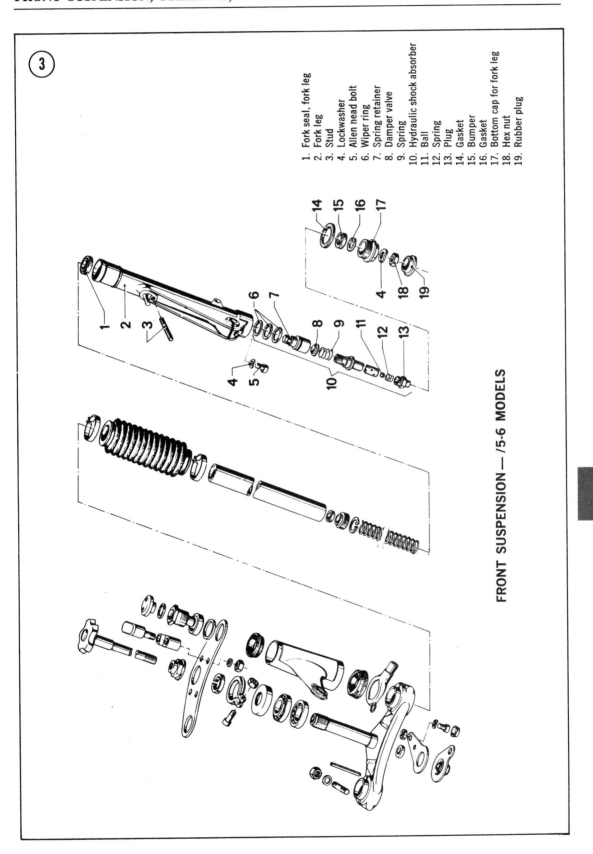

1. Fork seal, fork leg
2. Fork leg
3. Stud
4. Lockwasher
5. Allen head bolt
6. Wiper ring
7. Spring retainer
8. Damper valve
9. Spring
10. Hydraulic shock absorber
11. Ball
12. Spring
13. Plug
14. Gasket
15. Bumper
16. Gasket
17. Bottom cap for fork leg
18. Hex nut
19. Rubber plug

**FRONT SUSPENSION — /5-6 MODELS**

8

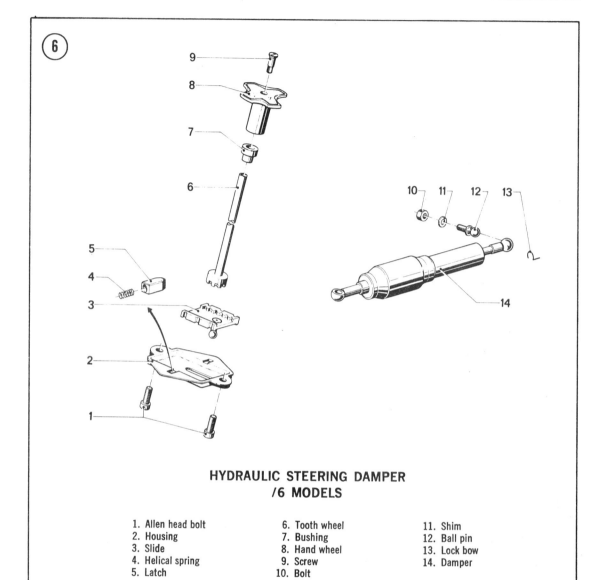

**HYDRAULIC STEERING DAMPER
/6 MODELS**

1. Allen head bolt
2. Housing
3. Slide
4. Helical spring
5. Latch
6. Tooth wheel
7. Bushing
8. Hand wheel
9. Screw
10. Bolt
11. Shim
12. Ball pin
13. Lock bow
14. Damper

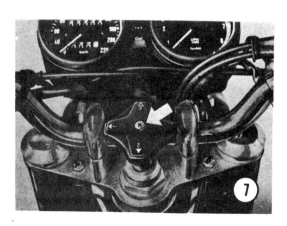

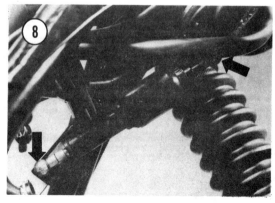

drop any of the pieces. Pull the assembly down and out of the steering head.

4. Reverse the above to install the damper assembly. Make sure the moveable ball is installed in the center of the adjuster plate (right end of the slot) and the knob is reinstalled with

the "O" facing forward. Lightly grease the balls before installing the damper and reconnect the clips. Check operation of the adjuster by indexing each position with the knob while checking movement of adjuster ball in slot.

## FRONT FORKS

### Removal

The procedure that follows covers complete removal and disassembly of the front forks. For routine seal replacement, the fork tubes need not be disturbed; only the sliders must be removed.

1. Place the motorcycle on the center stand and block up the front until the front wheel is off the ground (**Figure 10**).

2. On models equipped with a drum brake, disconnect the brake cable from the brake arm and the backing plate. Remove the nut from the brake anchor bolt and remove the bolt (**Figure 11**).

3. Unscrew the axle nut, loosen the pinch bolt, and pull out the axle (**Figure 12**). Remove the front wheel and brake assembly.

4. On models equipped with a disc brake, unscrew the axle nut, remove the washer, loosen the pinch bolt, and pull the axle out of the forks and wheel (**Figure 13**). Remove the wheel.

> NOTE: *Do not pull the brake lever when the disc is removed.*

5. Remove the bolt that attaches the brake line bracket to the fork leg (**Figure 14**). Remove the

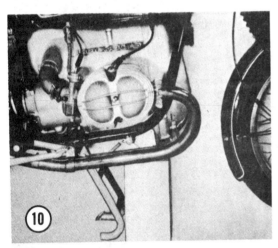

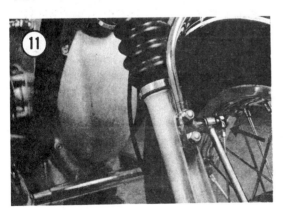

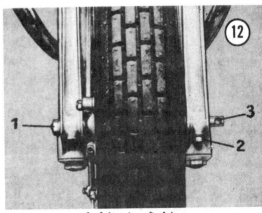

1. Axle nut    3. Axle
2. Pinch bolt

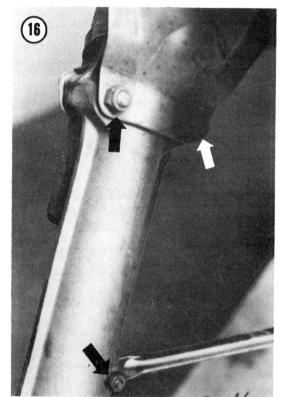

cap and spring from the bottom of the fork leg (**Figure 15**). Unscrew the eccentric adjuster pin located above the cap and remove the brake caliper from the fork leg. Tie the caliper out of the way and in such a manner that it does not hang on the brake hose.

6. Unscrew the nuts from the upper fender brace (**Figure 16**).

7. Unscrew the nuts and bolts from the lower fender braces and remove the front fender.

8. Remove the rubber cap from the bottom of each fork leg. Place a drip pan beneath one of

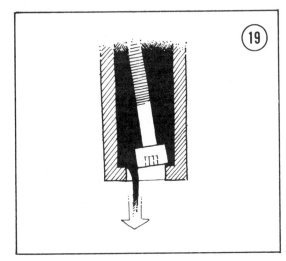

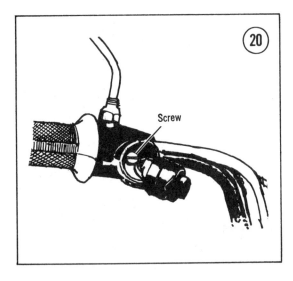

Screw

the fork legs. Hold the 4mm Allen bolt to prevent it from turning and unscrew the 13mm plug (**Figure 17**).

9. Unscrew the fill plug from the top of the fork leg using the pin wrench that is provided in the motorcycle tool kit (**Figure 18**). Push up on the Allen bolt and offset it so the oil will drain freely (**Figure 19**). Allow several minutes for the oil to drain and then drain the opposite leg in the same manner.

10. Loosen the clamping bands on the fork boots and slide the boots off the lower fork legs (sliders).

11. Pull the sliders off the fork tubes. If only the seals are being replaced, remove the old seals from the sliders and clean the sliders with solvent and blow them dry. Refer to *Seal Replacement* at the end of this chapter and install new seals. Reverse the preceding disassembly steps to assemble the front end. Refer to Chapter Three, *Front Forks*, and fill the forks with the correct grade and quantity of damping oil. If the upper fork legs are to be removed for inspection and service, continue on with the remaining disassembly steps.

12. Remove the steering damper.

13. Disconnect the battery ground cable.

14. Remove screws from the switch bracket and remove cable straps from the handlebars.

15. Pull the switch out of the bracket and remove the screw (**Figure 20**). Remove the opposite side switch the same way.

16. Remove headlight mounting bolts, washers, and grommets. Wrap the headlight in several thicknesses of newspaper, place a paper bag over it, and tape the neck of the bag closed around the wiring harness.

17. Cover the fuel tank with a clean cloth, remove the handlebar supports from the upper fork bracket (**Figure 21**), and carefully lay the handlebars on the fuel tank.

18. Remove the filler caps from the tops of the fork legs with a pin wrench.

19. Place a small block between the left side fork stops and unscrew the upper spring retainers (**Figure 22**).

20. Unscrew the nut from the top of the steering head (**Figure 23**) and remove the upper fork bracket.

8

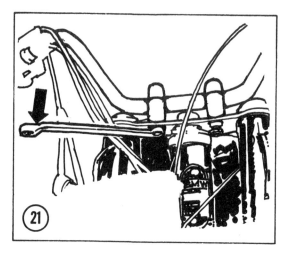

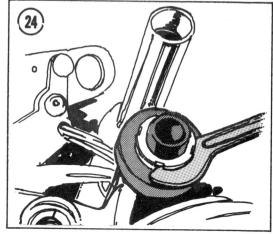

Allen bolt

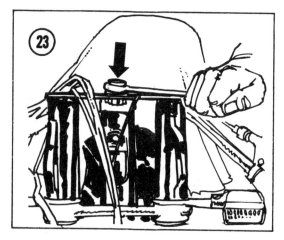

21. Remove the turn signal lenses and disconnect the wires.

22. Lift off the headlight brackets with their rubber rings, and at the same time pull out the turn signal wires.

23. Unscrew the crown nut (if fitted). See **Figure 24**. Remove the Allen bolt from the clamp ring and remove the ring (**Figure 25**). Remove the split ring nut and the upper dust cover from the steering head.

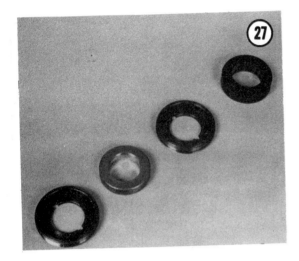

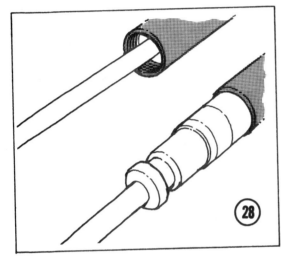

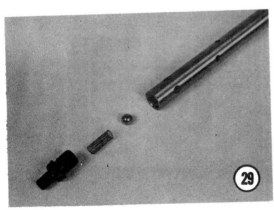

grooved wooden blocks between the vise jaws and the pivot tube.

> NOTE: *The remaining steps describe disassembly of the forks.*

26. Remove the dust cover.

27. Remove the gaskets from the bottom of the shock absorber bolts and remove the circlips from the bottom of the fork tubes (**Figure 26**). Then, remove the oil orifices with a pin wrench (**Figure 27**).

28. Pull out the shock absorbers, along with the bottoming rings and the springs (**Figure 28**).

29. Remove the springs.

30. To remove the fork tubes from the yoke, loosen the yoke pinch bolts, spread the tube bosses with a wedge, and withdraw the tubes.

31. Clamp the hex nut on the bottom of the shock absorber in a vise and unscrew the spring support and the piston rings. Remove the damper valve and its spring.

32. Clamp the shock absorber tube into a vise, using jaw protectors. Unscrew the retainer and remove the other ball and spring (**Figure 29**).

**Inspection**

1. If the front fork has been damaged in a collision, carefully examine the bottom fork yoke, top fork clamp, fork tubes, and lower legs for hairline fractures. Replace damaged parts as necessary.

2. Check the fork tubes for runout (**Figure 30**). The maximum allowable runout is 0.1mm (0.0039 in.). If the runout is more than this, replace the tube.

> WARNING
> *Do not attempt to straighten bent fork tubes. The likelihood of a fracture is very high in a tube which has been bent and straightened.*

3. Install true legs in the lower fork yoke. The distance from the top of the leg to the yoke (**Figure 31**) should be 160mm (6.3 in.).

4. Place 2 straightedges across the ends of the tubes (**Figure 32**) and visually check for distortion or misalignment.

5. With a large caliper, check to see that the tubes are parallel in the yoke.

24. Pull the fork assembly downward out of the steering head. It may be necessary to tap on the top of the pivot tube with a soft-face mallet.

25. Upend the fork and drain the oil from the legs. Clamp the entire assembly into a vise with

**8**

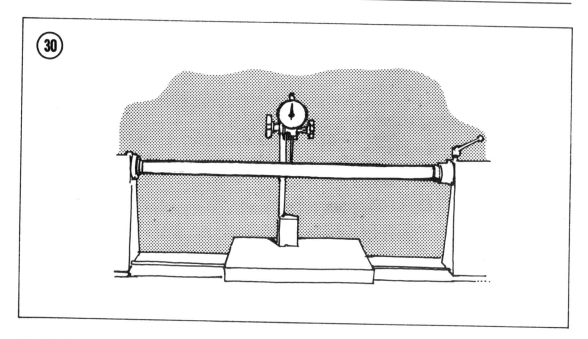

6. Check the alignment of the steering pivot tube with the fork tubes by installing the upper fork brace, the center nut, and the 2 spring retainers (**Figure 33**). The nut and retainers must screw on easily, without binding. If any of the above indicates that the lower fork yoke is bent, don't attempt to straighten it. Instead, replace it with a new unit.

7. With an inside micrometer, measure the inside diameter of lower fork leg at its upper end. It should be $28 \pm 0.15$mm ($1.10 \pm 0.006$ in.). With an outside micrometer, measure outside diameter of shock absorber piston. It should be $27.7 \pm 0.1$mm ($1.09 \pm 0.004$ in.).

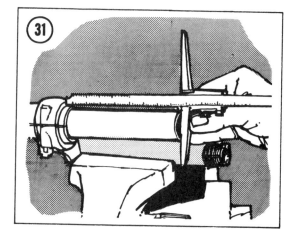

Subtract the piston diameter from the fork leg inside diameter to determine actual clearance. It should be between 0.05 and 0.55mm (0.0019 and 0.0217 in.). If the clearance is excessive, replace the worn component. Most likely, this will be the piston.

8. Check the damper valves for pitting and replace them if necessary. Check the valve springs for tension. If they offer little resistance, they should be replaced.

## Reassembly/Installation

1. Reassemble the shock absorbers in reverse order of disassembly.

2. Clamp the bottom retainer in a vise and tighten both ends of the shock absorber simul-

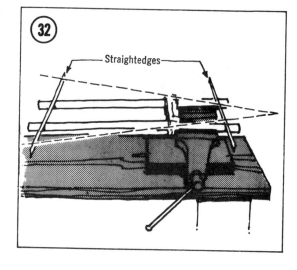

Straightedges

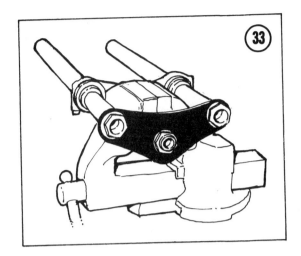

Rubber rings

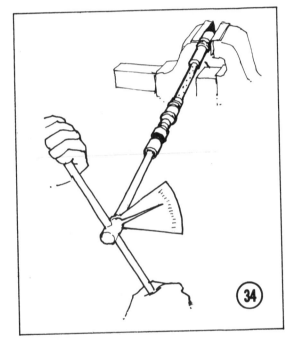

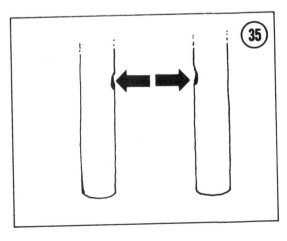

taneously (**Figure 34**) by turning the spring retainer nut with a torque wrench. Torque assembly to between 2.5-2.7 mkg (18-19.5 ft.-lb.).

3. Grease the steering head bearings and races. Set the top bearing into its outer race and slide bottom bearings over its inner race.

4. Reinstall the lower fork yoke and the top fork clamp in the steering head.

5. Reinstall the dust cover and the split ring nut. Tighten the nut until there is no play. Tap the tube and the yoke to take up any slack as you tighten the nut. Install the clamp ring and tighten the pinch bolt. The fork yoke and clamp assembly should move easily from side to side, with no play present, along the pivot axis.

6. Slide the fork tubes into the yoke. The holes in the tubes must face each other (**Figure 35**). Reinstall the turn signals and headlight brackets. Push the fork tubes up against the upper bracket (**Figure 36**). Install the upper spring retainers and torque them to 12 mkg (87 ft.-lb.). Tighten the pinch bolts.

7. Slide the dust covers onto the fork tubes, making sure the vent pipe in the fork yoke engages the vent hole in the cover (**Figure 37**). Tighten the cover clamping band.

8. Slide the springs and shock absorbers into the fork tubes.

9. Compress the shock absorber rings and insert the springs and shock absorbers, with the plastic ring in place, into the fork tubes.

8

10. Reinstall the oil orifice and circlip (**Figure 38**).

11. Install new gaskets on the bottom of the shock bolt and reinstall the lower fork legs. Hold shock absorber bolts with an Allen wrench and tighten retaining nuts. Torque nuts to between 2.3-2.6 mkg (16.6-18.8 ft.-lb.).

12. Slide the bottoms of the dust covers onto the legs and tighten the bands.

13. Reinstall the handlebars, switches, headlight, front fender and wheel, and steering damper in reverse order of disassembly. Refer to Chapter Three for filling the forks with oil, to Chapter Seven for adjusting headlight, and to Chapter Ten for adjusting front brake.

## SEAL REPLACEMENT

1. Remove the fork sliders as described earlier.

2. Carefully pry out the old seals from the top of the sliders. It may be necessary to heat the sliders to expand them and free the seals.

3. Clean the seal bores and tap in new seals, with the open face of the seal facing down. A large socket makes a suitable seal driver.

## STEERING HEAD BEARING ADJUSTMENT

### WARNING

*Steering head bearing adjustment is critical to the safe operation of the motorcycle. A specially calibrated wrench is available through the BMW distributors, Butler and Smith (see Sources list at the end of Chapter 11). If you do not have this wrench for the procedure which follows, refer this task to a BMW dealer.*

1. Unscrew the screw from the top of the steering damper knob (**Figure 39**) and remove the knob.

2. Loosen the handlebar mounting nuts (**Figure 40**) just enough so the handlebar can be pushed forward and the centering nut wrench can be put on the centering nut.

3. Loosen the centering nut and tighten the notched nut (**Figure 41**) with the special wrench until the fork will fall either right or left by its own weight. Hold the notched nut to prevent it from turning and tighten the centering nut.

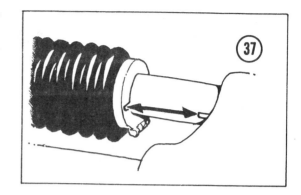

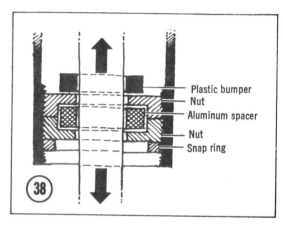

Plastic bumper
Nut
Aluminum spacer
Nut
Snap ring

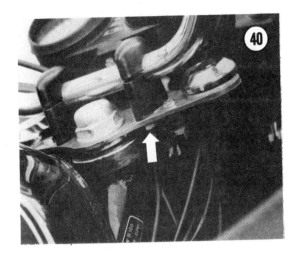

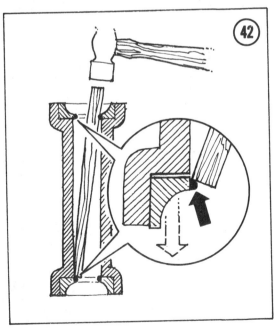

4. Grasp the fork legs and check for back and forth movement. If movement is present, readjust the steering head as just described.

5. If movement is still present or if roughness is felt as the fork is turned from side to side, the steering head bearings should be inspected and replaced if the races or balls are worn, pitted, or galled.

## STEERING HEAD BEARING REPLACEMENT

1. Disassemble the front end as described earlier.

2. Arc-weld a bead on each of the bearing races (**Figure 42**). Don't weld races to head.

3. Tap the races out of the steering head with a drift applied to the weld bead (**Figure 42**).

4. Clean the bearing race seats and drive in new races. Make sure the races are square with the bore and drive them in flush.

5. Reassemble the front end with new bearings. Grease the races and bearings with waterproof grease. Adjust the steering head as described in the previous procedure.

## FRAME

Frame service is limited to inspection for cracks in welds and tubes. If bending damage is suspected or apparent, the frame should be inspected and repaired as necessary by an authorized BMW service shop.

### Stripping the Frame

Refer to the appropriate chapters and remove the engine, transmission, controls, electrical system, seat, fuel tank, wheels, and suspension.

**Figures 43 and 44** are provided as general reference for the frame and for removal and installation of related components.

### Reassembly

Reassembly of the frame and installation of major components should follow the reverse order of disassembly.

Carefully label *every* piece for location as it is removed. Small, related parts should be kept together in small bags.

8

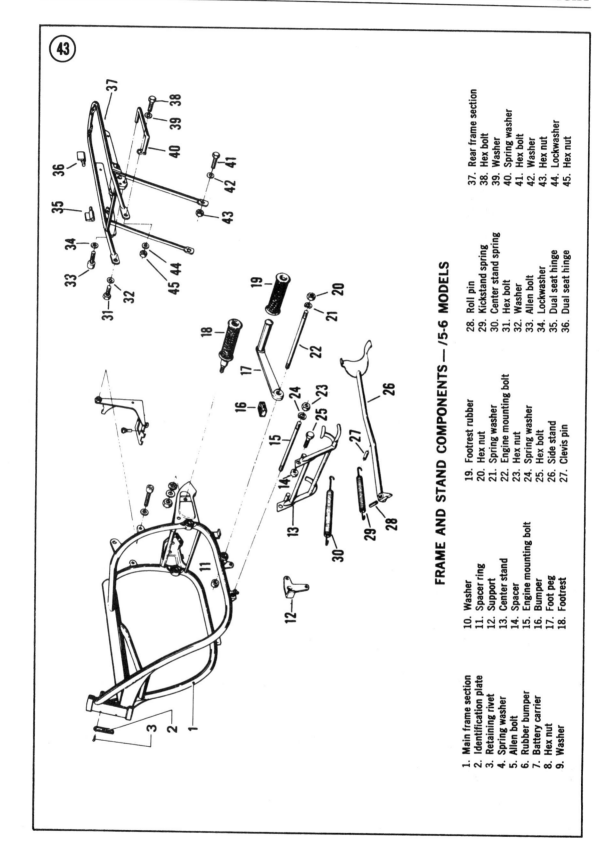

**FRAME AND STAND COMPONENTS—/5-6 MODELS**

1. Main frame section
2. Identification plate
3. Retaining rivet
4. Spring washer
5. Allen bolt
6. Rubber bumper
7. Battery carrier
8. Hex nut
9. Washer
10. Washer
11. Spacer ring
12. Support
13. Center stand
14. Spacer
15. Engine mounting bolt
16. Bumper
17. Foot peg
18. Footrest
19. Footrest rubber
20. Hex nut
21. Spring washer
22. Engine mounting bolt
23. Hex nut
24. Spring washer
25. Hex bolt
26. Side stand
27. Clevis pin
28. Roll pin
29. Kickstand spring
30. Center stand spring
31. Hex bolt
32. Washer
33. Allen bolt
34. Lockwasher
35. Dual seat hinge
36. Dual seat hinge
37. Rear frame section
38. Hex bolt
39. Washer
40. Spring washer
41. Hex bolt
42. Washer
43. Hex nut
44. Lockwasher
45. Hex nut

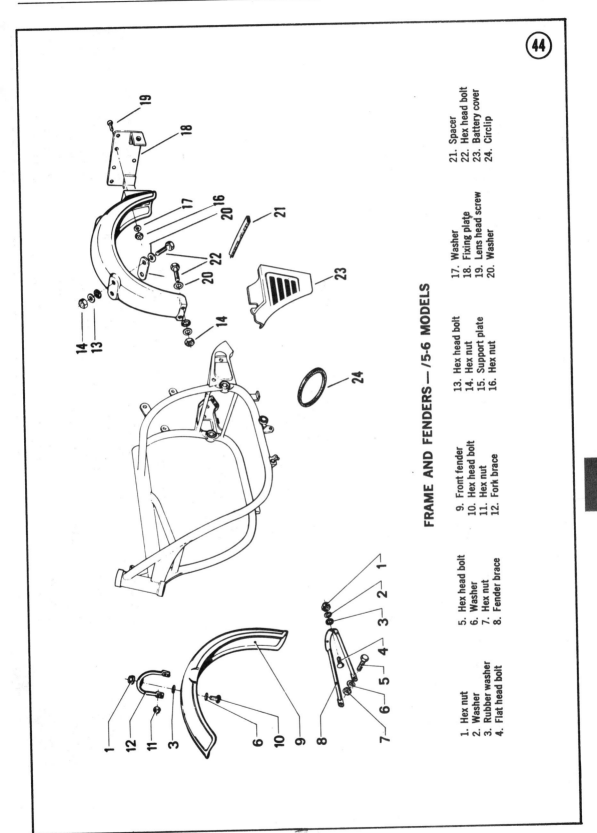

## FRAME AND FENDERS — /5-6 MODELS

1. Hex nut
2. Washer
3. Rubber washer
4. Flat head bolt

5. Hex head bolt
6. Washer
7. Hex nut
8. Fender brace

9. Front fender
10. Hex head bolt
11. Hex nut
12. Fork brace

13. Hex head bolt
14. Hex nut
15. Support plate
16. Hex nut

17. Washer
18. Fixing plate
19. Lens head screw
20. Washer

21. Spacer
22. Hex head bolt
23. Battery cover
24. Circlip

8

# CHAPTER NINE

# REAR SUSPENSION
# AND FINAL DRIVE

All models have a swing arm rear suspension with hydraulically dampened, coil-spring controlled rear spring/shock absorbers.

The hydraulic damping units on all models cannot be rebuilt. If they are found faulty, they should be replaced. Spring/shock absorbers are shown in **Figure 1**.

## REAR SHOCKS/SPRINGS

**Disassembly/Assembly**

1. Place the motorcycle on the center stand.

2. Remove the upper mounting bolts from the shocks (**Figure 2**).

3. Remove the lower right bolt, then elevate the swing arm slightly and remove the lower left bolt.

4. Move the selector on the shocks to its lowest tension setting, and install the shock compressor (BMW tool No. 550). See **Figure 3**. Clamp the upper shock eye in a vise and compress the shock. Place an open-end 9mm wrench on the 2 flats on the shock absorber shaft and unscrew the shaft from the eye.

> NOTE: *It may be necessary to heat the eye.*

5. Carefully release the shock compressor and disassemble the entire unit (**Figure 4**).

6. Assembly is the reverse of these steps.

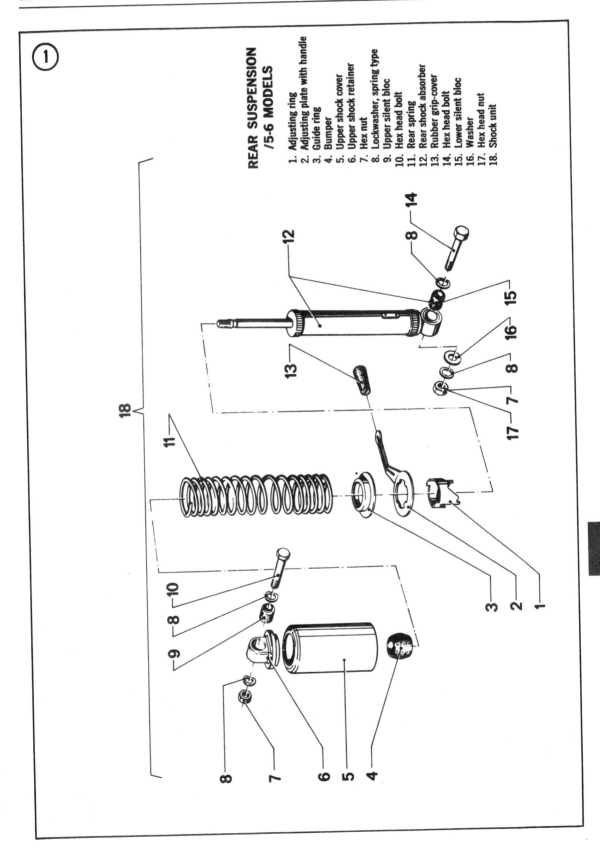

**REAR SUSPENSION /5-6 MODELS**

1. Adjusting ring
2. Adjusting plate with handle
3. Guide ring
4. Bumper
5. Upper shock cover
6. Upper shock retainer
7. Hex nut
8. Lockwasher, spring type
9. Upper silent bloc
10. Hex head bolt
11. Rear spring
12. Rear shock absorber
13. Rubber grip-cover
14. Hex head bolt
15. Lower silent bloc
16. Washer
17. Hex head nut
18. Shock unit

9

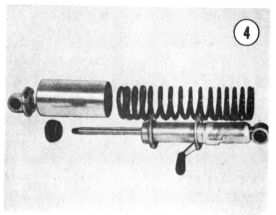

## Inspection

1. Measure the free length of the spring with a vernier caliper. If it measures significantly less than 251mm (9.88 in.), replace it.

2. Hold the shock absorber in its operating position and pump it in and out several times to displace the air into the upper chamber.

3. Test the relationship of compression and rebound damping by first compressing the shock absorber and then extending it. The force required for compression should be noticeably less than that for extension. The shaft should move smoothly and steadily, requiring the same force throughout the length of the stroke. If the

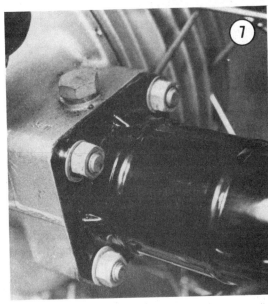

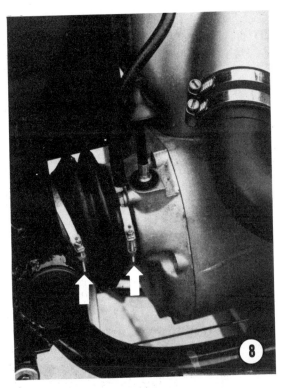

stroke is uneven, the shock is worn and should be replaced.

If the force required to compress the shock is about equal to the force required to extend it, or if the extension force is less, the shock is worn and should be replaced.

### CAUTION
*With the shock fully compressed, no more than one pound of pressure should be exerted on the shaft; more than this can cause internal damage to the unit.*

## FINAL DRIVE/SWING ARM

All BMW models employ a shaft drive to the rear wheel. The drive shaft is housed inside the right rear swing arm and runs in an oil bath. Power is transmitted through a lap-fitted pinion and ring gearset. The final drive is shown in cutaway in **Figure 5**.

### Disassembly

1. Remove rear wheel. See Chapter Ten.
2. Remove the bottom bolt from the right rear spring/shock.
3. Remove the filler and drain plugs from the drive unit (**Figure 6**) and allow the oil to drain.
4. Remove the wing nut from the end of the brake rod and withdraw the rod by depressing the brake pedal.
5. Remove the pin from the brake arm and reinstall it on the rod along with the wing nut.
6. Remove the 4 nuts which hold the rear drive to the swing arm (**Figure 7**).
7. Remove the rear drive from the swing arm.
8. Loosen the screw on the clamping band for the rubber boot at the universal joint (**Figure 8**) and push the boot back as far as it will go.

9

9. Lock drive shaft with BMW tool No. 508 and unscrew the 4 bolts from the drive shaft coupling (**Figure 9**). Discard lockwashers. New ones must be used anytime these bolts are loosened.

10. Remove the plugs from the swing arm pivot (**Figure 10**).

11. Loosen the locknut with a 27mm socket ground down as shown in **Figure 11**. The tool provided in the motorcycle tool kit is not strong enough. Remove the bearing pins with a 6mm Allen wrench (**Figure 12**).

12. Remove the bottom bolt and nut from the left side spring/shock (**Figure 13**) and remove the swing arm.

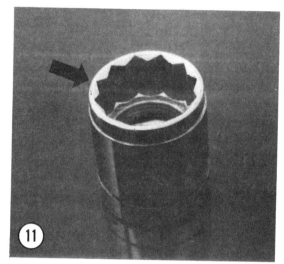

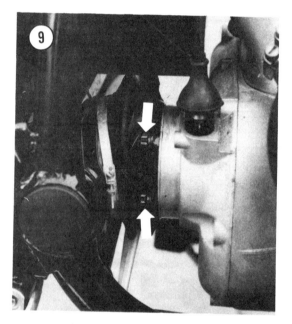

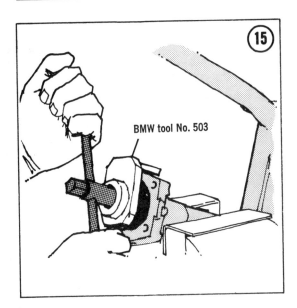

13. Refer to **Figure 14**. Remove rubber seals, thrust sleeves, bearings and the grease retainers.

14. Clamp the swing arm in a vise, using soft metal jaw protectors. Install the splined fixture (BMW tool No. 508), fitted with a 14mm socket, into the internal splines in the rear coupling. Unscrew the nut from the rear of the shaft (**Figure 15**).

15. Install a puller (BMW tool No. 204/2) on the rear coupling (**Figure 16**) and pull it off by turning the puller spindle clockwise. If necessary, rap sharply on the head of the spindle as it is turned.

16. Pull the drive shaft out of the forward end of the swing arm.

17. Mark the brake shoes "top" and "bottom" and remove them by first prying off the

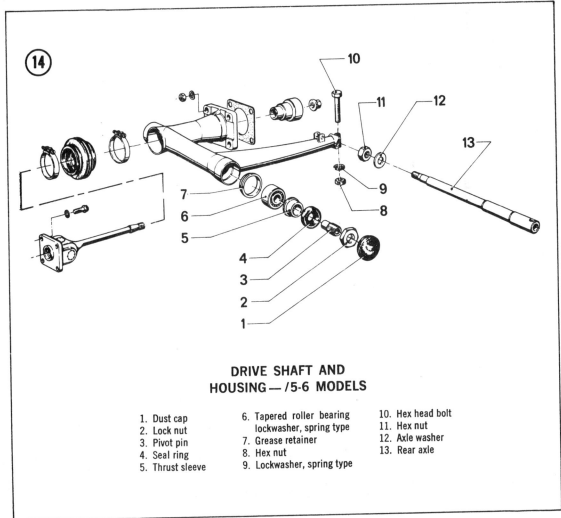

**DRIVE SHAFT AND
HOUSING — /5-6 MODELS**

1. Dust cap
2. Lock nut
3. Pivot pin
4. Seal ring
5. Thrust sleeve
6. Tapered roller bearing lockwasher, spring type
7. Grease retainer
8. Hex nut
9. Lockwasher, spring type
10. Hex head bolt
11. Hex nut
12. Axle washer
13. Rear axle

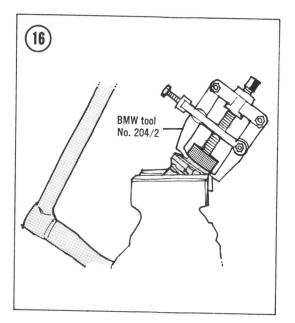

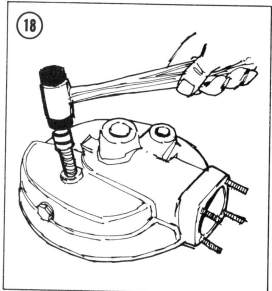

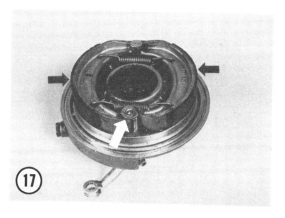

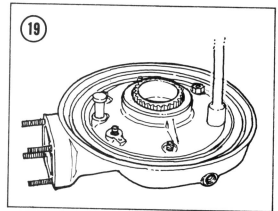

shoe that seats beneath the flattened side of the rear collar (**Figure 17**).

18. Unscrew the nut from the outer end of the brake cam and tap the cam out of the housing (**Figure 18**).

19. Unscrew the nuts from the housing cover (**Figure 19**).

20. Install BMW tool No. 505 over the splines on the ring gear hub. Screw 2 Allen bolts into the threaded (size M 6) holes in the housing cover and press it off by turning the bolts clockwise (**Figure 20**), evenly and progressively.

21. Refer to **Figure 21**. Heat the cover and lift it off the ring gear and bearing. The tool (No. 505) should be used to prevent damage to the seal. Remove the ring gear and the bearing inner race and shim.

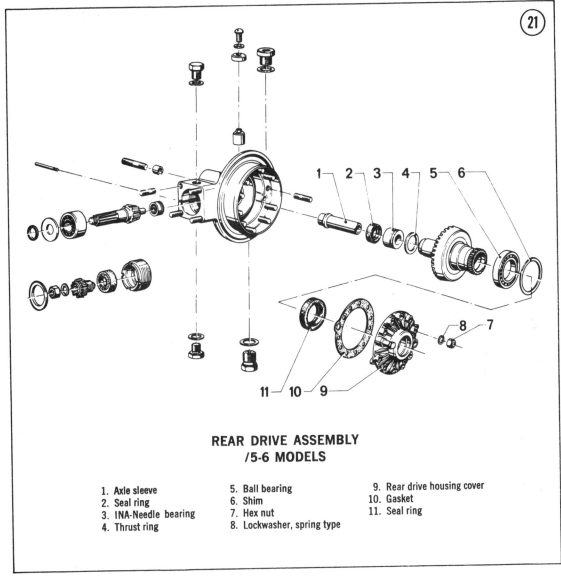

**REAR DRIVE ASSEMBLY
/5-6 MODELS**

1. Axle sleeve
2. Seal ring
3. INA-Needle bearing
4. Thrust ring
5. Ball bearing
6. Shim
7. Hex nut
8. Lockwasher, spring type
9. Rear drive housing cover
10. Gasket
11. Seal ring

22. Remove the large seal. Heat the cover again and tap it against a wood block or workbench top to knock out the bearing. Remove the shim from behind the bearing.

23. Heat the main housing to 180°F and pull out the needle bearing outer race. Drive out the seal located behind it. If the bearing set is to be replaced, pull the inner race off the ring gear shaft.

24. Straighten the coupling nut lock tab (**Figure 22**). Install a holder (BMW tool No. 507) over the swing arm studs to lock the gear and unscrew the coupling nut (**Figure 23**). Remove the nut, lock plate, and coupling hub.

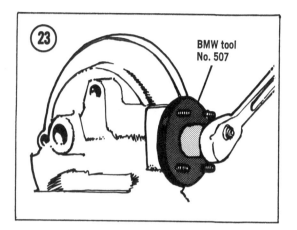

BMW tool
No. 507

It may be necessary to carefully pry coupling hub off with a 90-degree drift applied behind the hub.

25. Unscrew the threaded ring and remove the spacer. Remove the seal from the ring.

26. Heat the final drive housing to 180°F and install BMW puller No. 259/1 (**Figure 24**). Pull out the pinion and ball bearing assembly. Remove the bearing from the shaft and collect the shim behind it.

> NOTE: *It is necessary to remove the recessed pin (**Figure 25**) before removing the needle bearing assembly.*

27. Insert a soft metal drift through the holes in the ring gear (**Figure 26**) and off the ball bearing assembly.

## Inspection

1. Check all bearings, races, sleeves, seals, and the swing arm bearing pins for wear, pitting, and galling. Replace any pieces that are less than perfect. Check to see if the bearings have spun on the shafts, indicating a tight or frozen bearing. Slight damage to a shaft can be corrected with fine emery cloth; however, if the damage is severe, the shaft should be replaced along with the bearing.

2. Check the ring gear and pinion for excessive wear and for chipped or broken teeth. If any of these conditions are present, the ring gear and pinion must be replaced as a set. The dash number (e.g., 314-10 or 314+10) indicates, in hundredths of a millimeter, the deviation from standard of the position of the pinion. This will be important during reassembly.

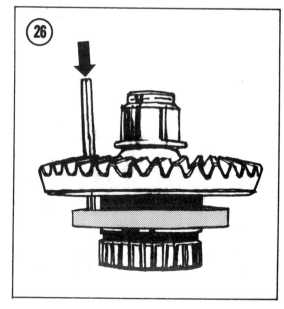

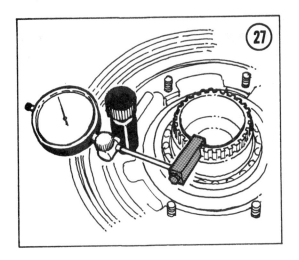

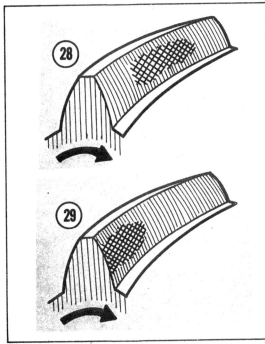

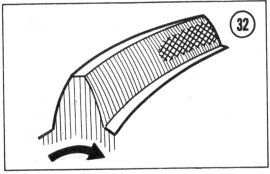

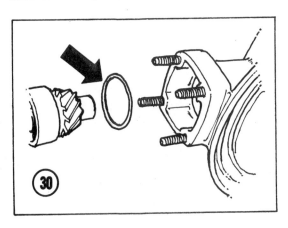

**9**

3. With the gearset installed in the housing (see *Final Drive, Reassembly*), check the backlash. Install a dial indicator and BMW tool No. 5104 and No. 260 on the outer edge of the ring gear. Refer to **Figure 27**.

4. Grasp the drive splines and gently turn the gear from one extreme of free play to the other, without turning the pinion. Correct backlash is between 0.15 and 0.20mm (0.0059 and 0.0079 in.).

5. Apply Prussian Blue dye to a tooth on the ring gear and rotate it to make contact with the pinion. Check the contact pattern on the tooth. If the contact pattern is in the center of the tooth or just slightly toward the forward end (**Figure 28**), the mesh of the gears is correct. If the contact pattern is at the forward end of the tooth (**Figure 29**), a thicker spacer is required between the pinion bearing and the housing (**Figure 30**). The backlash must be corrected by installing a thinner thrust washer between the ring gear and the needle bearing assembly (**Figure 31**). If the contact pattern is at the rear end of the tooth (**Figure 32**), a thinner spacer is

required between the pinion bearing and the housing. The backlash must be corrected by installing a thicker thrust washer between the ring gear and the needle bearing assembly.

> NOTE: *Each time the pinion is removed and reinstalled, the housing must be heated to 180°F.*

6. Double check the backlash and mesh.

7. Check the end play of the ring gear. Place 2 equal prisms on the mating surface of the cover (**Figure 33**), check the distance with a height gauge, and write it down.

8. Do not install the gasket in the housing. Place one of the prisms on the bearing (**Figure 34**), measure the distance with the height gauge, and write it down. Subtract this measurement (b) from the first (a). The result is the thickness of shim (thrust ring) required, because the end play is adjusted to 0 without the gasket. The gasket provides the required amount of side play.

**Reassembly**

1. Warm the large ball bearing assembly for the ring gear and reinstall it on the gear.

2. Heat the housing to 180° and reinstall the needle bearing assembly at the rear of the pinion shaft. Reinstall the bearing with a drift (BMW tool No. 252). See **Figure 35**. Replace the recessed pin (**Figure 36**) which holds the needle bearing in the housing.

3. See **Figure 37** and reinstall pinion and spacer.

4. Heat the housing to 180°F and reinstall the ball bearing assembly on the pinion with the open side of the bearing facing forward. Apply gasket cement to the inside spacer and install it. Install a new seal ring.

5. Press a new seal into the threaded ring (**Figure 38**). Install the ring with BMW tool No. 506a or No. 253. Torque the ring to 10-11 mkg (72-87 ft.-lb.).

6. Reinstall the coupling hub, a new lock tab plate, and the nut. Place the locking fixture on the hub and torque the nut to 10-11 mkg (72-87 ft.-lb). Bend the lock tab to lock the nut. Install the outer spacer.

7. Install the seal in the housing (**Figure 39**).

8. Install the spacer and inner bearing race on ring gear (**Figure 40**).

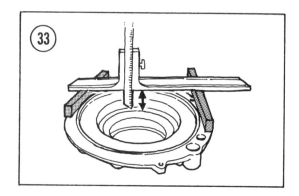

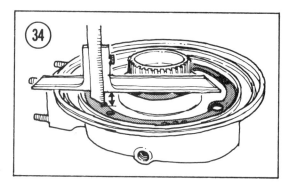

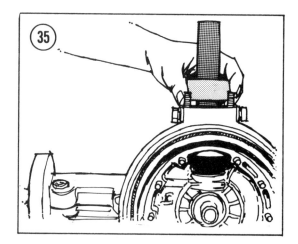

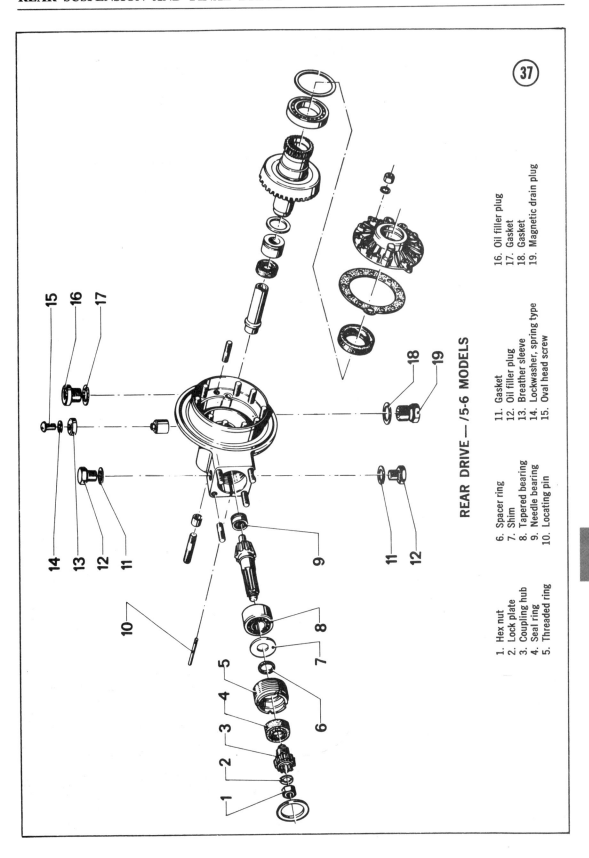

REAR DRIVE — /5-6 MODELS

1. Hex nut
2. Lock plate
3. Coupling hub
4. Seal ring
5. Threaded ring

6. Spacer ring
7. Shim
8. Tapered bearing
9. Needle bearing
10. Locating pin

11. Gasket
12. Oil filler plug
13. Breather sleeve
14. Lockwasher, spring type
15. Oval head screw

16. Oil filler plug
17. Gasket
18. Gasket
19. Magnetic drain plug

9

9. Heat the housing to 180°F, install the spacer, and press in the needle bearing (**Figure 41**).

10. Heat the cover to 180°F and press in the seal (**Figure 42**).

11. Heat the cover to 180°F, install the spacer, and press in the ball bearing.

12. Install the ring gear in the housing and place a new gasket on the sealing surface.

13. Put the cover in place and heat it to 180°. Put the sleeve (BMW tool No. 505) over the splines and carefully tap the cover down. Allow the cover to cool. Then, install the washers on the studs, screw on the nuts, and torque them to 1.8-2.1 mkg (13-14 ft.-lb.).

14. Reinstall the brake arm and brake shoes.

15. Degrease the conical end of the drive shaft and insert it into the swing arm.

16. Reinstall the coupling, screw on the nut, and tighten it to 24-26 mkg (175-188 ft.-lb.).

17. Grease the swing arm pivot bearings and races. Reinstall the grease retainers, bearing races, bearings, thrust sleeves and rubber seals in the swing arm.

18. Set the swing arm in place, between the pivot bosses on the main frame, and screw in the pivot pins but don't tighten them.

19. Reconnect the lower end of the left shock absorber to the swing arm.

20. Position the swing arm so the clearance between the ends of the pivot tube and the pivot bosses on the frame is the same on both sides (**Figure 43**).

21. Screw in the pivot pins while maintaining the clearance. When both pins are screwed in all the way, screw on the locknuts by hand. Tighten the pins to about 2 mkg (14 ft.-lb.) to preload the bearings. Then, loosen the pins and retighten them to 1 mkg (7 ft.-lb.). Tighten the locknuts to 10 mkg (70 ft.-lb.). Grease the bearings and install the plugs.

22. Recheck to make sure the clearance is equal on both sides and readjust if necessary.

23. Remaining assembly is in reverse order of disassembly.

CAUTION
*Use new lockwashers on the driveshaft coupling (U-joint) bolts.*

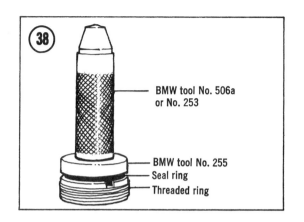

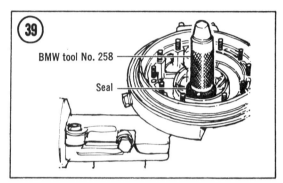

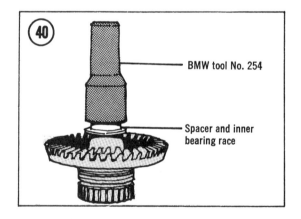

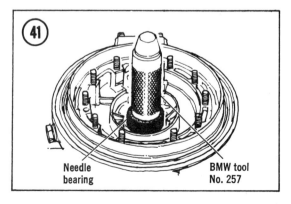

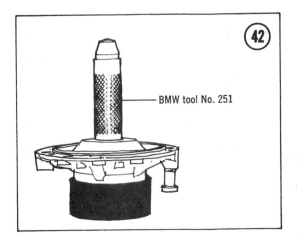

BMW tool No. 251

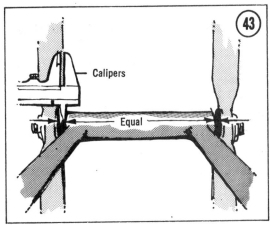

Calipers

Equal

9

# CHAPTER TEN

# BRAKES AND WHEELS

The only differences between front and rear wheels are rim diameter (the front is 19 inches, the rear 18 inches) and the fact that the front wheel does not have a drive spline. The wheels are shown in **Figure 1** and **Figure 2**. Refer to **Table 1** at end of chapter for recommended tires and pressures.

### WHEEL REMOVAL

**Front Wheel (Drum Brake)**

1. Place the motorcycle on its centerstand and set a block beneath the frame at the front of the engine to lift the front wheel off the ground.

2. Disconnect the brake anchor and cable.

3. Remove the axle nut, loosen the axle pinch bolts, and pull out the axle (**Figure 3**).

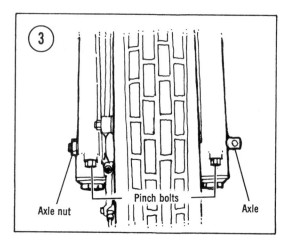

4. Remove front wheel and brake assembly.

**Front Wheel (Disc Brake)**

1. Place the motorcycle on its centerstand and set a block beneath the frame at the front of the engine to lift the front wheel off the ground.

2. Unscrew the axle nut, remove the washer, loosen the pinch bolt, pull out the axle, and remove the front wheel by pulling it down and forward to disengage the disc from the caliper (**Figure 4**).

**Rear Wheel (Drum Brake)**

1. Place the motorcycle on its centerstand and set a block beneath the frame behind the engine to lift the rear wheel off the ground.

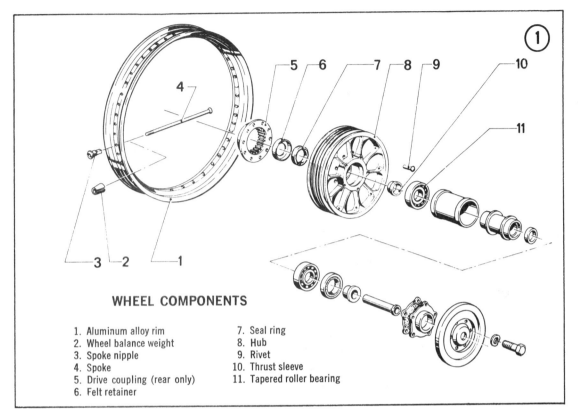

## WHEEL COMPONENTS

1. Aluminum alloy rim
2. Wheel balance weight
3. Spoke nipple
4. Spoke
5. Drive coupling (rear only)
6. Felt retainer
7. Seal ring
8. Hub
9. Rivet
10. Thrust sleeve
11. Tapered roller bearing

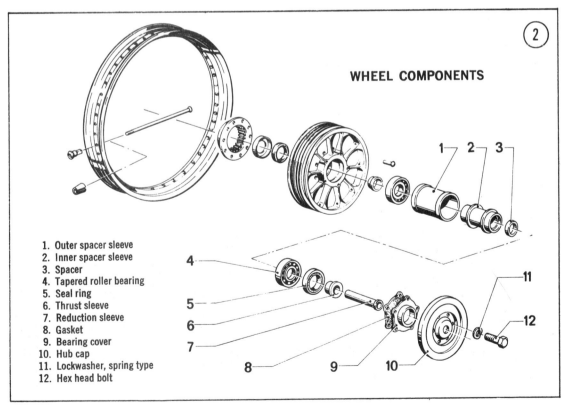

## WHEEL COMPONENTS

1. Outer spacer sleeve
2. Inner spacer sleeve
3. Spacer
4. Tapered roller bearing
5. Seal ring
6. Thrust sleeve
7. Reduction sleeve
8. Gasket
9. Bearing cover
10. Hub cap
11. Lockwasher, spring type
12. Hex head bolt

**10**

2. Unscrew axle nut on right side (**Figure 5**). Loosen the pinch bolt (**Figure 6**).

3. Place a drift pin in the hole in the left end of the axle and pull it out (**Figure 7**).

4. Pull the wheel to the left to clear the final drive and remove it to the rear. It may be necessary to lean the motorcycle to the right. It's a good ideal to have some assistance with this task.

### Rear Wheel (Disc Brake — 1978 R100 RS)

1. Place the motorcycle on its centerstand and set a block beneath the frame behind the engine to lift the rear wheel off the ground.

2. Unscrew the axle nut on the right side. Loosen the pinch bolt in the end of the swing arm on the left side.

3. Unscrew the caliper anchor bolt (**Figure 8**). Lift the caliper off the disc and suspend it from the frame with wire: don't allow it to hang on the brake line.

4. Place a drift in the hole in the left end of the axle and pull it out.

5. Pull the wheel to the left to clear the final drive and remove it to the rear. With assistance, lean the motorcycle to the right so the wheel will clear. Reverse the above to install the wheel.

### BEARINGS

The wheels on all models are fitted with tapered roller bearings on each side of the wheel.

5

7

6

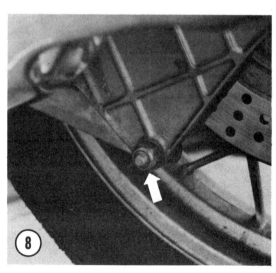

8

### Removal

1. Remove the left-side hubcap, if so equipped. The hubcap is held in place with 5 hex bolts.

2. Remove the spacer and bearing cover from the left side of the wheel (**Figure 9**).

3. Remove the washers, seals, and spacers (**Figures 10 and 11**).

4. Heat the hub to about 200° F. Insert the axle from the reverse side. Insert the spacer, washer and nut. Tighten the nut and pull out the races, bearings and spacer as an assembly. Tap out the left bearing outer race, outer spacer bushing, the right side bearing assembly and the spacer sleeve.

### Inspection

1. Install the complete bearing set on the axle (**Figure 12**).

2. Using jaw protectors, clamp the axle in a vise and install a spacer sleeve over the axle. Secure it with the axle nut and washer.

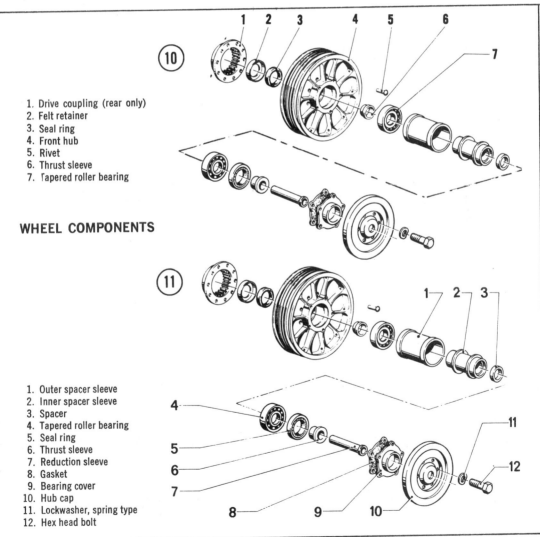

1. Drive coupling (rear only)
2. Felt retainer
3. Seal ring
4. Front hub
5. Rivet
6. Thrust sleeve
7. Tapered roller bearing

**WHEEL COMPONENTS**

1. Outer spacer sleeve
2. Inner spacer sleeve
3. Spacer
4. Tapered roller bearing
5. Seal ring
6. Thrust sleeve
7. Reduction sleeve
8. Gasket
9. Bearing cover
10. Hub cap
11. Lockwasher, spring type
12. Hex head bolt

**10**

NOTE: *Spacers can be made from tubing of the following sizes: Front—/5, /6 to mid-1975, 38.1mm (1⅓ in.) long x 14.3mm (⁹⁄₁₆ in.) ID; /6 from mid-1975 and /7, 50.8mm (2 in.) long x 17.2mm (¹¹⁄₁₆ in.) ID. Rear—all models and years, 85.73mm (3⅜ in.) long x 17.2mm (¹¹⁄₁₆ in.) ID. These spacers are substitutes for BMW tools No. 553 and 554.*

3. With the bearing assembly clamped firmly, there should be no apparent play and the large spacer should be able to be displaced with moderate pressure (**Figure 13**). If the play is excessive or insufficient, replace the left side spacer with one of appropriate size to correct the clearance.

### Installation

1. Heat the hub to about 200°F and tap in the outer bearing races with a drift (or BMW tool No. 5079 if available).

NOTE: *The reducer bushing must be installed in the front wheel.*

2. Repack the bearings with about 10 grams of bearing grease.

3. Reassemble the remainder of the components in reverse order of disassembly. Install them as an assembly in the wheel.

### SPOKE REPLACEMENT AND ADJUSTMENT

Spoke replacement and adjustment and wheel truing are jobs for an expert.

### WHEEL BALANCING

The instructions presented cover static balancing. Dynamic balancing requires the use of a special machine.

1. Remove the wheel to be balanced and support it on a free-turning axle as shown in **Figure 14**.

NOTE: *The standard axles fit too snugly to allow the wheel to turn freely during balancing.*

2. Rotate the wheel and allow it to come to rest. Make a mark on the tire with a piece of chalk at the 6 o'clock position. Rotate the wheel again and allow it to come to rest. Repeat this several times. If the mark stops at the 6

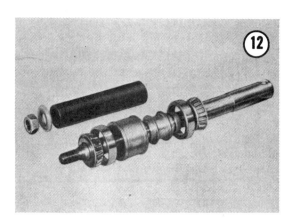

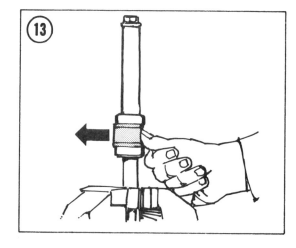

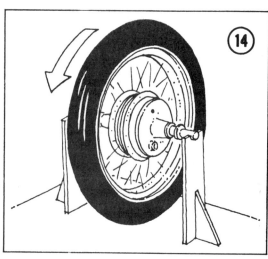

o'clock position each time the wheel obviously has a heavy side; go on to the next step. If the mark stops at a different point each time, the static balance of the wheel is correct.

3. Attach a weight to the spoke at the top of the wheel. Weights are available in 10 gram and 15 gram sizes, for either the 3.5mm (0.1379 in.) or 4mm (0.1576 in.) spokes.

4. Experiment with the weights until the wheel doesn't come to rest at the same point each time it's spun.

### DRUM BRAKES

The front brake is a double-leading shoe design and the rear brake is a single-leading shoe type. Brakes are shown in **Figures 15 and 16.**

### Front Brake Disassembly

1. Remove the front wheel as outlined earlier in this chapter.

2. Remove the circlips from the ends of the shoe pivots on the front brake. With a pair of pliers, unhook the springs from the brake shoes and remove them.

### Brake Inspection

1. Check the braking surface of the drum. If it's excessively worn or grooved, it will have to be turned down on a lathe. This is a job for an expert.

2. Check the brake lining for wear and remove foreign matter with a wire brush. If the linings on U.S. models are worn to a point where the

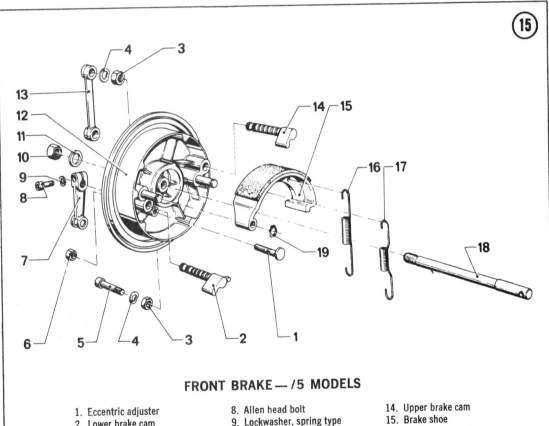

**FRONT BRAKE — /5 MODELS**

| | | |
|---|---|---|
| 1. Eccentric adjuster | 8. Allen head bolt | 14. Upper brake cam |
| 2. Lower brake cam | 9. Lockwasher, spring type | 15. Brake shoe |
| 3. Hex nut | 10. Hex nut | 16. Lower return spring |
| 4. Lockwasher, spring type | 11. Washer | 17. Upper return spring |
| 5. Allen head bolt | 12. Front brake plate | 18. Front axle |
| 6. Hex nut | 13. Brake torque spring | 19. Circlip |
| 7. Brake lever | | |

**10**

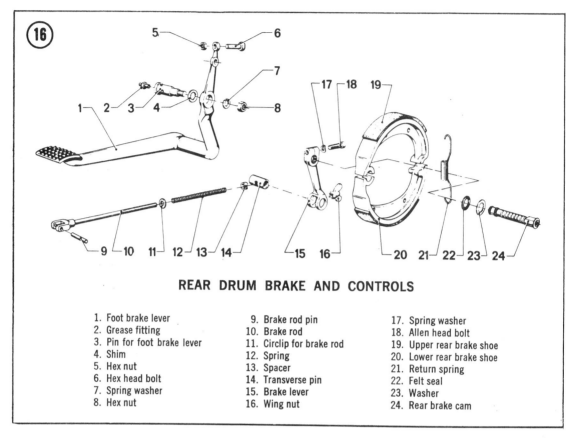

**REAR DRUM BRAKE AND CONTROLS**

| | | |
|---|---|---|
| 1. Foot brake lever | 9. Brake rod pin | 17. Spring washer |
| 2. Grease fitting | 10. Brake rod | 18. Allen head bolt |
| 3. Pin for foot brake lever | 11. Circlip for brake rod | 19. Upper rear brake shoe |
| 4. Shim | 12. Spring | 20. Lower rear brake shoe |
| 5. Hex nut | 13. Spacer | 21. Return spring |
| 6. Hex head bolt | 14. Transverse pin | 22. Felt seal |
| 7. Spring washer | 15. Brake lever | 23. Washer |
| 8. Hex nut | 16. Wing nut | 24. Rear brake cam |

rivets will soon come in contact with the drum, replace the linings.

If the lining is less than 1.5mm (0.059 in.) thick, replace the shoes and linings. Again, this is a job for an expert. New shoes and linings must be arced to match the drum, whether or not it has been turned down.

**Front Brake Reassembly**

Reassemble the brakes and reinstall them and the wheels in reverse order of disassembly.

**Front Brake Adjustment**

1. Adjust play in hand lever to 8-15mm (0.315-0.59 in.). Refer to **Figure 17**.

2. Refer to **Figure 18** and loosen the locknut on the adjustment cam. With an Allen wrench, turn the adjustment cam counterclockwise until it is tight. Then, turn it clockwise until the lower front brake acutating arm has 4mm (0.157 in.) free movement (measured at the cable anchor) before the shoe contacts the drum.

3. Hold the threaded cable sleeve at the rear of the lower brake arm with a 4mm wrench and turn the 10mm adjuster nut until the free movement of the upper brake arm is 4mm (0.157 in.) before the shoe contacts the drum.

**Rear Brake Adjustment**

1. Turn the wing nut on the end of the rear brake rod (**Figure 19**) clockwise until the brake shoes drag in the drum.

2. Back off the wing nut 3 to 5 turns. Free pedal movement should be ⅜-½ in.

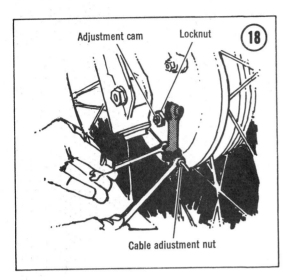

Adjustment cam    Locknut    (18)

Cable adjustment nut

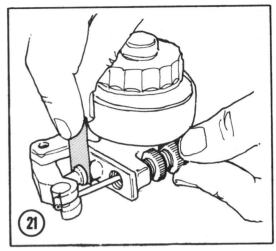

(21)

(19)

CAUTION
*Too little free movement in the brake
controls causes the brakes to lock during application.*

## DISC BRAKE

Service to the disc brake should be limited to
checking, correcting, and changing the hydraulic fluid, adjusting the cable, replacing the
pads, and removing and installing the caliper
and master cylinder. Rebuilding of the master
cylinder and caliper should be entrusted to a
BMW dealer.

The brake system is shown in **Figure 20**.

### Fluid Level

The brake fluid level should be checked and
corrected if necessary every 1,000 miles.
Remove the fuel tank and unscrew the cap from

the reservoir. If necessary, top up the fluid level
with fresh brake fluid. While the tank is off,
check the brake cable for excessive play. The
cable should be adjusted so that the feeler
gauge that is included in the tool kit can be inserted as shown in **Figure 21**. If the gauge is not
available, there should be a clearance of about
0.010 in.; however, it is essential that the piston
protrude a couple of thousandths of an inch out
of the brake body. This is essential so that the
ports are uncovered in the cylinder to permit
fluid to transfer from one chamber to the other.

If the arm is in contact with the piston it will
not permit it to return. In such case, screw the
adjuster in to increase the play. However, if the
piston still does not protrude slightly, the
master cylinder should be inspected and very
likely will require rebuilding.

In time, brake fluid will absorb moisture. As
a result, its boiling point will lower and it
becomes prone to boiling during hard brake application. For this reason, the brake fluid
should be replaced once each year. Connect a
bleeder hose to the bleeder valve on the caliper
and place the opposite end of the hose in a container. Open the bleeder valve and operate the
brake lever to expel the fluid from the system.
Keep a close eye on the fluid level in the master
cylinder reservoir and when the reservoir emp-
ties, fill it with fresh brake fluid.

### Bleeding

Connect the bleeder hose as shown in **Figure 22**. Pull in on the brake lever as far as it will

10

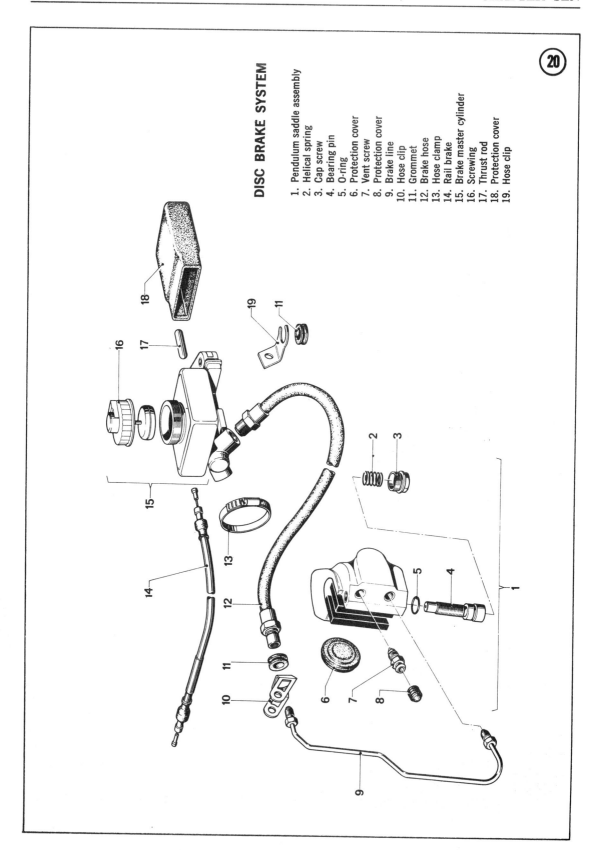

DISC BRAKE SYSTEM

1. Pendulum saddle assembly
2. Helical spring
3. Cap screw
4. Bearing pin
5. O-ring
6. Protection cover
7. Vent screw
8. Protection cover
9. Brake line
10. Hose clip
11. Grommet
12. Brake hose
13. Hose clamp
14. Rail brake
15. Brake master cylinder
16. Screwing
17. Thrust rod
18. Protection cover
19. Hose clip

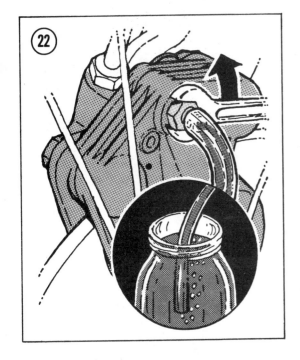

go and open the bleeder valve. Continue to maintain pressure on the lever and close the valve before releasing it. Failure to do this will draw air into the system.

Continue to bleed the system by pulling in on the lever, opening the valve, closing the valve, and releasing the lever until the fluid coming out of the bleeder hose is free of air bubbles. During bleeding, occasionally check the level in the reservoir and top it up with fresh fluid if necessary.

### Pad Replacement (Front)

The brake pads should be replaced when they have worn down to the colored lines. Both pads must be replaced as a set.

1. Place the motorcycle on the centerstand and support the front to raise the front wheel off the ground. Remove the wheel.

2. Remove the retainer from the inside pad and pull it out of the caliper (**Figure 23**).

3. Carefully push the brake piston back into the caliper. Lightly grease the guide pin of the outer pad with Molykote. Install the O-ring and then install the pads (outer first) in the caliper. Install the retainer on the inside pad with the angled end facing down. Install the front wheel.

4. Remove the cap from the adjuster bore in the bottom of the fork leg (**Figure 24**). Turn the eccentric adjuster until the inside pad is parallel with the inside surface of the disc. Check to make sure the entire surface of the pad contacts the disc. Grease and reinstall the spring, screw in the cap, and tighten to 6.0-6.5 mkg (44-47 ft.-lb.).

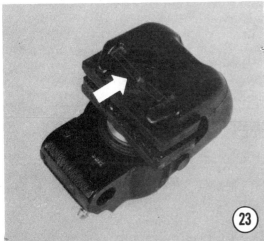

### Pad Replacement (Rear)

The brake pads must be replaced when they have worn down to the colored lines. Both pads must be replaced as a set.

1. Remove the dust cap from the reservoir and remove the pad retaining pins (**Figure 25**).

2. Remove the cap from the reservoir and cover it with a clean shop rag. Pull the old pads out of the caliper with needle-nose pliers. Slowly press the pistons back into the caliper to provide additional room for the new, thicker pads.

3. Install the new pads, pins, clips, and dust cover.

**10**

4. Correct the fluid level in the reservoir if necessary and install the cap.

## Caliper Removal/Installation (Front)

1. Place the motorcycle on the centerstand and support the front to raise the front wheel off the ground. Remove the wheel.

2. Draw off the fluid from the master cylinder reservoir. Be careful to keep brake fluid off painted surfaces.

3. Unscrew the brake line at the caliper (**Figure 26**).

4. Remove the plug from the bottom of the fork leg. Screw an 8mm x 1.25 x 50mm bolt into the eccentric adjuster and pull it down and out of the fork leg. Remove the caliper from the fork leg.

5. Reverse the above to install the caliper. Fill and bleed the system, adjust the cable, and align the inside brake pad with the disc as described previously.

## Caliper Removal/Installation (Rear)

1. Draw off the fluid from the master cylinder. Be careful to keep brake fluid off painted surfaces.

2. Unscrew the brake line at the caliper (**Figure 27**). Wrap the end of the brake line in a clean shop rag to catch dripping fluid and keep dust and dirt out of the line.

3. Unscrew the caliper anchor bolt (**Figure 28**).

4. Unscrew the caliper mounting bolts (**Figure 29**) and pull the caliper off the disc.

5. Reverse the above to install the caliper. Fill and bleed the system as described earlier.

## Master Cylinder Removal/Installation

1. Remove the fuel tank. Drain the fluid from the system with the aid of the bleeder valve on the caliper.

2. Remove the rubber cap from the master cylinder (**Figure 30**). Disconnect the cable from the arm (**Figure 31**). Unplug the electrical connector. Unscrew the brake line fitting from the cylinder (**Figure 32**). Unscrew the clamp and remove the master cylinder.

3. Reverse the above to install the cylinder. Fill and bleed the system, adjust the cable, and check the operation of the caliper as described earlier.

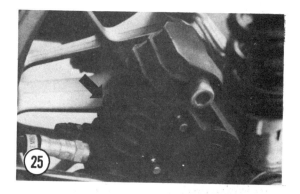

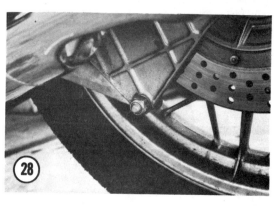

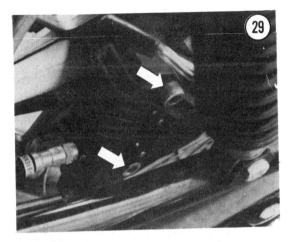

Table 1    TIRE SIZES AND RECOMMENDED PRESSURES

| | Tire Size | |
|---|---|---|
| Model | Front | Rear |
| R50/5 and R60/5 | 3.25 x 19 | 4.00 x 18 |
| All other models | 3.25H x 19 | 4.00H x 18 |

| | Pressure* | |
|---|---|---|
| | Psi | Kg/cm$^2$ |
| Front tire (all except R60/6 and R90S) | | |
| Solo | 24 | 1.75 |
| Dual | 24 | 1.75 |
| Rear tire (all except R60/6 and R90S) | | |
| Solo | 26 | 2.00 |
| Dual | 28 | 2.50 |
| Front tire (R60/6 and R90S) | | |
| Solo | 27 | 1.75 |
| Dual | 28-30 | 1.75 |
| Rear tire (R60/6 and R90S) | | |
| Solo | 28 | 2.00 |
| Dual | 30-32 | 2.50 |

*NOTE: All recommended tire pressures are for average conditions. Minor adjustments in pressures may be necessary due to rider/passenger weight, touring accessories and tire composition.

**10**

# CHAPTER ELEVEN

# PERFORMANCE IMPROVEMENT

Before the 1970's, most American riders considered the BMW to be somewhat motorcycling's equivalent to the Chevy straight-6 or the Model T: a totally reliable, dependable machine with adequate performance for any normal riding conditions, available in any color so long as you wanted black.

A fine machine—but hardly a superbike and certainly not a hotrod. Those riders (most European) who did hotrod the early 500's or 600's discovered that they had lost one of BMW's strongest virtues—its incredible reliability. The old-style 3-piece crankshafts simply wouldn't stand the strain. So those riders who wanted a performance machine looked elsewhere.

Then the situation changed radically. BMW began a very active and successful roadracing program in America, under the direction of Butler & Smith, the U.S. distributor. Most of the victories were scored by a young English rider, Reg Pridmore.

The second change was BMW's "new image." Not only were Beemers available in a rainbow of shades, but they weren't the old medium-displacement, medium-performance engines. The engine options increased to 750cc's, then 900, and finally 1000. Styling included not only the traditional BMW, but the radical S and RS series. Suddenly BMW was a performance machine. Riders who wanted even more than stock were pleased to discover that BMW would accept hotrodding quite easily, without any part being overstressed.

There are many good reasons to want more performance from a BMW, besides wanting to look on the far side of 130 mph: the owner of a 750 may want to keep up with his friend's 900 or 1000, without spending the money for a larger bike; an R90S owner may wish to have better mid- and low-range highway performance; a touring rider may wish to have the same performance on his gear-laden bike as he did on his bare stock machine; or the proud owner of an R100RS may simply want to have performance as superior to anything else on the road as his bike's appearance.

Fortunately, the BMW in any configuration has several advantages over other marques. Stock parts are of far higher quality on the BMW than on most other makes, suggesting that they were chosen less for inexpensive cost than for their functionalism. BMW's are rather over-engineered in most areas, hence able to take more performance without needing too much reinforcement of other components. Also BMW's overall approach seems far more oriented toward practical, human engineering than the far more common sterile testlab approach.

Some modifications may be performed by the owner/mechanic, others may require more tooling and sophistication. Emphasis must be placed on the need for careful and skilled work in this area. One reason that competition machinery performs so much better than stock is the care with which it is assembled and maintained. For this reason, an owner who isn't sure of what he is doing would be better off having the work done by a shop experienced with BMW's than to experiment himself. This potential problem may be compounded in some areas by a reluctance by dealers to become involved in high-performance modifications. Some of this may be ascribed to natural conservatism, some to reluctance to work in an area where experience and skill may be lacking, and some of it to the knowledge that a performance bike will be ridden harder (and therefore be more prone to break) than a stock machine.

Both Reg Pridmore's shop, RPM Motors, and Brown Motor Works are fully prepared to handle performance work on a mail order basis. Generally the cost of such work is no more than that charged for the equivalent job by a dealer, plus the cost of shipping and crating.

**Table 1** at the end of the chapter lists shops and suppliers.

## ENGINE MODIFICATIONS

Since the BMW's handling and reliability are so superb in stock configuration, most riders begin with more horsepower. Engine modifications are best handled on a step-by-step basis: first, for financial reasons and, secondly, to avoid building an engine which may be too

much for the rider's needs or desires. The rider who merely needs better 50-80 mph passing times has no need for a flat-out production roadracer — and almost certainly wouldn't be happy with it in his daily riding.

By far the easiest way to get more performance throughout the engine's powerband is with increased displacement and compression. There are several modifications available for the various models of BMW.

### Displacement Changes (R75/5, /6, /7)

The first option most 750 owners consider is to simply increase their engine's displacement to 900cc's and continue using stock components. Since the 750 and 900 share a common crankshaft, bearings, stroke, and cases, this should be simple.

Unfortunately, this can't be done with the existing cylinders. It is necessary to replace at least the cylinders with larger-sized components.

This is a bolt-up operation, with no engine reinforcement necessary. However, it's extremely expensive — just about as much as trading your 750 in for a newer 900.

Pridmore's additional recommendation, should this project be attempted, is to replace the 750 heads with 900 heads. However, if only minor performance improvements are sought, the 750 heads may be retained. If they are kept, under no circumstances should higher than stock compression pistons be installed — with the increased displacement putting more volume into the stock-sized combustion chambers, compression will automatically be increased.

A far less expensive step is to install an 840 kit, available from RPM Engineering (**Figure 1**). The retail cost of this kit, which consists of a cylinder bore, new pistons, pins and rings, is less than the retail cost of one stock 900 cylinder. Pridmore offers this kit on a "cylinder-bore-by-his-shop-only" basis because he feels that all too often bore jobs are inaccurately performed. After the cylinders are bored they are returned to the owner together with the rest of the big bore kit. Installation using the kit instructions may be easily performed by any moderately skilled owner/mechanic or shop.

The 840 kit not only increases displacement,

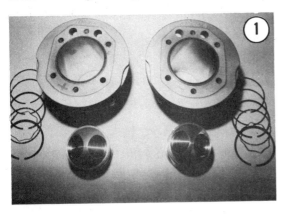

**11**

but ups compression as well to 10.5:1. While this may seem excessive for street use, particularly considering the very low quality of gas available today, there have been no complaints. Engine life should not be affected by this increase; Pridmore says that several of these kits have over 60,000 miles on them with no reported failure.

### Displacement Changes (R90/6, S)

Since there is only 4mm difference in the piston diameter between the 900 and 1000cc engines, some riders have considered simply boring their stock cylinders and installing the bigger pistons.

This may be done. However, the cylinder liner becomes excessively thin, and consequent heat buildup and lack of strength will almost certainly guarantee that this modification will have a short life expectancy.

Once again, the only way to get the larger displacement is to replace the cylinder (and, for maximum results, heads) with the newer parts. On BMW's manufactured prior to mid-1976, the cases will also have to bored out to accomodate the larger cylinder spigots.

A slight increase in performance is possible on 900cc engines by installing high compression pistons (**Figure 2**). These BMW-manufactured pistons will raise the compression to 10.8:1. However these pistons, assuming no other changes are made to the engine, won't seriously improve performance — probably nothing more than 0.1 improvement in the quarter mile elapsed time should be expected.

### Displacement Changes (R100/7, S, RS)

Since BMW performance parts are somewhat oriented toward roadracing and only secondar-

ily toward street performance, and since there is no roadracing class above 1000cc's, it is unlikely that big bore kits for the engine will become available. As on the 900, the only change which may be made is to install a set of 10.8:1 pistons, available from BMW dealers or from RPM or Brown. The same small benefits will be experienced on the 1000 as on the 900.

### FLYWHEEL

With all engine models, significant benefits not only in performance but in reliability and rideability are realized with a lightened flywheel.

In stock configuration, the flywheel weighs approximately 10 pounds. For street use, it may be cut down almost 50% in weight, to 5.2-5.3 pounds (**Figure 3**).

To avoid problems on reinstallation, this should be done to the engine's existing flywheel. The lightening is done either by Butler and Smith through a local dealer, or, as with any other modification in this chapter, it may be handled through either RPM Motors or Brown Motor Works.

Removal and reinstallation are done to stock specifications with the procedures in Chapter Four.

This weight reduction will drastically reduce engine inertia. After modification, the engine will rev more rapidly and, when the throttle is chopped, decelerate under drive more readily.

Engine torque will not suffer with the lightened flywheel. As a matter of fact, since the engine will now wind far more rapidly, acceleration throughout the powerband will be significantly improved.

Other side benefits are lessened driveline strain and consequently longer engine life, and an increase in shifting ease — one way to lessen that seemingly omnipresent "klunk" that all BMW's have when shifting.

This lightening will not affect the flywheel's lifespan — Pridmore has been installing these for over five years on every configuration of BMW from touring-only bikes to full-on roadracers, with no failures.

## CARBURETION

The stock Bing constant-vacuum carburetors have proven themselves to be highly reliable fuel mixers over the years. For normal street use, including moderate performance applications, they are more than adequate.

However, for high-performance, the next stage in engine build-up is a carburetor change. Riders of 1970-71 BMW's should consider changing carburetors even for stock applications, since the Bings used in those years are particularly troublesome and there is no way to modify them acceptably.

A highly satisfactory change is the use of 2 Mikunis (**Figure 4**), available in kit form and closely pre-jetted, from either RPM or Brown Motor Works.

Installation is quite simple — the Bings are removed and the Mikunis installed, together with new throttle cables. The stock intake manifold, air hose, and air cleaner assemblies are used.

Still better flow is possible by removing the stock airhoses and using Uni sock-type filters over each carburetor mouth. For competition use, open airhorns (bellmouths, vacuum stacks) are used, since racers are more interested in the last bit of performance than they are in the possibility of sucking contaminants into their engines.

For the 750 or 840 BMW, Pridmore recommends use of 32 mm venturi Mikunis; for the 900/6, the 34 mm throats. The 38 mm Dell'Ortos found as stock on the R90S should not be changed.

With the 1000cc engine, BMW began using Bings on all its models, including the performance-oriented S and RS series. This was done for various reasons, including the sometimes- unreliable Italian parts supply and the steadily more severe noise pollution requirements in America. For these engines, installation of the 38mm Mikunis is recommended.

> NOTE: *It is far less expensive in the long run to purchase a pre-set complete kit from RPM or Brown, rather than to buy bare carburetors and begin to jet from scratch — the Mikuni has an awesome variation in jetting potential and requires extreme skill to set up from ground zero.*

Several advantages will be gained with this carburetor change. Although in theory a carburetor with a variable venturi (diaphragm-type) should be more exactly responsive to an engine's fuel requirements, in practice there seems to be a lag between engine intake requirements and carburetor response. Using the Mikunis, response is much crisper and power is increased through the engine's entire range, most noticeably at full throttle. Mileage should also increase by 1-2 miles per gallon.

For the fully committed performance enthusiast, Pridmore offers a set of 38mm Dell' Ortos (**Figure 5**), set up for either the 90/6 or

any 100-series engine. These, with their integral accelerator pumps, will give significantly better response on acceleration.

These carburetors are prefitted with tuned bellmouth intakes; no air filtering system is used. According to Pridmore, no engine damage has been traceable to use of these open carburetors, even from prolonged street use; however, you would be wise to avoid obviously dusty areas.

## HEADWORK

Once better carburetors have been installed on the engine, the flow characteristics of the heads should be improved.

No mass-produced cast part can be exactly like the next one. Even with careful inspection, there will still be casting marks, dimples, and rough patches. This is especially significant on heads.

Headwork — porting, polishing, precision valve jobs, etc. — will not only markedly increase performance (around 10-15%) but will also increase gas mileage. In addition, porting work performed by a skilled expert will tailor the flow characteristics, and hence power output, to the requirements of the rider. Under no circumstances should this work be done by anyone other than a skilled and professional motorcycle head porter, such as Branch Flowmetrics or RPM.

RPM offers 3 stages of headwork for BMW's. Stage I, the simplest and least expensive, consists of opening up the intake and exhaust passages, improving the flow characteristics of those passages, and doing a very careful valve job.

Stage II is much the same porting job as Stage I, plus the installation of heavy-duty valve springs and titanium retainers. These will improve valve function at high rpm, thus enabling the engine to rev higher and last longer than the stock components. Normally the Stage II porting job is done in conjunction with the installation of a high-performance, street or strip camshaft.

Stage III is far more elaborate, since it's intended for the "performance-is-king" enthusiast. The inlet ports are reangled and the carburetor manifolds (Mikunis or Dell'Ortos only) are set so that the carburetors mount facing slightly outward and upward (at an angle of 12° from horizontal). See **Figure 6**. After this extensive modification, the normal Stage II work is performed.

All three of these configurations may be run on the street successfully; each offers increasingly greater performance, with an increasingly greater price tag.

The Stage III for the R90S also includes a slight narrowing of the inlet ports at a certain point, thus giving a venturi effect to increase mixture speed.

An R90S-only option that fits well with this is the RPM extended manifolds. These manifolds, made of either aluminum or steel, mount into the stock heads and move the carburetors slightly further away from the head. This increases the speed of the mixture entering the head, boosting performance.

Other options are available, such as stainless steel valves, oversize valves, etc. Used on the street, the only advantage stainless valves will offer is increased lifespan. Oversize valves will be of prime benefit to those interested in more top-end performance.

## CAMSHAFT

The stock BMW camshaft is relatively mild. For the next stage in increased performance the shaft should be replaced. Two options are available—either the No. 336 street cam or the No. 904 strip/street cam. Both cams are ground from billets from Germany by Sig Ergson and sold by Butler and Smith to authorized dealers.

The milder No. 336 offers the same lift as the stock cam, but increased duration. The No. 904

increases lift from 0.336 to 0.500 and consequently requires valve notching the pistons. The No. 904 should be considered barely streetable, since it offers most of its benefits between 4500-8500 rpm — somewhat radical for most street riders.

To get the full benefits from any performance camshaft, follow the manufacturer's recommendations not merely on installation procedures but for recommended lifters, pushrods, and valve springs.

RPM, for instance, installs its cams with hardened and modified lifters, plus special pushrods (**Figure 7**). These pushrods are of a high-quality steel and, while slightly heavier than the late-model alloy rods, will not flex under load. They're also slightly shorter than stock.

Any camshaft should be degreed when installed, rather than simply installed by lining up the timing marks. There's more than enough variation in parts to cause a marked loss of power.

Cam degreeing is fairly simple, requiring only normal tools plus a dial indicator gauge and an inexpensive degree wheel. It should be done when the cam is initially installed and the engine is out of the frame. See Chapter Four, *Camshaft Disassembly*.

1. Install the new camshaft using the manufacturer's instructions and stock procedures. If the camshaft manufacturer's instructions differ from stock, always follow the camshaft instructions.

2. Reassemble the engine, leaving off the front engine cover and the stator housing assembly.

3. Install the degree wheel on the crank. It will be necessary to improvise a mounting cone to securely hold the degree wheel on the crank. Position a wire somewhere on the engine and use its tip as an indicator.

4. Turn the engine through until one cylinder is at TDC on the compression stroke. The OT mark on the flywheel should be lined up with the reference mark in the inspection hole. Both valves, should be closed.

5. Position wire pointer so that it is over the 0° reading on the indicator gauge.

6. Consult the camshaft specification sheet, which was sent with the cam, for intake valve opening point and for the amount of lift at which this is obtained (normally this will be at zero lift, but not necessarily). It may be necessary to contact the manufacturer for this last figure.

7. Position the dial indicator gauge on the cylinder at TDC and set the indicator directly on the intake valve. Zero the dial indicator gauge.

8. Turn the engine through until the intake valve begins to open (or, if intake opening specifications are measured at a certain amount of lift, until that amount is reached on the dial indicator). Consult the degree wheel. The degree read on the wheel should exactly match the camshaft manufacturer's specified opening point. If not, it will be necessary to remove the camshaft and reinstall it, using an offset Woodruff key (**Figure 8**) to replace the stock key between the camshaft and front camshaft bearing. These offset keys may be custom-ordered from Brown Motor Works.

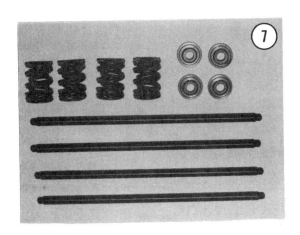

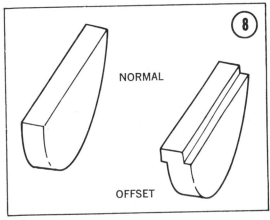

NORMAL

OFFSET

## EXHAUST SYSTEMS

The final improvement to the engine's breathing is one which a number of riders may not wish to make. For complete efficiency, the exhausts must also be modified. Since one of the strong points of BMW is the quietness, and since an exhaust more efficient than stock will be slightly louder, this is a comfort sacrifice that may not be desireable for some owners.

There are three options. The first is a modification to the stock exhaust and involves removing a certain amount of the stock muffler's internal baffling for better flow.

The second is to replace the stock mufflers with accessory items, such as those sold to dealers by MCM.

Still a third is to use RPM's two-into-one exhaust (**Figure 9**). A header system, with the pipes using a common collector, will markedly improve exhaust flow, since each exiting exhaust pulse creates a small vacuum behind it, thus dragging the next pulse forward at a greater rate of speed.

All three of these methods will improve power, with the header system being the most efficient. All of them will require rejetting of the carburetors — normally only an increase in the size of the main jet.

All three of these will also be slightly louder than stock. The header system, for instance, is rated by Pridmore at an estimated 84-86 db (A). This is certainly not enough to warrant a ticket, nor will it be obnoxious to the rider, passenger, or passing motorists.

For those who want the looks of the header system, yet stock noise level, Pridmore will make a quiet version of the system. Since muf-fling is handled by layers of fiberglass cloth wrapped around the muffler core, all that the quiet pipe consists of is extra layers of glass cloth.

With the quiet system, a BMW will have slightly greater power than stock.

## IGNITION

Replacing the stock ignition system with the Boyer Bransden Transistorized Ignition produces some improvement in power, plus a large improvement in maintenance ease and reliability (**Figure 10**).

This is an easily installed kit, requiring only the removal of the stock points plate assembly, the installation of a new plate and rotor in its place, and the mounting of a small transistorized sending unit somewhere on the bike's frame.

Rather than conventional metal points, the Boyer ignition uses magnetic pickups mounted on the points plate. As the magnet on the rotor passes sensor coils on the stator plate, current is produced, then amplified and transmitted to the coils and the plugs.

With no metal-metal contact, there is no point wear at all. Once installed and set, the Boyer system may be sealed and forgotten.

Installation of the system will add about 1½ to 2 horsepower, according to Pridmore. It also will increase low rpm smoothness, since the transistorized ignition won't advance fully until 4200-4400 rpm.

Another advantage of the Boyer is that, with the stock mechanical advance system removed from the end of the camshaft, there will be less

⑨

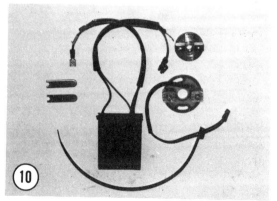
⑩

whipping. On many BMW's, this whip causes damage to the cam seal and consequent oil leakage into the points compartment.

Some twin-cylinder riders have found that their ignition may be improved by replacing the stock coils with automotive coils, which are vastly more efficient than most motorcycle parts. However, BMW coils, like most other things on the motorcycle, are superior items. Some slight improvement is gained by replacing the coils with the Bosch Blue coils long used by Volkswagen performance enthusiasts.

Additional electronic ignition systems are marketed by Gerex, Martek, Prestolite and Dyna for models through 1978. These ignition kits replace the breaker point assembly but are used with the stock mechanical advance mechanism. Prestolite and Dyna produce kits with single and dual output ignition coils. The kits with dual output coils are designed especially for models with cylinder heads modified for dual spark plugs. Mounting brackets for the special coils are supplied with the kits. The Dyna III and Prestolite dual output units both use 12 volt coils.

A Camtron electronic ignition system is available for 1979 and 1980 models. This kit uses an optical sensor to replace the breaker points but uses the stock mechanical advance mechanism. Dual output Andrews ignition coils can be used with this system for dual spark plug conversions.

## DUAL SPARK PLUG CYLINDER HEAD MODIFICATION

The dual spark plug cylinder head modification has become very popular as a performance improvement and provides several benefits for all types of BMW riders. The installation of a second spark plug in the lower half of each cylinder head provides hotter and quicker combustion within the cylinder. This hotter and quicker combustion results in improved fuel economy, quicker cold starts, improved performance, lower exhaust emissions and most importantly, decreased premature detonation (pinging). Most machines modified for dual spark plugs and equipped with a dual output electronic ignition

can burn regular-grade leaded gasoline without pinging.

The dual spark plug modification is accomplished by machining a threaded hole in the lower half of the cylinder head for a 12 mm or 14 mm short reach (1/2 in.) spark plug. The 14 mm threaded hole is considered by most sources to be more desirable since spark plugs of the same brand and heat range as the upper plug are more readily available in the 14 mm size. The durability and serviceability of the 14 mm threaded hole has been thoroughly proven under severe road racing conditions.

Installing the lower spark plug does not decrease the road clearance. The rocker cover will contact the road long before the lower spark plug.

With some changes, the dual spark plug modification can be used with a stock breaker point ignition. To use the stock ignition, an igniton amplifier such as the Accel (No. 35355) and dual output coils such as Andrews coils (black color), must be used. However, to obtain maximum benefits from the conversion as well as generally improve engine reliability, it is recommended that a dual output ignition such as the Dyna III or Prestolite (kit No. 70-67) be installed at the same time (on models through 1978). On 1979 and 1980 models the Camtron electronic ignition system with Andrews dual output coils is recommended.

To fully realize all the benefits from the dual spark plug conversion the ignition timing must be retarded several degrees. The exact timing changes and how the electronic triggers are set will vary based on the type of ignition system used. For best results, follow exactly the instructions provided by the company performing the cylinder head machine service as well as any additional instructions supplied with the special ignition system components. On models with an electronic tachometer a special diode is often necessary, as is the case with the Prestolite ignition system, to maintain tachometer accuracy. With the Prestolite system, use Prestolite 65-172 electronic tachometer adapter.

Several reputable firms throughout the country are experienced with dual spark plug conversions and can provide services varying

**11**

from simple machine work to complete kits, including the ignition systems (**Table 1**). Contact one or more of these supplier/dealers for information and prices. The cost of the cylinder head machine work and additional ignition system components is generally $200 to $300 depending on the type of ignition system chosen.

## OIL SUMP

With increased engine displacement and compression the BMW engine will run slightly hotter. This may be compensated for by installing a high-capacity oil sump (**Figure 11**).

This sump is available through many dealers or from RPM. It is black anodized cast aluminum and easily bolts to the engine in place of the stock sump. It does not interfere with cornering clearance or ease of maintenance.

With the sump installed, oil capacity is increased by one full quart. In addition, the sump is designed to accept an oil pressure sending unit. RPM offers a pressure gauge and line which may be fitted to the handlebars.

## OIL COOLERS

Oil temperature may be further reduced by using an oil cooler. This, particularly in a very hot climate or when the bike is ridden at a sustained high speed, will prolong engine life by reducing oil breakdown.

RPM recommends the Hayden cooler. Lockhart Industries also markets an excellent unit. Either of these will not only reduce temperature but also increase oil capacity by about half a quart.

One caution with coolers: During winter riding or in cooler climates they may overcool the oil. If an engine has been equipped with a cooler it may be necessary to block off a portion of the cooler with duct tape during fall or winter riding. Lockhart Industries is the only company offering a built-in solution to this slight problem—their high-performance cooler is available with a built-in thermostat. In the event of the thermostat failing the oil will not be blocked but merely recycled through the engine without passing through the cooler.

## OVERALL ENGINE

With the above modifications the BMW engine of whatever size is pretty well at its ultimate for practical street performance. Further performance increases, oriented toward the track, greatly increase the expense and unfortunately seriously lessen the engine's dependability.

But modified as described above, any model BMW will not only have greatly increased power for all street or even street/strip conditions but will be more reliable, require less maintenance and be more fun to ride for the performance-oriented enthusiast.

## GEARING
## (R90S, R100S AND R100RS)

The top-of-the-line BMWs seem to be geared for wide-open, no-speed-limit European *autobahns* rather than for maximum performance under American speed limits.

Acceleration capabilities throughout the power range may be improved by replacing the S and RS final drive with that used on the /6 and /7 models, thus reducing the secondary ratio from 3.0:1 to the more practical 3.09:1. However, this modification, while simple, is not inexpensive.

## FRAME

Unlike most other superbikes, BMWs need very little in the way of modification to make them handle. Most of the other performance machines require extensive changes merely to bring frame and suspension capabilities up to par with engine performance. In some cases, this cannot be done.

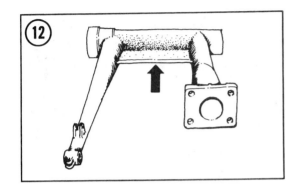

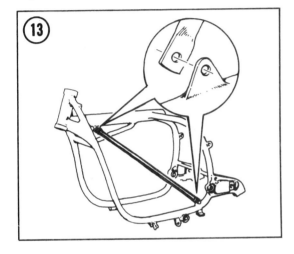

But BMW has always built a sturdy, non-flexy frame that will function perfectly under any street and even most street/strip conditions.

In 1977 the already beefy frame was further strengthened, as was the swing arm, thereby making an already superb handler better. But even earlier /5 and up models will need no frame alternations for street use.

However, for a tiny percentage of riders who exploit their high-performance machines to the limit, two things may be done.

1. The swing arm may be crossbraced with steel tubing welded between the swing arm pivot and rear wheel (**Figure 12**).

2. Sturdy tabs may be welded to the frame near the steering head on the frame toptube and near the bottom of each center frame downtube. To these tabs are bolted fabricated steel crossbraces to reduce frame flexing while cornering. This modification may be custom-ordered from RPM (**Figure 13**).

Obviously these modifications are pointless for street riding. The latter crossbracing requires running without air cleaners. Also, these sections must be removed before the engine may be pulled from the frame. Worst of all, these modifications won't offer any benefits, even under strenuous street riding.

## SUSPENSION

Road bikes, particularly touring machines, are built with ultra-soft suspension intended to keep the rider comfortable for long, weary miles. Performance cycles, on the other hand, have stiff, responsive, precise suspension.

BMW is the only manufacturer that has spent a great deal of engineering time and effort trying to give the best of both worlds to the owners of its machines.

The stock BMW suspension is plush and comfortable for about half its travel, but when pushed farther becomes increasingly stiff and exact.

### Shocks

For normal street riding the stock BMW suspension is more than adequate. The rear shocks—European-built Boges—are excellent.

Touring riders or those who want a variable suspension might consider replacing the Boges, when worn out, with S&W airshocks.

In these shocks the conventional spring is replaced by an air reservoir. Conventional oil damping is retained. Mounting these shocks is simple; they are almost bolt-ons. After the shocks themselves are installed all that remains is to run a small air line from each shock to a centrally-mounted tire-type valve.

As air pressure is added to the shocks they become progressively stiffer. Because the pressure may be varied anywhere from about 20 to over 50 pounds, the rider can chose from an unlimited number of adjustments; he can suit the ride not only to the road conditions but to his comfort requirements or load. Further adjustments to damping may be made by varying the amount of oil in the shocks.

These shocks not only work superbly but they also have an extremely long lifespan—sets are in use with well over 70,000 miles on them and no trouble has been experienced. The only cautionary note on the airshocks is that the

**11**

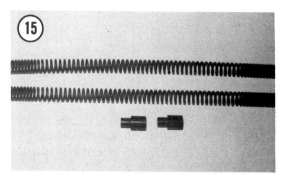

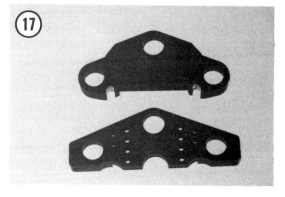

rider should very carefully ensure that there is adequate clearance to the sides and bottom of the shock—the rubber cushion has far more of an expansion rate under load than do conventional shocks.

For the uncompromising performance rider, use of a very stiff, precise shock may be desired. RPM offers their own set of Koni shocks (**Figure 14**) for experts who ride high-horsepower BMWs. Spring rates can be tailored to the individual rider's needs.

A second, extremely durable shock is the S&W conventional shock. It not only provides precise action under hard riding conditions, but also offers an extremely long lifespan.

### Front Forks

For sustained hard riding the stock front forks should be slightly modified.

Those first few inches of travel, while comfortably plush for the touring rider, are too soft for the high-performance rider.

The stock fork springs should be replaced with RPM heavy-duty fork springs (**Figure 15**)

to stiffen up the ride. RPM offers spring spacers in conjunction with their fork springs. These are available in three different lengths, to preload the springs to the desired degree of stiffness.

It is important that the buffer spring (**Figure 16**) also be replaced if stiffer fork springs are used. Otherwise the internal spring bumper will be quickly destroyed.

When extremely hard cornering or braking takes place, the stock forks may have some slight shimmy. RPM manufactures two different upper triple clamps (**Figure 17**) designed to end this problem.

requires the use of a rear disc and is consequently the more expensive of the two.

RPM offers the Morris wheel already set up with a complete rear disc brake (**Figure 20**). The disc unit may be either Grimeca or, at a greater cost, Lockheed.

## BRAKES
## (ALL-DISC EQUIPPED MODELS)

For those interested in reducing unsprung weight to the absolute minimum, RPM offers plasma-coated light-weight replacement discs. However, considering that these are quite expensive and will offer little benefit to most street riders, they should be considered as essentially a competition-only item.

## TIRES

High-performance motorcycles and high-performance riding require a careful choice of tires.

Most street riders must compromise between a tire that is soft enough to provide maximum traction and one which is hard enough to have a rational lifespan.

There are some differences of opinion in tire selection for the BMW. Pridmore recommends a Continental K112 4.25x18 on the rear and a Michelin M45 3.50x19 on the front. Although the Continental RB2 also works well on the front, Pridmore claims that hard braking will wear a cupped pattern on the Conti but not on the harder composition Michelin.

Brown recommends Dunlop K81s front and rear for the average rider and Continentals (K112 rear, RB2 front) for the more

The Type I, which is designed for use with the R100RS, but may be modified to fit all 1974 and later BMWs, not only stiffens the front forks but adds a slight amount of ground clearance for increased cornering ability.

The Type II (**Figure 18**) maintains standard clearance and is designed to fit all 1970 and up BMWs. It also will reduce front end flexing and wobble.

## WHEELS

Two styles of cast-alloy wheels are available for BMWs. Both Morris Industries and Lester Wheels make bolt-on wheels for Beemers.

Improved appearance is not the only advantage the cast wheel has over the conventionally-spoked one. Because of its higher rigidity, a cast wheel will improve high-speed and cornering stability.

In addition, the deeply dished rim lessens the possibility of a tire coming off in the event of a blowout.

The Lester wheel is the heavier of the two and it retains the stock rear brake assembly. The Morris Industries wheel (**Figure 19**)

11

experienced rider. He feels that the Dunlops are far more forgiving than the Contis to the less experienced rider who overcooks a turn.

Clymer did considerable testing of the Dunlops pair and the Continentals. The K81s saw about 7,000 miles of touring and 500 miles of hard canyon riding before the wear bands on the rear tire appeared, indicating 2 mm of tread remaining. The center section was worn flat while the sides had plenty of tread. The front tire tread was down to about 4.5 mm (it had 7 mm of tread when new).

The K81 is an excellent tire known for its handling and it is very popular for production racing. However, the soft rubber wears too rapidly for a touring motorcycle.

The Continentals (K112 rear, RB2 front) are currently on the test bike. They have logged 9,000 touring miles and 750 street performance miles. There is no cupping of the front tire, probably indicating that we don't brake as hard as Reg Pridmore—but you might. The rear tire tread measures 3 mm, indicating the useful life down to the wear bands will be about 12,000 miles. The Contis handled beautifully wet or dry and should be the first choice for installation on a BMW that will tour or see multi-use.

Both the Dunlops and the Continentals handled well on the notorious rain grooves found on many concrete highways around the country. The Dunlops squirmed a bit for about 500 miles but once they scrubbed-in they settled down. The Continentals ignored the rain grooves right out of the box. On the test bike it was possible to turn the steering damper off and take our hands off the bars at higher than prudent speeds without our noticing any wiggle.

Metzeler tires come stock on the BMW and are also good tires. If you are primarily a touring or commuting rider, leave them on for their useful life. Then consider replacing them with Continentals. If you are primarily a hard, fast rider, give the Metzelers a try, then switch to either the Continentals, Dunlops or the Continental/Michelin combination that was recommended earlier.

None of the tires mentioned here require rim locks or sheet metal screws through the rim for any sort of street riding. For competition, get advice based on your requirements from Reg Pridmore or Bob Brown.

## OVERALL

Of course, other options exist for the BMW; you can make your bike anything from a super-competitive production class roadracer to a highly modified BMW R100RSE like Reg Pridmore's factory hot rod—a high-powered machine which might cost almost double what the RS runs.

However, considering not only the cost of the modifications but the actual needs of the street rider, very little more than what is outlined here should be done to the BMW.

High performance, not only in engine modifications but in handling and suspension, can make the German shaft-drive machine not only a bike that is far superior to its stock counterpart and others of its size, but one which loses none of its justly famed mechanical reliability and ease of maintenance.

Table 1    PERFORMANCE SUPPLIERS

| | |
|---|---|
| BMW Staten Island<br>421 Richmond<br>Staten Island, NY 10302 | Dual spark plug kits,<br>accessories |
| Branch Flowmetrics<br>7051 Village Drive<br>Buena Park, CA 90621 | Cylinder head work |
| British Marketing<br>P.O. Box 219<br>San Juan Capistrano, CA 92693 | Boyer-Brandson<br>electronic ignitions |
| Brown Motor Works<br>885 West Mission Blvd.<br>Pomona, CA 91766 | Engine building,<br>machine work, dual<br>spark plug kits |
| Freeman Cycles, Inc.<br>50 Federal St.<br>Beverly, MA 01915 | Dual spark plug kits, accessories |
| Hayden Trans-Cooler Inc.<br>1531 Pomona Road<br>Corona, CA 91766 | Oil coolers |
| Lester Tire and Wheel Co.<br>26881 Cannon Road<br>Bedford Heights, OH 44146 | Alloy wheels |
| Lockhart Industries, Inc.<br>15707 Texaco Ave.<br>Paramount, CA 90723 | Oil coolers,<br>thermostat |
| MCM Manufacturing Co.<br>601 South East Street<br>Anaheim, CA 92805 | Exhaust systems,<br>racks, engine guards |
| Morris Industries<br>2901 West Garry Ave.<br>Santa Ana, CA 92704 | Alloy wheels |
| One Stop Head Shop<br>8211 Belclaire Lane<br>Austin, TX 78745 | Engine machine work,<br>dual spark plug kits |
| RPM (Reg Pridmore Motors)<br>1946 E. Thompson Blvd.<br>Ventura, CA 93003 | Engine building, machine<br>work, performance accessories |
| San Jose BMW Motorcycle Center<br>1886 West San Carlos St.<br>San Jose, CA 95128 | Dual spark plug kits,<br>race equipment,<br>accessories |
| S&W Engineered Products<br>13415 Marquardt<br>Santa Fe Springs, CA 90670 | Springs and<br>suspension units |
| Terrycable<br>P.O. Box 1321<br>Hesperia, CA 92345 | Control cables |
| Walus Engineering<br>P.O. Box 84<br>Beecher IL 60401 | Dual spark plug kits |
| Boyer-Brandson Electronics<br>38 London Road<br>Bromley, Kent BR1 3QR, England | Electronic ignition |
| Gus Kuhn BMW Centre<br>275-277 Clapham Road<br>London, SW9 OBJ, England | Spares, performance<br>equipment |
| H and S Accessories Ltd.<br>Unit 14, Bordon Trading Estate<br>Bordon, Hampshire GLL35 9HH, England | Parts and accessories |

11

SUPPLEMENT

# 1979 AND LATER SERVICE INFORMATION

The following supplement provides additional information for servicing the 1979 and later models listed in **Table 1**.

Other service procedures remain the same as described in the basic book, Chapters One through Eleven.

The chapter headings in this supplement correspond to those in the main portion of this book. If a chapter is not referenced in this supplement, there are no changes affecting that chapter; follow the procedures described for the comparable model in the basic book.

If your BMW is covered by this supplement, carefully read the appropriate chapter in the basic book before beginning any work.

**Table 1 NEW MODEL LISTING (1979-ON)**

| 1979-1980 | 1981 | 1982 |
|-----------|--------|--------|
| R80/7 | R100T | R100T |
| R100T | R100RT | R100RT |
| R100RT | R100S | R100RS |
| R100S | R100RS | R100S |
| R100RS | R100 | |
| R100T | R100CS | |

CHAPTER THREE

# PERIODIC MAINTENANCE AND LUBRICATION

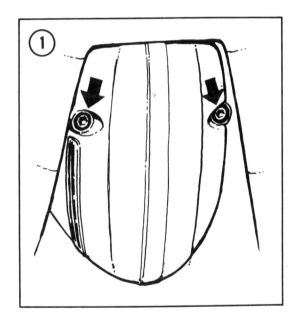

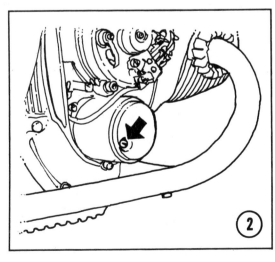

Refer to **Table 2** for recommended fuel and lubricants and to **Table 3** for approximate refill capacities for 1979 and later models.

## TUNE-UP

Refer to **Table 4** for tune-up specifications and to **Table 5** for recommended spark plugs for 1979 and later models.

## ROTARY IGNITION TRIGGER DISTRIBUTOR (1979 AND 1980 MODELS)

A new ignition distributor was introduced on 1979 models. It has mechanical contact breaker (points) like the earlier units. The points and condenser are replaceable and the points are adjustable.

### Points Replacement

1. Disconnect the battery ground cable.

> CAUTION
> *If the battery ground is left connected when the front engine cover is removed, a short is very likely to occur. In such case, the diodes in the rectifier may well be damaged, requiring replacement of the entire diode board.*

2. Unscrew the Allen head screws that attach the front cover to the engine (**Figure 1**) and remove the cover.

3. Unscrew the screw from the distributor cap (**Figure 2**) and remove the cap.

4. Unscrew the screws that attach the support bracket (**Figure 3**) and remove the bracket.

**12**

5. Disconnect the electrical leads (**Figure 4**), unscrew the point lockscrew, and remove the point assembly.

6. Reverse the above to install a new points assembly. Refer to *Ignition Timing* and adjust the point gap and the ignition timing.

7. Install the cap on the distributor. Install the front engine cover, and reconnect the battery ground lead.

### Ignition Timing

1. Remove the front engine cover and the distributor cap as described above.

2. Unscrew the spark plugs from the cylinder heads. Refer to Chapter Three — *Spark Plugs, Inspection,* and check the condition of the plugs to help assess engine and ignition condition.

3. With an Allen wrench, rotate the engine clockwise (**Figure 5**) until the points are fully open.

> *CAUTION*
> *Turn the crankshaft, not the distributor shaft on the end of the camshaft.*

4. Check the point gap with a flat feeler gauge (**Figure 6**). It should be 0.016 in. (0.4mm). If the gap is not correct, losen the contact breaker lockscrew (**Figure 7**), insert the tip of a screwdriver between the two nubs on the contact breaker plate and move the plate until the gap is correct. Then, without further moving the plate, tighten the lockscrew. Recheck the gap.

5. Connect a dwell meter to the ignition in accordance with the instrument manufacturer's instructions. Reconnect the battery ground lead and start the engine. At 1,000 rpm, the dwell angle should be 120°. If the dwell angle is less, reduce the point gap. If it is greater than 120°, increase the point gap. Shut off the engine and disconnect the dwell meter. disconnect the dwell meter.

6. Connect a strobe timing light in accordance with the instrument manufacturer's instructions. Start the engine and allow it to idle (800-1,000 rpm). Direct the strobe at the timing hole on the left side of the crankcase. The "S" mark should align with the indicator

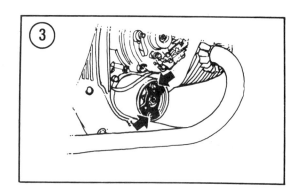

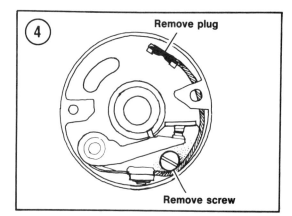

Remove plug

Remove screw

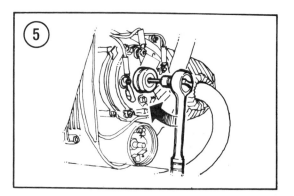

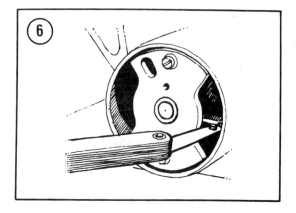

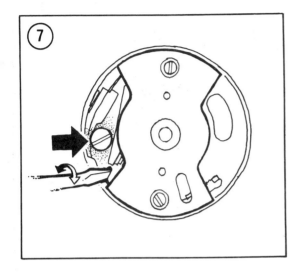

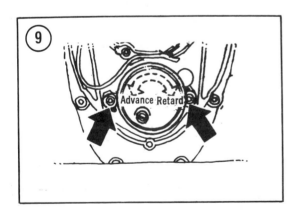

(**Figure 8**). If the mark appears below the indicator, the timing is retarded; if it appears above the indicator, the timing is too advanced.

To correct the timing, loosen the Allen bolts on each side of the distributor (**Figure 9**) and rotate the distributor while watching the timing mark. To retard the timing, turn the distributor clockwise, and turn it counterclockwise to advance the timing. When the timing is correct, tighten the Allen screws.

7. When the basic timing is correct, increase the engine speed to 3,500 rpm and check the timing in the full advanced position. The "Z" mark should align with the indicator (**Figure 10**). If it is more than just a couple of degrees off and the basic timing is correct, inspect and clean the distributor mechanical advance.

## ELECTRONIC IGNITION (1981-ON)

All 1981 and later models are equipped with an electronic ignition system. There are two ways to time the engine—the static method (engine stopped) and the dynamic method (engine running).

### Static Timing

Because of the high voltage associated with the electronic ignition system, checking the static timing with a test light or buzz box is not possible. Instead, BMW has designed and made available a special timer with a light-emitting diode and built-in 9-volt battery. Checking static timing on models with electronic ignition is only possible by using this special tool. It may be ordered from your BMW dealer. The part number is 88 88 6 123 650.

*CAUTION*
*The ignition switch must **not** be turned ON when performing this test.*

1. Remove the Allen screws and remove the front engine cover (**Figure 1**).
2. Remove the spark plugs.
3. Remove the plug from the flywheel inspection hole. See **Figure 11**.
4. Disconnect the 3-pin plug at the distributor and connect it to the BMW timing

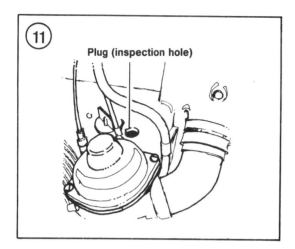

Plug (inspection hole)

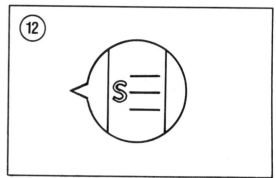

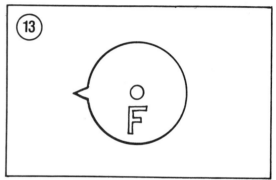

box following the manufacturer's instructions.

5. Turn the engine clockwise using the rotor nut (**Figure 5**) or the kick starter. Ignition timing is correct if the BMW timing box lights up when the center line "S" mark on the flywheel aligns with the notch in the flywheel inspection hole. See **Figure 12**. If the static timing is incorrect, loosen the distributor screws and turn the distributor until the timing is correct. See **Figure 9**.

6. After the ignition timing is properly set, reconnect and install all parts.

**Dynamic Timing**

Dynamic timing is set by using a timing light.

1. Connect a timing light to the engine following the manufacturer's instructions.

2. Remove the plug from the flywheel inspection hole (**Figure 11**).

3. Start the engine and run it at 950 ±150 rpm.

4. Point the timing light at the flywheel inspection hole. The ignition timing is correct if the center line "S" mark on the flywheel aligns with the notch in the flywheel inspection hole (**Figure 12**). If the bottom stripe is visible, ignition timing is retarded; if the top stripe is visible, the timing is advanced.

5. Increase engine speed to about 3,500 rpm. The "F" mark on the flywheel should align with the notch in the flywheel inspection hole. See **Figure 13**.

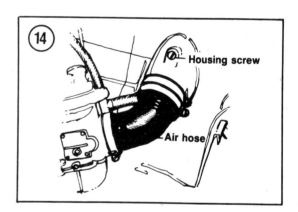

Housing screw

Air hose

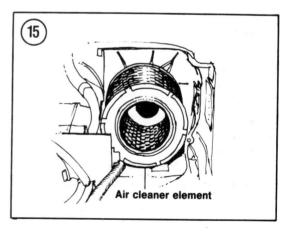

Air cleaner element

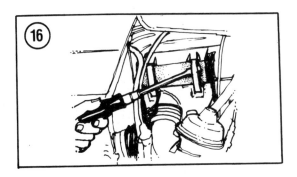

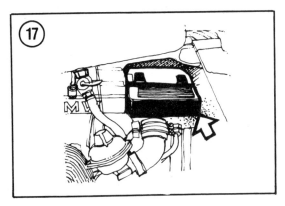

6. If the ignition timing is incorrect in Step 4 and Step 5, loosen the distributor screws and turn the distributor until the timing is correct. See **Figure 9**.

*NOTE*
*If the "S" mark lines up at idle correctly but the "F" mark does not line up at advance, the spark trigger may be*

*faulty. Have a BMW technican check it for you. If the spark trigger tests okay, the ignition timing should be adjusted in favor of the "F" mark at ignition advance.*

## AIR CLEANER

A properly functioning air filter is essential to engine efficiency, long engine life and good gas mileage.

### Removal/Installation (1979 Models)

1. Remove the fuel tank.
2. Remove the starter cover.
3. Disconnect the engine breather hose at the air cleaner housing.
4. Disconnect and remove the air filter housing-to-carburetor air hose (**Figure 14**).
5. Remove the air filter housing screw (**Figure 14**). Then pull the air filter element (**Figure 15**) out of the housing shell.
6. Installation is the reverse of these steps.

### Removal/Installation (1980-on)

1. Pry the air filter clips off of the filter housing with a screwdriver. See **Figure 16**.
2. Pull the filter element out (**Figure 17**) and replace it. During installation, be sure the filter fits in the housing properly and that the clips are secured tightly.

### Table 2 RECOMMENDED FUEL AND LUBRICANTS

| | |
|---|---|
| Fuel | 91 octane |
| Brake fluid | DOT 4 |
| Final drive gear oil | |
| Above 41° F (50° C) | SAE 90 |
| Below 41° F (50° C) | SAE 80 |

### Table 3 APPROXIMATE REFILL CAPACITIES

| | |
|---|---|
| Fork oil | |
| 1979-1980 | 265 cc (8.96 oz.) |
| 1981-on | 220 cc (7.44 oz.) |
| Engine oil* | 2.46 liters (2.6 qt.) |
| Final drive** | 350 cc (11.83 oz.) |

* Check engine oil level with dipstick resting on top of threads.
** On models equipped with the torsion damper driveshaft, it is impossible to check the oil level in the driveshaft housing. Instead, drain and refill with 150 cc (5.07 oz.) with the correct weight hypoid gear oil.

12

**Table 4 TUNE-UP SPECIFICATIONS**

| | |
|---|---|
| Ignition timing | "S" (middle line) mark @ idle |
| | "Z" mark @ 3,500 rpm |
| Valve clearance | |
| Intake | 0.10 mm (0.004 in.) |
| Exhaust | 0.15 mm (0.006 in.) |
| Idle speed | |
| 1979 | 800-1,000 rpm |
| 1980-on | 800-1,100 rpm |

**Table 5 RECOMMENDED SPARK PLUGS***

| Model | Bosch | Champion |
|---|---|---|
| 1979-1980 | | |
| R80/7 | W7D | N10Y |
| R100S, R100RT, R100RS, | W5D | N6Y |
| R100T | | |
| 1981-on | W6D | N10Y |

* Higher number in Bosch spark plugs indicates a colder heat range. Higher number in Champion plugs indicates a hotter heat range.

CHAPTER FOUR

ENGINE

Engine specifications for 1979 and later models are in **Table 6** and **Table 7**.

### CYLINDER HEAD (1980-ON)

Procedures used to remove and install the cylinder head are the same as for 1979 and earlier models, except that you must disconnect the intake line at the cylinder head before removal (**Figure 18**). During installation, tighten the intake line securely.

### CAMSHAFT AND CRANKSHAFT SERVICE

This procedure describes removal and installation of the timing chain cover, timing chain and sprockets on 1979 and 1980 models with the rotary ignition trigger distributor.

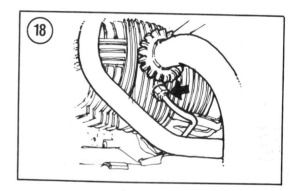

### Removal/Installation

1. Perform Steps 1-4 under *Camshaft and Crankshaft Service, Disassembly* in Chapter Four of the main body of this book.
2. Referring to **Figure 19**, disconnect the electrical connector at the distributor. Then

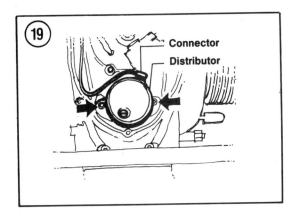
Connector
Distributor

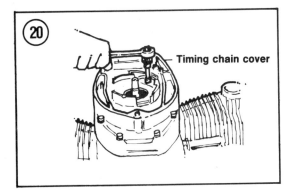
Timing chain cover

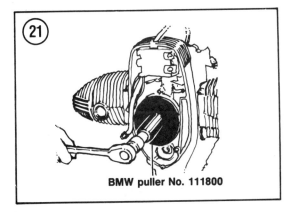
BMW puller No. 111800

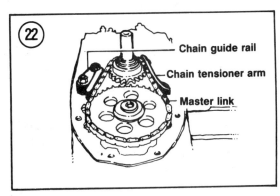
Chain guide rail
Chain tensioner arm
Master link

remove the 2 distributor mounting screws and remove the distributor.

3. Remove the Allen screws and nuts securing the timing chain cover to the engine housing. See **Figure 20**.

4. Attach BMW puller No. 11 1 800 to the tapped holes used previously for the alternator housing with 3 M5 Allen screws. Tighten the puller bolt (**Figure 21**) and pull off the timing chain cover.

5. Referring to **Figure 22**, remove the bolts securing the chain guide rail to the crankcase housing and remove it. Then remove the chain tensioner arm.

6. Remove the master link clip (**Figure 22**) and separate the timing chain.

7. Using 2 large screwdrivers, pry off the camshaft chain sprocket as shown in **Figure 23**.

8. Using BMW puller No. 11 2 600, pull the crankshaft chain sprocket off of the crankshaft together with its bearing (**Figure 24**).

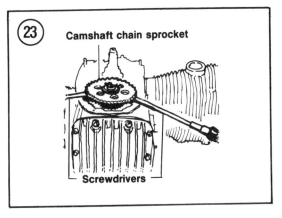
Camshaft chain sprocket
Screwdrivers

BMW No. 112600

12

## Installation

1. Heat the crankshaft chain sprocket and bearing to approximately 175° F (80° C). Wearing thick work gloves to protect your hands, push the sprocket/bearing assembly onto the crankshaft.
2. Install the camshaft chain sprocket.
3. Turn both sprockets until their index marks align. Then install the timing chain and join the ends of the chain with a new master link. Secure the master link so that the closed end of the link faces in the direction of chain drive.

*CAUTION*
*Incorrect installation of the timing chain master link could cause the chain to disconnect during engine operation and result in expensive engine damage.*

4. Install the chain tensioner arm (**Figure 22**).
5. Install the chain guide rail (**Figure 22**) and tighten the attaching bolts securely. Be sure the chain guide rail is parallel with the run of

the chain. If not, reposition the chain guide rail.
6. To install the timing chain cover, first heat the ball bearing seat area in the cover to 175° F (80° C). When the correct temperature is reached, quickly place the cover onto the engine. Install the Allen screws and nuts and tighten them securely, starting with the center screws. BMW does not specify a tightening sequence.
7. Install the distributor by inserting it into the timing chain cover (**Figure 19**). Install and tighten the Allen screws securely.
8. Install the alternator assembly as described under Step 26 and Step 27 under *Camshaft and Crankshaft Service, Reassembly* in Chapter Four of the main body of this book.
9. Check the ignition timing as described in the Chapter Three section of this supplement.

## CLUTCH

New clutch specifications for 1979 and later models are found in **Table 8** (specifications) and **Table 9** (tightening torques).

**Table 6 ENGINE SPECIFICATIONS (1979-ON)**

| Item | mm (in.) |
|---|---|
| Cylinder bore | |
| R80/7 | 84.8 (3.34) |
| R100 models (all) | 94 (3.70) |
| Maximum cylinder taper | 0.02 (0.0008) |
| Piston stroke | 70.6 (2.78) |
| Compression ratio | |
| R80/7 | 9.2:1 |
| R100 models (all) | 9.5:1 |
| Oil pump | |
| Outer rotor diameter | 57.1 (2.248) |
| Housing inner diameter | 57.2 (2.252) |
| Outer rotor/pump clearance | 0.10-0.17 (0.0039-0.0067) |
| Inner-to-outer rotor gap | 0.12-0.20 (0.0047-0.0079) |
| Valves | |
| Length | 98.4-98.8 (3.874-3.890) |
| Valve head diameter | |
| Intake | |
| R80/7 | 42 (1.654) |
| R100 models (all) | 44 (1.73) |
| Exhaust | |
| R80/7 | 38 (1.496) |
| R100 models (all) | 40 (1.575) |
| Stem diameter | 7.934-7.950 (0.3124-0.3130) |
| (continued) | |

## Table 6 ENGINE SPECIFICATIONS (1979-ON) (continued)

| Item | mm (in.) |
|------|----------|
| Valve head deflection | 0.025 (0.0010) |
| Valve seat angle | 45° |
| Valve seat width | |
|   Intake | 1.5 (0.059) |
|   Exhaust | 2.0 (0.079) |
| Valve guides | |
|   Outer diameter | 14.050-14.061 (0.5479-0.5483) |
|   Inside diameter | Use BMW reamer 8H7 |
|   Cylinder head bore | Use BMW reamer 14H7 |
|   Interference fit | 0.032-0.061 (0.0012-0.0023) |
| Valve springs | |
|   Free length | 43.5 (1.712) |
|   Install direction | Green mark facing cylinder head |
| Camshaft | |
|   Camshaft bearing journal diameter | |
|     Alternator end | 24.96-24.97 (0.9828-0.9833) |
|     Flywheel end | 23.97-23.98 (0.9438-0.9442) |
|   Flange bearing bore | |
|     Diameter in crankcase | 40.00-40.04 (1.5750-1.5765) |
|     Outer diameter | 39.98-40.00 (1.5740-1.5750) |
|     Bore diameter | 25.00-25.01 (0.9840-0.9845) |
|   Radial clearance | 0.02-0.046 (0.0008-0.0018) |
|   Base circle diameter | 28 (1.102) |
|   Cam lift | 6.756 (0.2660) |
|   Tappet outer diameter | 21.975-21.955 (0.8651-0.8643) |
|   Tappet bore in crankcase | 21.985-22.006 (0.8655-0.8663) |
|   Tappet radial clearance | 0.01-0.051 (0.0004-0.0020) |
|     Maximum wear | 0.075 (0.0030) |
|   Pushrod length | 274.7-275.3 (10.814-10.838) |
| Piston rings | |
|   End gap | 0.30-0.45 (0.117-0.0175) |
|   Side clearance | 0.04-0.07 (0.0016-0.0027) |
|   Installation direction | ID mark facing upward |

## Table 7 PISTON SPECIFICATIONS (1979-ON)

| Cylinder | R80/7 mm (in.) | R100 mm (in.) |
|----------|----------------|---------------|
| Standard size | | |
|   Grade A | 84.765 (3.3372) | 93.960 (3.6992) |
|   Grade B | 84.775 (3.3376) | 93.970 (3.6996) |
|   Grade C | 84.785 (3.3380) | 93.980 (3.7000) |
| First oversize | | |
|   Grade A | 85.015 (3.3470) | 94.210 (3.7090) |
|   Grade B | 85.025 (3.3474) | 94.220 (3.7094) |
|   Grade C | 85.035 (3.3478) | 94.230 (3.7098) |
| Piston clearance | | |
|   New | 0.023-0.047 (0.0009-0.0018) | 0.028-0.047 (0.0011-0.0018) |
|   Wear limit | 0.08 (0.0031) | 0.08 (0.0031) |

12

#### Table 8 CLUTCH SPECIFICATIONS (1979-ON)

| Item | mm | in. |
|---|---|---|
| Diaphragm spring thickness | | |
| R80/7 | 2.6 | 0.102 |
| All R100 models | 2.8 | 0.110 |
| Clutch plate thickness | | |
| New | 6 | 0.0098 |
| Wear limit | 4.5 | 0.177 |
| Clutch plate external diameter | 180 | 7.087 |

#### Table 9 CLUTCH TIGHTENING TORQUES (1979-ON)

| Item | N•m | ft.-lb. |
|---|---|---|
| Clutch nut @ flywheel | 23 | 17 |
| Clutch lever adjusting screw locknut | 20-23 | 14.7-17.0 |

CHAPTER FIVE

# TRANSMISSION

New transmission specifications for 1979 and later models are found in **Table 10** (specifications) and **Table 11** (tightening torques).

## TRANSMISSION (1980-ON)

### Removal/Installation

Removal and installation of the transmission on 1980 and later models is the same as for 1979 and previous models, except that it is necessary to first remove the air filter housing. See the Chapter Six section of this supplement for details.

**Table 10 TRANSMISSION SPECIFICATIONS (1979-ON)**

| Item | mm | in. |
|------|-----|-----|
| Drive shaft end play | 0-0.1 | 0-0.0039 |
| Input shaft end play | 0-0.1 | 0-0.0039 |
| Output shaft end play | 0-0.1 | 0-0.0039 |
| Free-running pinions end play | 0.15-0.30 | 0.006-0.018 |
| Output shaft bushing clearance | 0.005-0.035 | 0.000-0.0013 |

**Table 11 TRANSMISSION TIGHTENING TORQUES (1979-ON)**

| Item | N•m | ft.-lb. |
|------|-----|---------|
| Oil drain plug | 23-26 | 14.7-19.2 |
| Transmission mount on engine | 20-24 | 14.7-17.7 |
| Output shaft | 200-220 | 147-162 |
| Gearbox case-to-cover bolts | 7-8 | 5-6 |
| Kick starter lever nut | 20-23 | 14.7-17.0 |

CHAPTER SIX

# FUEL SYSTEM

## CARBURETOR (R80 MODELS)

The 32 mm Bing constant-vacuum carburetor used on R80 models is shown in **Figure 25**. It is similar to other CV carburetors except that it has a near-flat cover, it does not have a throttle slide tube and the diaphragm and throttle slide are bonded together.

Service this unit as described for other CV carburetors (see Chapter Six in the main body of this book).

## AIR FILTER HOUSING (1980-ON)

### Removal/Installation

1. Place the motorcycle on its centerstand.
2. Remove the air filter element as described in the Chapter Three section of this supplement.

3. Loosen and remove the nuts securing the intake valve to the air cleaner housing. See **Figure 26**. Then pull the valve out of the housing.

4. Remove the battery and the battery box.

5. Pull the crankcase breather T-adapter (**Figure 27**) out of the air cleaner housing.

6. Referring to **Figure 28**, remove the nut (1) and bolt (2) securing the air cleaner housing to the frame. Then press the discharge line (3) with your finger to disconnect it from the housing.

7. Pull the air cleaner housing up and remove it from the frame.

8. Reverse Steps 2-7 to install the housing. After completing installation, check all air line connections to make sure they are properly secured.

12

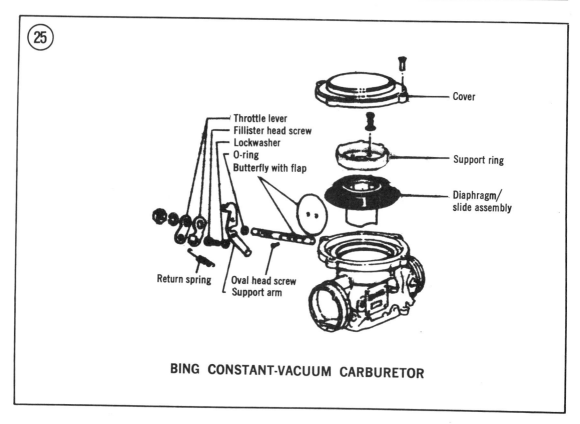

Cover

Throttle lever
Fillister head screw
Lockwasher
O-ring
Butterfly with flap

Support ring

Diaphragm/
slide assembly

Return spring

Oval head screw
Support arm

**BING CONSTANT-VACUUM CARBURETOR**

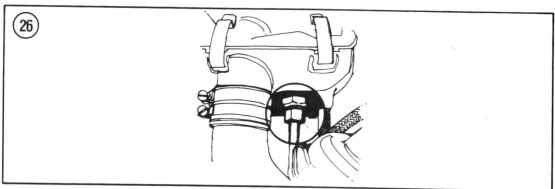

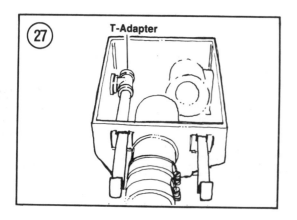

T-Adapter

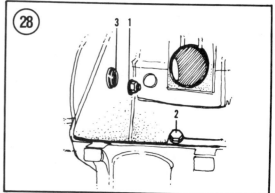

CHAPTER SEVEN

# ELECTRICAL SYSTEM

All 1981 and later BMW models are equipped an electronic ignition system. The system consists of 2 spark plugs, 2 ignition coils, a command module (black box) and a Hall impluse transmitter. The BMW electronic ignition system is similar to a contact breaker point ignition system, with these differences:

a. Mechanical contact points are replaced by the Hall impulse transmitter unit. The elimination of contact breaker points means that periodic adjustment of point gap and ignition timing are no longer required. Once set properly, initial timing should not require adjustment unless the unit is removed.

b. An intermediate electronic switch, the command module, receives the weak signals from the Hall impulse transmitter and uses them to turn the ignition coil primary current on and off.

c. The ignition coil has a special low resistance primary winding that helps it produce a powerful spark at high rpm.

## Service Precautions

Improper service could cause permanent damage to the ignition components. Observe the following precautions during service.

1. The spark plug cables are not to be shortened in length for any reason.

2. Do not disconnect the spark plugs cables while the engine is running.

3. Do not use an ohmmeter to test the distributor or the command module.

4. When installing or replacing the command module, apply a heat transfering anti-corrosive material (such as GE Silicone Compound No. Z5 or Dow Corning Heat Sink Compound No. 340) to the backside of the module. This will prevent module overheating due to insufficient heat transfer between the module and its mounting base (heat sink).

12

# INDEX

**13**

# WIRING DIAGRAM KEY

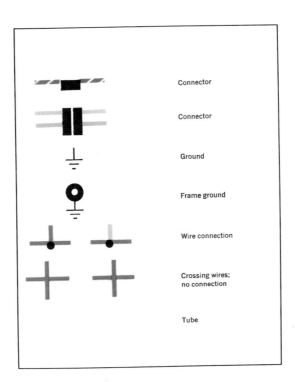

| | |
|---|---|
| | Connector |
| | Connector |
| | Ground |
| | Frame ground |
| | Wire connection |
| | Crossing wires; no connection |
| | Tube |

**NOTE:** Wiring diagrams for 1981 & 1982 models were not available at the time this book went to press.

# 1970-1972 R50/5 — R75/5 (without Fuses)

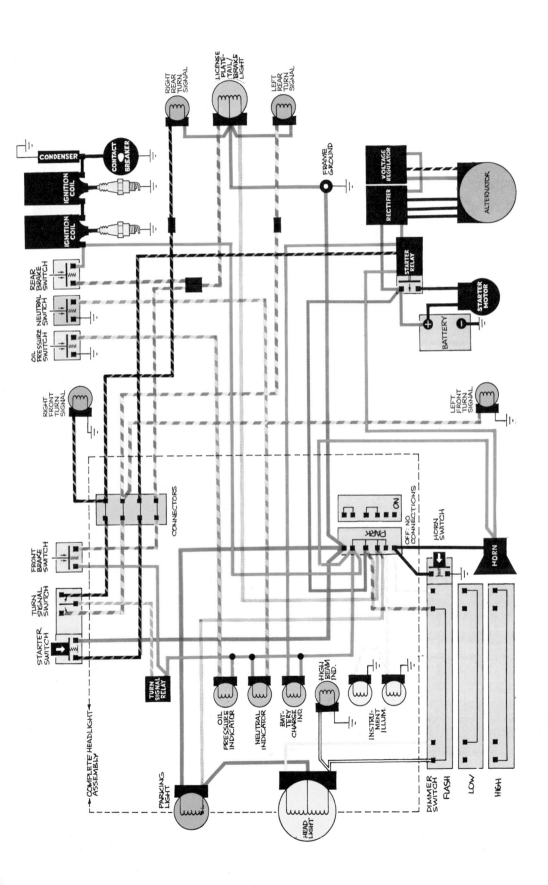

# Late 1972-1973 R50/5 — R75/5 (with Fuses)

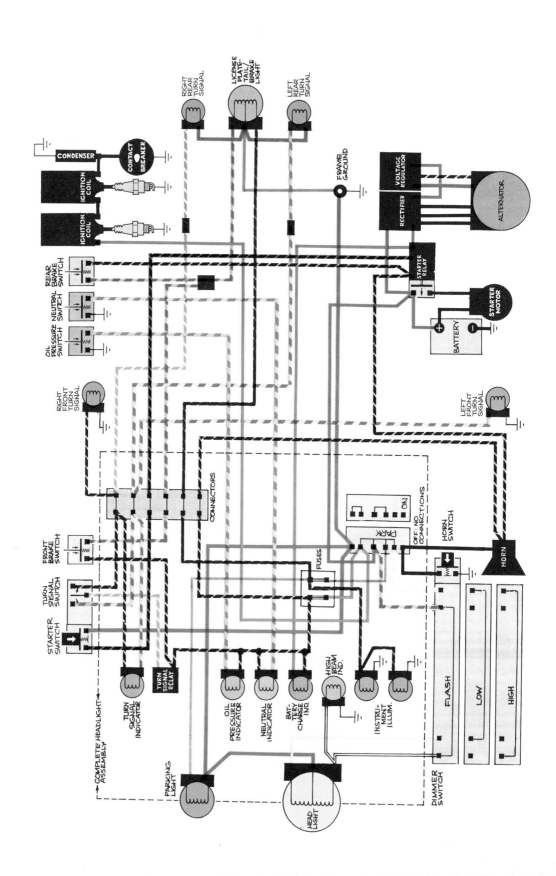

# 1974 R60/6 — R90S

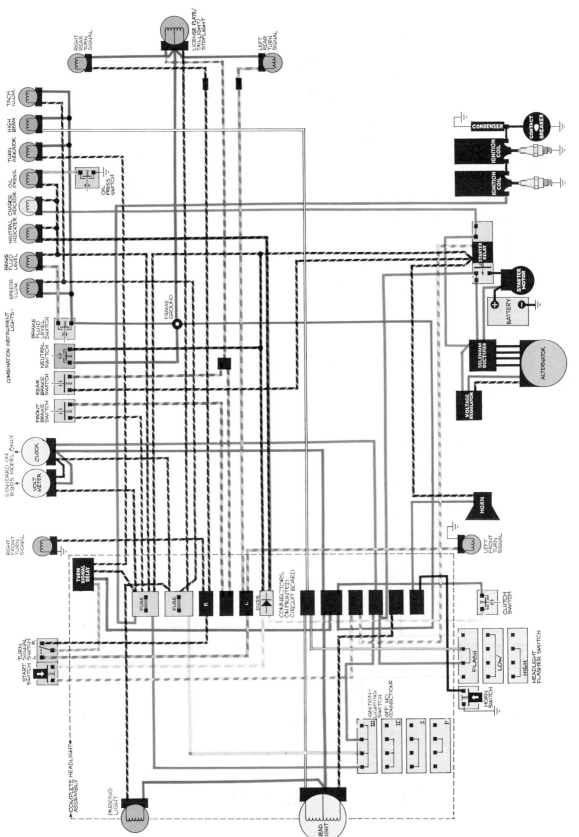

# 1975-1976 R60/6—R90S

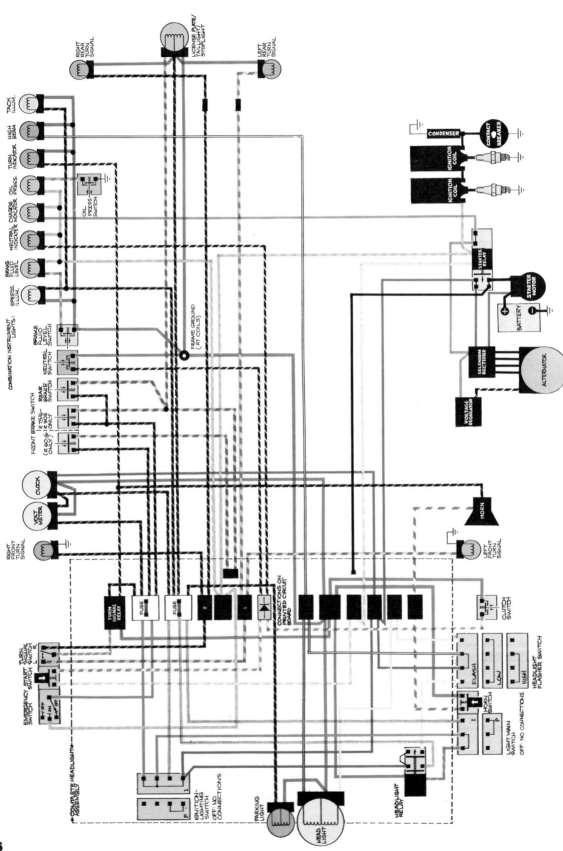

# 1977 R60/7 — R100S

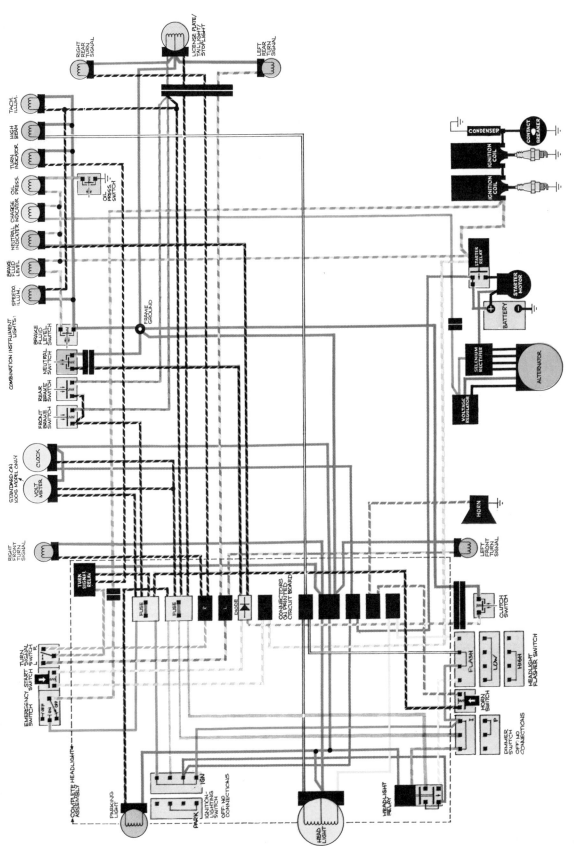

# 1977 R100RS

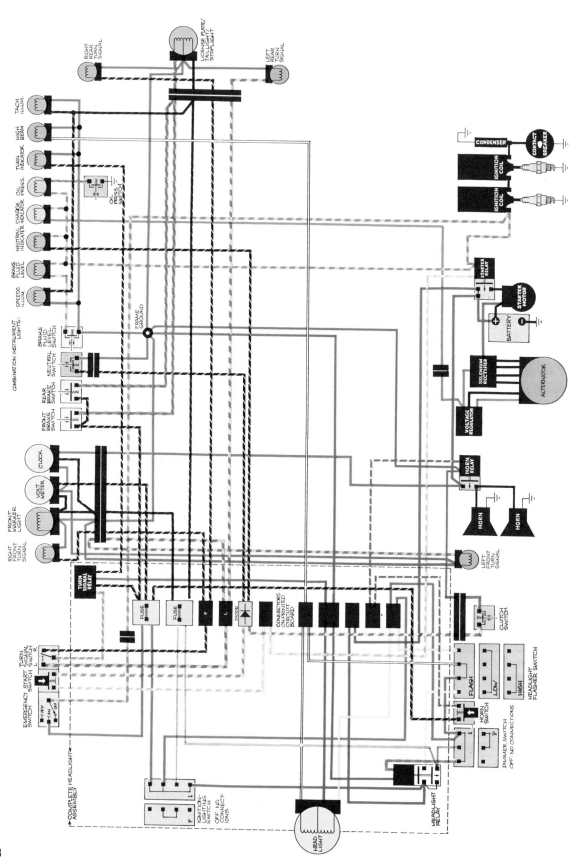

# 1978 R80/7 — R100S

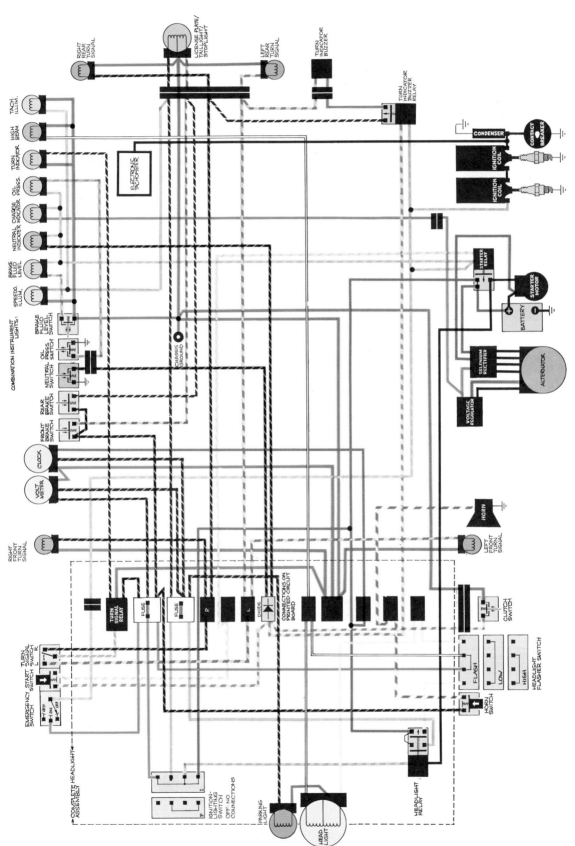

# 1978 R100RS

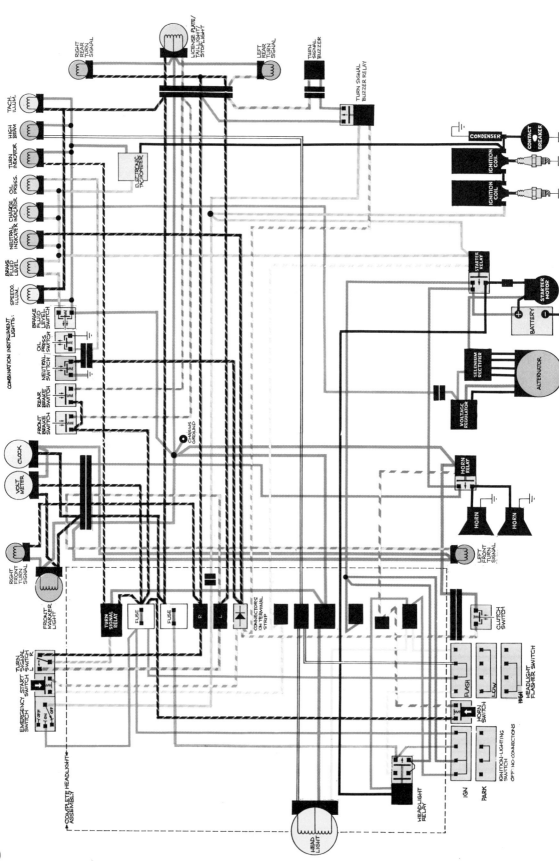

# 1979-1980 R80/7, R100T, R100S

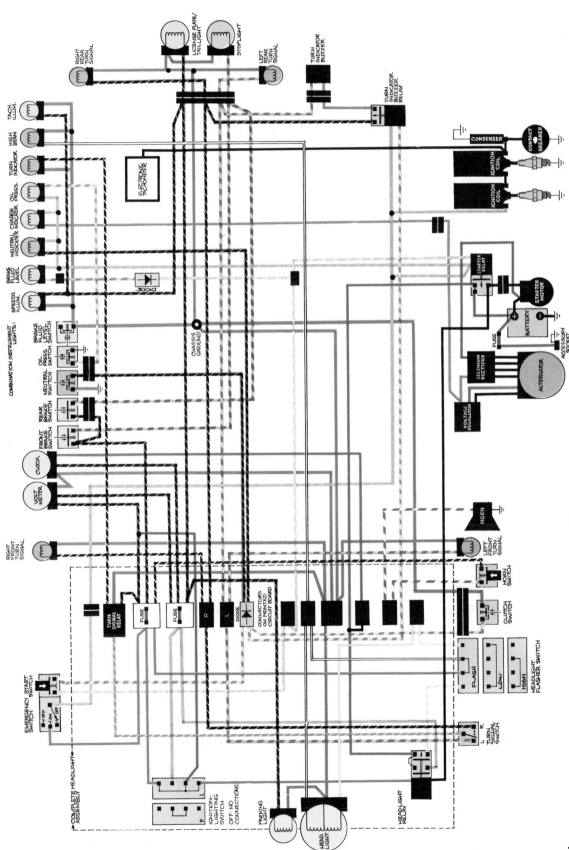

# 1979-1980 R100RS, R100RT

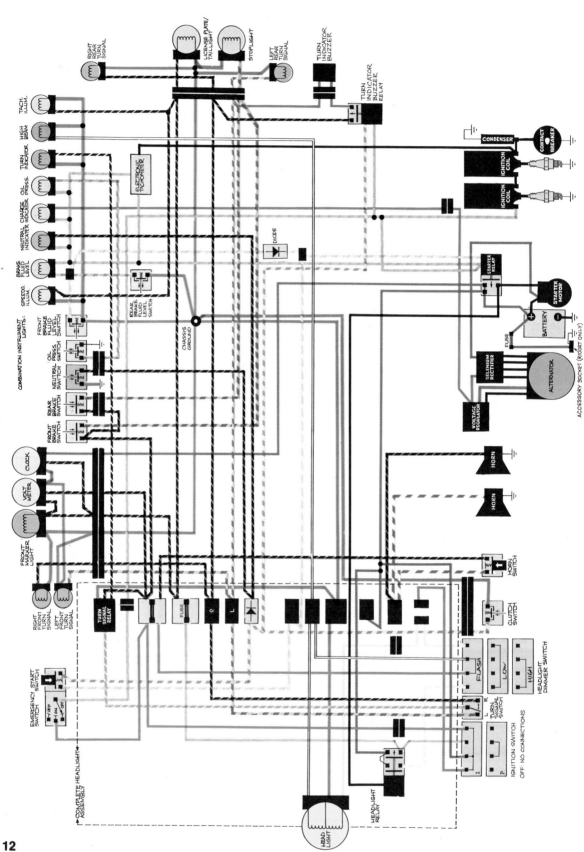